JOHN BINNS is Visiting Professor at the Institute for Orthodox Christian Studies and Vicar of Great St Mary's the University Church, Cambridge. He serves also as Chairperson of the charity Partners for Change Ethiopia. His previous publications include *An Introduction to the Christian Orthodox Churches* (2002) and *Ascetics and Ambassadors of Christ: The Monasteries of Palestine, 314–631* (1994).

'John Binns has a long and deep acquaintance with the Ethiopian church – its liturgy, prayer, ancient ascetic practice and unique art and architecture. In this lush and authoritative book he leads the reader on a journey into the spiritual world of those he has so often visited, and does so with a striking sensitivity to their theological world and fractured political milieu. Much more than a travel book, this volume is more truly a whole spiritual education.'

SARAH COAKLEY, Norris-Hulse Professor of Divinity,
University of Cambridge

'This remarkable book helps its readers not only to learn about the Ethiopian Orthodox Church – its history, theology and spirituality – but also to live its amazing journey over the centuries. John Binns has poured all his experience and deep love of the church into his volume, which is unique in its breadth, scope and sympathy. I cannot recommend it highly enough.'

MOUNEER HANNA ANIS, Archbishop of the Episcopal/Anglican
Diocese of Egypt with North Africa and the Horn of Africa;
Primate of the Episcopal/Anglican Province of Jerusalem
and the Middle East

THE ORTHODOX CHURCH OF ETHIOPIA

A History

JOHN BINNS

LONDON • NEW YORK • OXFORD • NEW DELHI • SYDNEY

T&T CLARK
Bloomsbury Publishing Plc
50 Bedford Square, London, WC1B 3DP, UK
1385 Broadway, New York, NY 10018, USA
29 Earlsfort Terrace, Dublin 2, Ireland

BLOOMSBURY, T&T CLARK and the T&T Clark logo are trademarks of Bloomsbury Publishing Plc

First published in Great Britain 2017 by I.B. Tauris & Co.

A catalogue record for this book is available from the British Library.

A catalog record for this book is available from the Library of Congress.

ISBN: HB: 978-1-7845-3695-4
PB: 978-0-5676-9502-4
ePDF: 978-1-7867-3037-4
eBook: 978-1-7867-2037-5

Typeset in Stone Serif by OKS Prepress Services, Chennai, India

To

Sue

William and Sally

Thomas and Joshua

Contents

List of Illustrations

MAPS

FIGURES (All images courtesy of the author)

TABLES

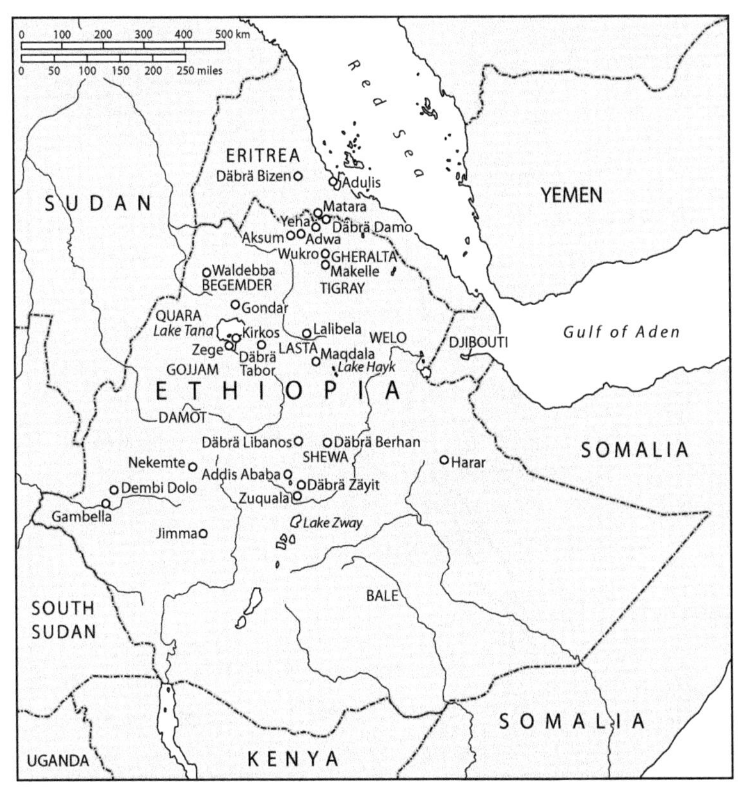

MAP 1 Map of Ethiopia

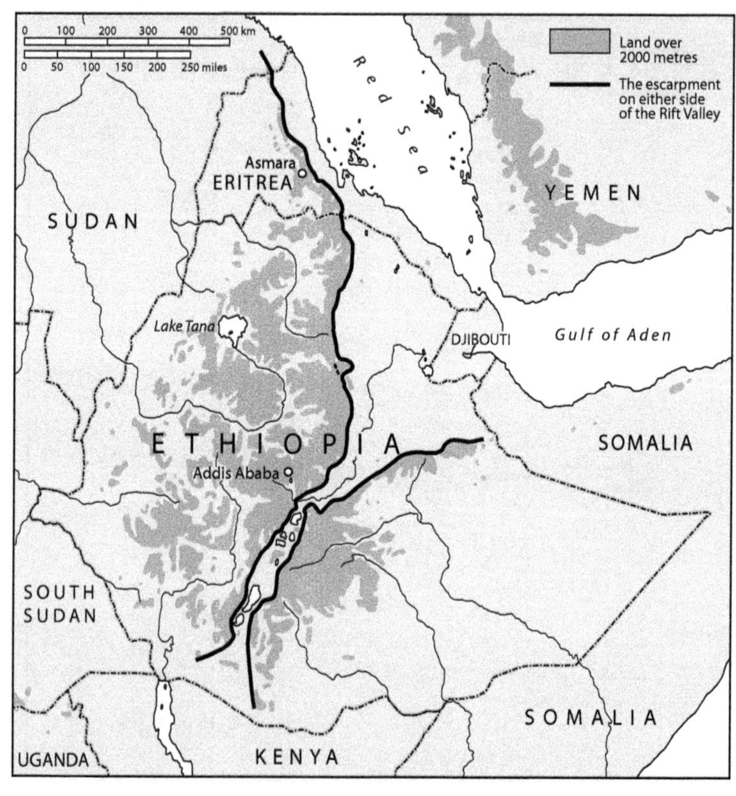

MAP 2 Map of high ground in Ethiopia

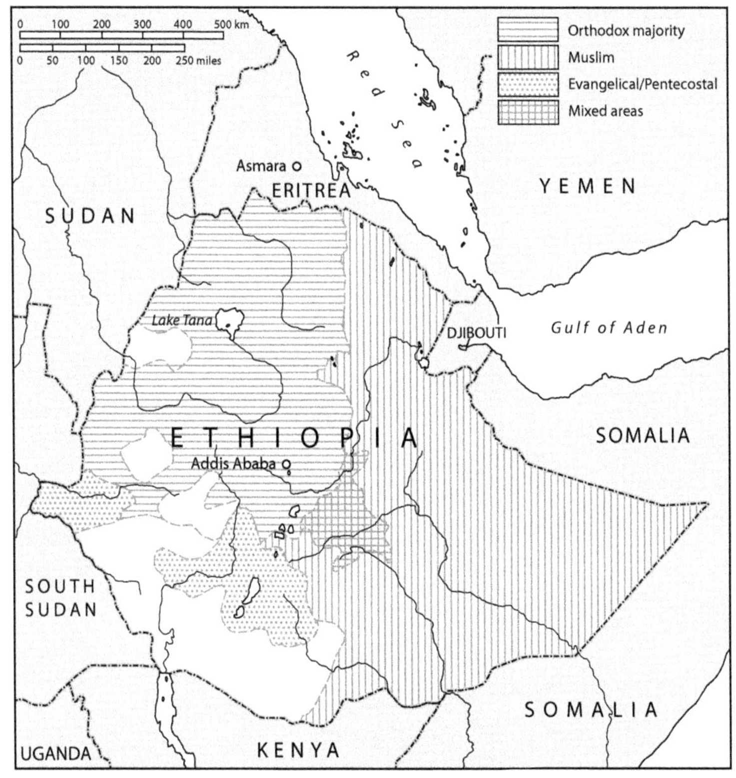

MAP 3 Map of religion in Ethiopia

Acknowledgements

The first day I spent in Ethiopia was Christmas Day in 1993. Ethiopia was one of eleven countries I was visiting while carrying out research for a study of the history of the Christian Orthodox Churches. I had talked to many monks, married priests and lay people, had worshipped at countless liturgies and been amazed at the underlying unity of faith along with many very diverse ways of living it out. I thought I knew Orthodox Christianity – at least a little – and would be on familiar ground. But it became immediately and startlingly clear to me that Ethiopia was different. It did not fit easily into categories I was used to. I went to churches – and there were many of them; I talked to anyone who would explain their church to me – and they were generous with their time; I absorbed the atmosphere of this generous and surprising country. From this experience this research project took shape. My purpose was to explore and describe a rich and unexpected tradition of Orthodox Christianity.

Since that first Christmas visit, I have returned most years, and have carried out three longer research projects. These included a three-month visit to Gondar where I spent many hours with teachers and students in traditional church schools and a further three-month visit meeting people from various churches to discover more about the contemporary situation. The people I met and got to know have provided much of the material in Chapters 8 and 10.

There are many people who have shared in creating this account – although of course they can't be held responsible for my failures to understand. My special thanks to my guide and collaborator Melaka

Selam (a title meaning Messenger of Peace) Qumelachew Muluneh, who has given me generous support, and to his family Kassanesh, Lidiya and Selamawit who always welcome me to their home; Ato Mulugeta Gebru whose leadership of the Jerusalem Children and Community Development Organisation, with which I have worked through this period, has been nothing short of inspirational; Dom Colin Battell OSB who was then chaplain to St Matthews Anglican Chaplaincy and introduced me to the country; and to Professor David Frost, former Principal of the Institute of Orthodox Christian Studies Cambridge, where I was appointed Visiting Professor. There are many others who have guided and advised me and shared their knowledge and wisdom with me. They include Ralph Lee, then of Trinity Theological College Addis Ababa; Bishop Grant leMarquand, Anglican Bishop of the Horn of Africa, and Bishop Mouneer Anis in Cairo and Bishop Andrew Proud; Ayele Tarakegn whose researches have taken him to all corners of the country; Peter Jones, Director of Partners for Change Ethiopia; Clive Oppenheimer, fellow traveller; the teachers and students of Gondar whom I pestered with questions, including Sisay Molla, Hailemariam Dessalegn, Mamher Nekatabab, Yeneta Gebre Mika'el, and I especially revere the memory of Mamher Le'ul, a gentle and wise teacher who was tragically murdered a few months after I had known him. While I was researching this book I was serving as Vicar of Great St Mary's, the University Church in Cambridge. The Bishop of Ely Stephen Conway and colleagues at the church have been sympathetic and patient in encouraging me to persist in combining work in Ethiopia with parish ministry in central Cambridge. I have also enjoyed and valued my contacts with Alex Wright, Sara Magness and their colleagues at I.B.Tauris, and hope that they are as pleased as I am to see this project through to a conclusion.

The person who has been most affected by my long-term commitment to this project and to the people of Ethiopia and to whom I am most grateful is my wife, Sue, and dedicating this book to her and to William and Sally, Thomas and Joshua, is a small recognition of how much they have given me over the years.

Note on Transliteration

A book on Ethiopian history has to address the problem of writing. There are over 250 characters in the Ethiopian writing system, called *fedäl,* which is based on syllables rather than single letters. There are seven vowel sounds, which are called orders, and I use diacritical marks to distinguish two to show how these words are spoken.

First order: symbol is 'ä'; this is 'a' as in care.
Second order: symbol 'u'; this is 'u' as in prudent.
Third order: symbol 'i'; this is 'i' as in ravine.
Fourth order: symbol 'a'; this is 'a' as in father.
Fifth order: symbol 'é'; this is 'e' as in prey.
Sixth order: symbol 'e'; this is a short vowel often hardly sounded, like the 'i' in sit or 'e' in horses.
Seventh order: symbol 'o'; this is 'o' as in go.

I do not distinguish the various different consonants since the diacritical marks most frequently used are not likely to be familiar.

I do not use these marks for the vowels in cases where an Anglicised equivalent is familiar, or for most place names which a reader may have become familiar with in guide books or maps. So I use Addis Ababa rather than Addis Abäba; and Haile Sellassie rather than Haylä Selassé.

Ethiopian people are given a name, to which they add the name of their father. There are no surnames or family names. So I will refer to the scholar Taddesse whose father's name was Tamrat as Taddesse Tamrat, or just Taddesse, rather than Tamrat, T.

I hope this solution combines accessibility for a general reader with reasonable accuracy for those more familiar with Amharic, as well as introducing some of the features of Ethiopian speech.

Abbreviations

AÉ	*Annales d'Éthiopie*
CSCO	Corpus Scriptorum Christianorum Orientalium
EA	*Encyclopedia Aethiopica*
JEthSt	*Journal of Ethiopian Studies*
PG	Patrologia Graeca
PL	Patrologia Latina

INTRODUCTION

A Tradition of Faith

The Ethiopian Church began its life a thousand years before the birth of Christ. At that time the queen from Ethiopia came to Jerusalem to visit King Solomon. She was amazed at his wisdom, and stayed listening to all he said. When she returned to Ethiopia she brought with her the books of the Old Testament. Before the time of Solomon the people of Ethiopia worshipped God but now they had the books to guide them.

Menelek was in the womb of the queen. He was born and grew up. When he was twenty years old he went to visit his father in Jerusalem. All who knew him were amazed at his wisdom. When the time came for him to return Solomon asked the people of Israel whether he should go back alone or whether he should give him honour and support by sharing authority with him. The people of Israel recommended that he should be given support as he was chosen by God. So he returned with the Ark of the Covenant going with him and accompanied by 318 church scholars, who also brought with them the holy books of the Old Testament.

They took the Ark to the monastery of Tana Kirqos – because at that time there was a synagogue there and there was sacrifice according to the rule of the laws. It remained at Tana Kirkos for five hundred years and then it was taken to Aksum. So for 950 years worship was according to the Old Testament. Then Christ was born. This took place 5500 years after the creation of the world.

After Christ was born Herod sent his soldiers to kill the newborn king. Mary and Joseph and the child fled to Egypt. The angels Gabriel, Michael and Urael helped them and so they arrived in Egypt. After a while in Egypt they continued to Ethiopia led by a pillar of light. Jesus showed to his mother Aksum, Waldebba, Mahabere Selassie and Tana Kirqos. They stayed for six months at Kirqos where the people respected them greatly, and provided all they needed for their stay. The marks of the feet of Christ can still be seen in the rock at Tana Kirqos. These are still there to this day. The holy family also visited many holy monasteries, Däbrä Libanos, Zuquala, led by a pillar of light. Holy people were living in monasteries.

Jesus told Mary that in Ethiopia there are holy places and hospitable people. Mary loved Ethiopia and asked her son to give it to her as a tithe offering – or *asrat*. Ever since this covenant there has been a great love for Mary by the people of Ethiopia.

Every year Ethiopian people used to go to Jerusalem. One year a eunuch from the court of the queen went to Jerusalem and was baptised by the apostle Philip. He returned to Ethiopia and the apostle Matthew also went to Ethiopia and brought the gospel to the people. It was in AD 43 that Christianity came to Ethiopia.

Some years later a Syrian merchant came to Ethiopia. He was shipwrecked and come to the court of the kings Abreha and Atsbeha. He brought with him the books of the New Testament because until then the people only had the Old Testament books. This was in 341. Then Frumentius went to Egypt where he was made bishop by St Athanasius who sent him to teach the people of Ethiopia.

Then in 457 the nine Syrian Saints came. The people of Ethiopia were hospitable and welcomed them warmly. The king received them as guests, and they preached all over the country, bringing the gospel to all places, and also built up many monasteries.

Among their followers was Yared. He composed music, prepared *qené* and expounded the Bible. One day he was singing to King Gäbrä Mäsqäl. As he sang the king lifted his stick which had a cross on the top and a spear at the bottom. He lifted it and then set it to the ground. As he did this it pierced his foot but he was so caught up in the music that he did not feel this.

This is the story of how the Christian faith came to Ethiopia. It is narrated by a distinguished scholar of the church as we sit in a small flat in Addis Ababa not far from the Patriarchate. As he tells it, I'm aware that he stands in a long tradition which has passed the story through generations and centuries. It's rooted in history but has been enriched by the insights and the prayers of those who have passed it on. It's a story not only of a church but of a nation. It gives to Ethiopia, that people inhabiting a mountainous area in East Africa, an identity and a sense of a place in the purposes and choice of God.

It's a story which shows that Ethiopia was formed out of three main experiences. There is the beginning of a monarchy which traces its origin back to the Old Testament King Solomon. Then there is its Semitic roots which gave it a language, spoken by the people who brought the faith from the Middle East. Then there is its Christian faith, which penetrated the country over centuries. So monarchy, language and faith constituted the state which survived and expanded in the high mountainous plateau of the Horn of Africa.

This story was told and retold not only by the Ethiopians themselves but also by foreign observers and historians. Its approach is summarised by Edward Ullendorff in his review of Ethiopian life and history, who wrote of 'Abyssinians proper, the carriers of the historical civilisation of Semitized Ethiopia [...] who live in the central and northern highlands'.[1] These were the unchangeable characteristics which made Ethiopia what it was. The biographer of the nineteenth-century emperor Yohannes, Zewde Gebre Sellassie, includes this assessment: 'It is difficult for Ethiopian commentators or foreign historians to imagine the geography, religion or politics of the country in any other setting but monarchy.'[2] He would have assumed the use of the Amharic language and adherence to the Orthodox Church.

But the inconceivable happened. Zewde's book was published in 1975, and in the preceding year an army coup had toppled the emperor Haile Sellassie, and so brought to an end a dynasty which had ruled Ethiopia since 1270, and traced its roots back several centuries before that. It brought about a new form of government and changed Ethiopia. A recent survey of modern Ethiopia begins by reflecting on this event: '1974 was the year of destiny (and) for many lovers of Ethiopian culture, 1974 was the year of doom. King Solomon had died a second death and Ethiopia had landed in the modern world with a painful thud. Seldom has a date been so significant in the history of a people and of a nation.'[3] A further stage of the move into modernism came in 1991 when another new government took power.

A policy of ethnic federalism asserted the place of a variety of national and ethnic groups, and their languages, in the new modern Ethiopia. At the same time, a new constitution established freedom of religion, and all churches and faiths were recognised and given the right to worship and to carry out a life and mission. The state of Ethiopia defined by its monarchy, language and faith had been dismantled. The Ethiopian Orthodox Tawehedo Church found that it was no longer a national church but one of a number of religious communities in a multi-ethnic republic.[4]

The new state needed a new story. Or rather, since the full variety of ethnic groups and faith communities gained a new recognition and place in society, it needed new stories. These were provided by researchers who wrote the histories of other ethnic groups. Then the systems of Islam, Evangelicalism and Pentecostalism, and traditional religions as well, gained a new position and became the subject of many studies.

Alongside these political changes came a renewed interest in the study of the large, populous and changing nation in the Horn of Africa. The discipline of Ethiopian studies has grown and extended. The Centre Française des Études Éthiopiennes was set up in its present form in 1991, and occupies a peaceful site in the Kebena district of Addis Ababa. Then the Hiob Ludolf Centre was established in Hamburg in 2002, which has published much new research, including the five-volume *Encyclopedia Aethiopica*, which can only be described as magisterial. The acceleration in the process of research has made new understandings possible, questioned many previously accepted assumptions and submitted material and evidence to critical scientific examination.[5]

The texts and other evidence for the history of the church have benefitted from this historical analysis. An example of this approach, although not by a researcher at either of the institutions mentioned, is the series of articles and books by the historian Stuart Munro Hay. Munro Hay placed written sources from the medieval period alongside other forms of evidence, such as land grants and coin finds, and concluded that the accounts of some of the people and events which had been seen as having foundational importance in fact rested on flimsy historical evidence and had to be treated with great caution.[6] This raised questions about the story of the church, and he has proposed a more tentative approach and concluded that much of the record of older events may be the product of later ages, and so less reliable than was once thought. The rich tradition set out for me by the scholar of the church has been examined with newly critical historical analysis.

A different kind of challenge to the story of the church came from authors from Western church traditions. Much of the recent scholarship about the church has been written by scholars who have been associated with Catholic and Evangelical churches. These begin with the presupposition that there's something wrong with the Orthodox Church of Ethiopia, which would be put right if either the church accepted the authority of Rome or, alternatively, allowed reform according to biblical Protestant principles. Here, to give just one example, is the judgment of Jeronimo Lobo, a Portuguese Jesuit who lived in Ethiopia in the first half of the seventeenth century, and who wrote of 'the gospel that they [the Ethiopians] still preserve, although mingled with an infinite tangle of weeds of Jewish and Muhammadan errors and countless heresies, amid thorns that smother it so much'.[7] These presuppositions were bound to affect the recounting of the story.

In the pages that follow I have set out to write a history of the Ethiopian Church which presents both the historic traditions which sustained it through its long period of monarchy, and also which explores how the church has responded to the challenges of its sudden arrival in a modern world.

There are ten sections, each relating to a specific period of history. Each of these begins with a short passage to introduce the historical events. This is followed by a longer discussion which shows how the church developed in that period. As well as describing how the church took shape during the period under review, I draw on examples from other periods, to show that the tradition took shape through the full course of its history, and provided the distinctive characteristics which have continued to shape its life and identity. I also include stories of the people and the things they did, which are not only colourful and dramatic but give a sense of the passions and hopes which moved the personalities involved.

These show that the church in Ethiopia represents an important and distinctive strand of Christian history. It demonstrates the form that the Christian faith took in this environment which lies on the frontier of the Semitic Middle East and the vast stretch of sub-Saharan Africa. It is, to use a cumbersome but accurate phrase, the only pre-colonial Christian church in sub-Saharan Africa. It is not, like some Christian traditions of Africa and Asia, a historical relic, but it remains a large and thriving community with about 40 million members. The churches of Africa have grown fast during the last fifty years. This new prominence of the Christian faith over the continent gives renewed importance to the experience of its only traditional church.

CHAPTER 1

Place and Idea: Identifying Ethiopia

THE PLACE: A GEOGRAPHY AND A HISTORY

The Federal Democratic Republic of Ethiopia is a nation state located in the Horn of Africa. It is surrounded by Sudan, Kenya, Somalia, Somaliland, Djibouti and Eritrea. It covers an area of over a million square kilometres. It has a rapidly growing population, which has now passed 90 million inhabitants, and so is the second most populous country in Africa, after Nigeria.[1] It is a land of contrasts, divided between a high plateau, with a spectacular mountain landscape in the north and west, and some of the lowest and hottest regions of the world in the south and east. For many it is still remembered as a place of poverty, war and famine, with images imprinted on the conscience of the world during the tragic years of 1984–5 and the international response which followed. But these are now being replaced by reports of economic growth, with some figures showing it to be the third fastest-growing economy in the world.

The Ethiopia described by these statistics is a new country, with its current borders set out in the late nineteenth century through a series of treaties with the colonial powers of Europe. It reached this point after a long and sometimes turbulent history. The first reference to Ethiopia as a nation comes from the fourth century. The king of the city state of Aksum, near the coast of the Red Sea was Ezana. A Greek inscription describes him as *basileus aithiopion* – king of Ethiopians. Ezana himself became Christian and this set in place the history of the Christian kingdom of Ethiopia, which was to be maintained until the fall of Haile Selassie in 1974. The kingdom of Ethiopia was characterised by its monarchy, its Semitic language and its Christian Orthodox faith. Its extent and location shifted in reaction to the changing political circumstances and the balance of military power. It was forced by the rise of Islam away from the coastal plain and towards the interior; then the restored Solomonic kings who reigned from the late twelfth to early sixteenth centuries expanded the size of the kingdom to the south. There was a brief but devastating invasion by the Muslim armies of Ahmad ibn Ibrahim al Ghazi known as 'Grañ' the left-handed, between 1527 and 1543, which reduced the size of the kingdom and threatened its continuing independent existence. This was followed by a more prolonged expansion by Oromo tribesmen, which also reduced the power of Christian Ethiopia. The modern state of Ethiopia was formed as part of the imperialist division of Africa in the late nineteenth century when the invading Italians were defeated and the emperor extended the borders to their greatest extent. The region below the high ridge of Entoto in Shewa with its hot springs grew into the capital city of Addis Ababa or 'new flower'. Founded in the 1880s, it is the third highest – and one of the most recently founded – capital cities in the world. Ethiopia had become a modern kingdom, with agreed borders, and a complex ethnic mix with over eighty languages spoken. Thus after a process of expansion, contraction, then renewed expansion and southward movement, the modern Ethiopia came into being.

This kingdom grew in the mountains, which remained its heartland even after it extended into the plains. Its location at a high altitude led to its importance, not just in the history of the region but in the history of the human race. These mountains and their significance take us back beyond the city state of Aksum to the beginnings of the human story.

Mountains matter, and these mountains have shaped the history of Ethiopia and of the people who inhabit them. Most of the African continent is flat. The vast majority of its land surface is less than 1000 m above sea level. Only a small part is higher than 2000 m, just 1.35 per cent, and of this only 0.1 per cent is higher than 3000 m above sea level. Most of this African high ground is in Ethiopia. Although Ethiopia comprises only 4 per cent of the African continent, it contains half of the land above 2000 m and four fifths of the land above 3000 m. This has led to the favourable conditions which enabled the human race to begin and then to thrive. Many disease-bearing insects do not survive at high altitudes, and as a result malaria and bilharzia are absent from the highlands of Ethiopia, as is the tsetse fly, which ravages the cattle herds of pastoralists in the lower-lying areas. As well as being a healthy place to live it is also fertile. High land attracts rain. Hot damp air is blown inland from the sea, and while it brings heat and discomfort on the coastal plains, it falls as rain when it comes into contact with land at higher altitudes. The monsoon winds of the Indian Ocean to the east reverse direction in the autumn, and this change brings a second rainy season, so that farmers can expect two harvests in a single year.[2]

To add to these natural advantages, the Ethiopian highlands are surrounded by steep escarpments to the north, west and east; and dry desert land to the south. These have made it inaccessible to invaders, and it has been a well-defined and well-defended highland enclave for many millions of years. The natural frontiers have set the high plateau apart from the lower regions around it and enabled its kingdom to remain distinct and to survive. There have been a succession of peoples who have attempted invasion – Muslims and Oromo in the sixteenth, British and Sudanese Mahdists in the nineteenth, and Italians in the twentieth centuries. But these incursions have generally been short-lived and the Christian Amhara kingdom of Ethiopia was able to withdraw, regroup and re-establish itself.

In these mountains, both animals and plants have thrived. Elephant and lion, leopard and zebra, as well as many other African animals, birds and plants have flourished in the high ground of Ethiopia during its history. Some species have survived only in Ethiopia. It is estimated that 12 per cent of the East African region's mammal species and 3 per cent of its birds are found only in Ethiopia.[3]

Many plants are endemic to Ethiopia. Ethiopians are especially proud of their coffee, a familiar name for a plant which is grown in, among other places, Ethiopia. The Kaffa district provided the name by which the plant is known in many parts of the world, although, strangely, not including Ethiopia itself, where it is called *bunna*. It is generally agreed that the beans of this plant were first harvested and domesticated in Ethiopia. Then there is *tef*, a form of millet, with tiny seeds, each of which is smaller than a pinhead, with one hundred and fifty *tef* seeds equal in size to one grain of wheat. Its yield is lower than other crops, but it is suited to the high terrain and can germinate when other crops fail. It is highly nutritious, and a single daily portion provides enough protein to sustain a reasonably healthy diet. Today *tef* is grown throughout the highlands and gives that gentle undulating green character to the landscape during the growing season. When harvested it can be mixed with water, left to ferment, and then cooked to form the wide flat pancake, *enjära,* the staple food of the Ethiopians.

Enjära and coffee are the great facilitators of Ethiopian social interaction. The coffee ceremony is a regular domestic ceremony at the end of the working day or as a welcome to guests. Coffee beans are roasted, ground and boiled on a carpet of grass scattered around the charcoal stove, and brewed in the traditional *jerber* coffee pot, surrounded by the perfume of incense in the air. It is served in small cups, with three cups drunk before the group breaks up. The eating of *enjära* is also of a part of highland 'culture'. The large flat pancakes are placed on a basket, called a *mesob,* served with piles of spicy sauce or *wat,* piled on the *enjära,* and thus form a shared communal dish. People will refer to the eating of *enjära* as their culture, and see it as an essential part of ethnic identity.

This highland culture belongs in a long history of human development. A little over three million years ago, a young woman was living in the verdant forest which then covered the high plateau. She was 122 cm in height and weighed 8 kg. She was able to stand upright and, while she could still climb trees, she had to find a safe place where she could sleep by night – unlike other carnivores who used the cover of darkness for hunting. By day she foraged for food. After she had died her bones – or to be precise about 40 per cent of her bones – were preserved over millennia and were discovered in 1974 in the Afar depression north-east of Addis Ababa by a team led by Donald Johanson of the Cleveland Museum, Ohio. He called her Lucy since they happened to be playing the Beatles' song 'Lucy in the Sky with Diamonds' when they found her, but Ethiopians are more respectful and call her *Dinkinesh* meaning 'you are wonderful'. Her technical classification is *Australopithecus afarensis*, and she was then the earliest known example of a hominid, and is a candidate for the position of the ancestor for the human race. A plaster cast can be viewed in the National Museum in Addis Ababa. Older hominid remains have been discovered in Ethiopia and elsewhere since then, but *Dinkinesh* remains as a moving reminder that we, as humans, originated and then evolved, in Ethiopia. As was put in a recent TV broadcast by Brian Cox, every one of us has an Ethiopian ancestor if we go back a mere 200,000 years.[4] Or, as the archaeologist David Phillipson notes, 'Ethiopia has the longest archeological record of any country in the world.'[5]

This high mountain land was the place where the human race began. Later it was the backdrop to the growth of the oldest written culture in sub-Saharan Africa, and the centre of one of the great empires of the ancient world, an evolving state and a church.

ETHIOPIA IN LITERATURE

The name Ethiopia had been used for well over a millennium before it was associated with the land we know today as Ethiopia. It is not surprising that the location to which the name was applied was vague and non-specific, since the pre-scientific geographical picture of the world lacked accurate definition. People thought that there was a land bridge connecting Africa and Asia – as indeed there once was. The word Ethiopia was used by the Greeks, and is found in Homer. It occurs in several places in the *Iliad* and *Odyssey*, and later in Herodotus' histories. The Greek word *aithiops* means, literally, 'burnt face', and was applied to people living over a wide area. An Ethiopian could be anyone with dark skin who lived south of Egypt, and so Ethiopia could be Arabia, or India, or Africa south of the Sahara. Some medieval maps show an eastern Ethiopia south of the Nile and a western Ethiopia to the south of Mauretania. By the sixteenth century, the location of Ethiopia was narrowing down to be directed to the Upper Nile and Nubia, but it was not until the late nineteenth century that the name was firmly attached to the modern state. Since there had previously been no specific location of Ethiopia, it could be used in a general way to describe a kind of people. It is more accurate to describe Ethiopia as 'a concept rather than a geographical location', an idea rather than a place.[6]

Ethiopia was not the only name which could be used of this rather broad area inhabited by dark-skinned people. Some maps and texts prefer to speak of Abyssinia, which was applied to the same area until the nineteenth century. This alternative title can be traced back to Arabic/Sabaean inscriptions of the first millennium BC. Here there is a name written in the un-vocalised form HBST, which became Habashat or *al-Habash* in Arabic. This eventually became Abyssinia. The word is often understood as deriving from an Arabic root meaning mixed, although this derivation is questioned. The association with mixture could be derived from either the composite racial character of people living in the mountains or the variety of ethnic groups in the area. The name Abyssinia was used to refer to present-day Ethiopia until the mid-nineteenth century, and the last occurrence of the word in a formal political context is the person called the *negus habashat* or king of Abyssinia in a treaty between Ethiopia and England signed in 1843.

Another term which started life as a general description and later adhered to a specific place was Sudan. Sudan is an Arabic term meaning black. Arabic texts write of *Bildad es Sudan* or land of the blacks to apply to a large swathe of western and central Africa, south of the Sahara. As late as the nineteenth century, this general title was used by a group of American Evangelicals who founded a missionary society in 1873 to bring the gospel to the people of Africa, to the 'great Soudan'. They called their society the Sudan Interior Mission, or SIM, and set up its first headquarters in Nigeria. They later changed the name to Serving in Mission. In due course the name Sudan was taken by the new African state formed in 1956.

The word Ethiopia evokes what it means to be African. Travellers from the West have been drawn by the attractions of Africa, and they often expressed this mysterious magnetism in use of the word Ethiopia. Nineteenth-century missionaries felt themselves called to evangelise Africa, and for them it was often Ethiopia. The missionary T.J. Hutchinson published an account of his endeavours in 1861 entitled *Ten years wandering among the Ethiopians from Senegal to Gabon*, and in 1885 Daniel Flickinger wrote *Ethiopia or Thirty years of missionary life in western Africa* – he meant Sierra Leone.[7]

The names Ethiopia, Abyssinia and Sudan began as general descriptions. They indicated that unknown space south of the Sahara where people with burnt faces or black features, or mixed origins, live. For those using it in Europe, the name Ethiopia resonated with a sense of mystery, antiquity, riches and abundant natural resources. The word Ethiopia retained this evocative character and came to be used in the last two centuries to articulate and express the growing hopes and longings of those born on the continent and those who came to it, as a sense of African identity was discovered.

These longings and aspirations have been reinforced by historical events. As Europeans advanced over Africa occupying large areas as colonies, Italians began to extend their power over northern Ethiopia. In January 1896 the Ethiopian king Menelek advanced northwards with his huge army of 100,000 soldiers, and dependents, until they came to the mountains around Adwa in Tigray. They faced a much smaller but better-equipped Italian force, with less than 8500 Italian troops and 10,700 Eritreans. Both sides delayed the battle as long as they could, partly because the terrain gave the advantage to the defender, but also, from the Italian point of view, because Menelek faced huge difficulties in supplying and feeding such a large army. When the Italians finally advanced on 1 March, the battle was over in three hours. The Italians divided into three columns and advanced on the Ethiopians, but one lost its way, and they found themselves on level ground with attacks launched by the Ethiopian army who had stayed in the hills and so had the advantage of height. Seventy per cent of the Italian army was either killed, wounded or captured, leaving it unable to continue the campaign. It is estimated that Menelek lost between 4000 and 7000 troops, leaving his army as an effective force while what was left of the Italian army withdrew.[8] As a result of this engagement at Adwa, Ethiopia became the only part of Africa which retained its independence from the imperialist powers of Europe.

When the nationalist movements across Africa slowly gained independence it was Ethiopia they looked to. The Organisation for African Unity, now called the African Union, was set up in Addis Ababa in 1963, and its headquarters are still there. Eight of the newly independent states of Africa favoured the Ethiopian colours of green, red and yellow when selecting a design for their national flag.

ETHIOPIA IN THE BIBLE

Religious faith is bound up in this ideal of Ethiopia. Ethiopians are people of faith, with a special relationship with the gods, and possessing qualities of virtue and justice. This is a claim made by Ethiopians today who often consider themselves to be a naturally religious people. Census findings show that over 95 per cent of Ethiopians affirm that they have a religious faith, and many affirm its importance to them.

This religious claim is traced back to classical times. Homer, in the *Iliad*, describes a primeval human ancestor, Aithiops, who lived in the far east of known lands. He was a perfect man with a special relationship with the gods. Zeus led other gods to make a twelve-day visit to his descendants 'the blameless Ethiopians', and later, in the *Odyssey*, Poseidon 'lingered delighted at the banquet side' of the Ethiopians. The Greek historian Diodorus Siculus, writing in the first century, said that the Ethiopians considered that they were the first nation to worship the gods, a view which was repeated by others. Later, Lactantius Placidus, writing in the fifth century, wrote that 'the Ethiopians are certainly the justest men and for that reason the gods leave their abode frequently to visit them'.[9] It was a reputation which has stayed with them, and is repeated in later literature. Samuel Johnson's Prince Rasselas was upright and, like the Ethiopians of Homer, just. One of his friends says 'oppression is, in the Abissinian domain neither frequent nor tolerated'. Ethiopians often claim not only to have a high level of religious commitment, but also that they have always believed in God.[10] Faith was there from the beginning and it was gradually refined and directed until the proclamation of Christ completed the process.

The Bible also testifies to the faith of Ethiopians. There are many references to Ethiopia in the Bible – all but one of them in the Old Testament. The name Ethiopia, when used in English translations, is taken from the Greek Septuagint translation, and is equivalent to the Hebrew Cush. The most frequently cited reference to Ethiopia is the psalm verse, 'Let Ethiopia hasten to stretch out its hands to God' (Psalm 68.31). This shows that the faithfulness of the Ethiopian Church is prophesied by the psalmist David, and as a result this chosen nation is placed decisively within the divine plan.

An early genealogical passage links Ethiopia and Arabia. A section of the first book of the Bible, Genesis, provides a record of the names of the descendants of Noah. 'These are the descendants of Noah's sons, Shem, Ham and Japheth [...]. The descendants of Ham: Cush, Egypt, Put and Canaan. The descendants of Cush: Seba, Havilah, Sabtah, Raamah, Sheba and Sabteca' (Genesis 10.1, 6–7). The clue to making sense of this obscure list of names is to recognise that they are also names of places and that the genealogy makes connections between peoples and presents a pattern linking separated parts of the human family. The list of names shows a connection between Canaan, which is in modern Israel, and Cush, Egypt and Put, three regions of Africa. Then there is a further connection made between Cush, or the Hebrew Ethiopia, and the regions of Seba, Havilah, Sabtah, Raamah, Sheba and Sabteca, which are in Arabia. All this suggests that the compiler of the list knew something about Africa, and thought that the people of Asia were descended from the people of Africa. His contention is confirmed by modern linguistic studies which show that Semitic languages were first spoken in Africa, and then moved across the Red Sea into Arabia and Asia Minor probably around 2000 BC.[11] From there Semitic speakers migrated back to Africa a thousand years later. There is a further passage which makes the same connection between north-east Africa and Arabia. It recounts a military alliance between Arabia and Ethiopia against Judah. 'The Lord aroused against Jehoram the anger of the Philistines and of the Arabs who are near the Ethiopians. These came up against Judah and invaded it' (2 Chronicles 21.16–17).[12]

The most celebrated of the biblical characters connected with this region is the Queen of Sheba, a place included in the genealogy just mentioned, or the queen from the south. She visited King Solomon, an expedition to be remembered and described as an essential foundational moment in the religious life of Ethiopia.

Two more biblical Ethiopians are encountered in the pages of the Bible. There is Ebed-Melech, a servant in the court of King Zedekiah who is part of the story of the prophet Jeremiah. After the prophet has displeased the king and is thrown into a pit, Ebed Melech shows him compassion and support (Jeremiah 38.7–13). Then there is the Ethiopian eunuch, a court official who meets the apostle Philip and is baptised by him (Acts 8.26–27). He is described as 'an official of the Candace queen of the Ethiopians'. The title Candace means 'mother of the king' and is a title of the Meroitic kings of Nubia. It indicates that he came from what is today Sudan.[13] This is the only occurrence of the word Ethiopia in the New Testament.

Islam too had its pious Ethiopians. Bilal ibn Rabah is recorded as one of the first companions of the prophet and was renowned for the beauty of his voice. Although he was a slave born in Mecca his mother was Ethiopian, and he was remembered for his African features.

While none of the famous biblical Ethiopians can plausibly be considered to have lived in the land mass which is modern Ethiopia, they are Ethiopians in that more general sense which was current at that time of people living in the area south of Egypt and bordering on the Red Sea. They show that there was good communication between the Israelites of the Old Testament and the peoples of the Red Sea region. This common heritage is reflected in the Ethiopian tradition that the Queen of Sheba was in fact queen of both Saba and Aksum. We do not need to demonstrate the precise origin of these figures to show that Ethiopia, and the region around, was part of the cultural world of the Bible.

CONCLUSION

This account shows that there are many Ethiopias. These are both physical and conceptual, making Ethiopia both an idea and a place. As a place it is the land mass which benefitted from a congruence of favourable physical features. It became a kingdom which produced a written language and literature, and a Christian church. Ethiopia also has a much wider meaning to refer to more general characteristics. Ethiopia as idea arises out of the use of the word as a general name for anyone living south of Egypt, and so can be appropriated by those who want to express the rich character and identity of the country south of the Sahara. Its presence in classical and biblical literature also conveys a sense of faith and an instinctive closeness to the divine. These different Ethiopias have converged in the mountains in the Horn of Africa to form a culture and identity of a large and strategic nation state with a long religious and Christian tradition of faith. This conjunction produced a church, and a form of Christianity which was different from that in any part of the world. The ancient Greeks who pointed to the creativity of Ethiopians in forming religious rites and practices may have been given prophetic foresight of what was to come.

CHAPTER 2

Semitic and Cushitic: A Meeting of Cultures

HISTORY: PRE-AKSUMITE CIVILISATION

Two ethnic and cultural groups converged to occupy the coastal regions of northern Ethiopia during the first half of the first millennium BC, and from this meeting a civilisation was formed. The two groups who encountered one another were, first, farmers, speaking a Cushitic language and living in the fertile area of north Tigray and south Eritrea, and then, second, new arrivals coming from the north of the Red Sea and speaking a Semitic language.

Both these two cultural strands can be traced back to a common origin in the area covered today by Ethiopia and Sudan. Some time before 2000 BC the people of this region were speakers of a language group which linguists call Afro-Asiatic or Hamitic-Semitic. This larger group split into several smaller language families. One of these language groups was Semitic, and the Semitic language speakers then separated again. Some remained in their region of origin in Africa while others migrated into Asia, either across the Red Sea or by land through Egypt and Sinai. Meanwhile the Cushitic branch had stayed in their African homeland and from them the extensive family of Cushitic languages, which include Oromo and Afar, descended. This slow division and dispersion across north-east Africa and into Asia took place over a long period, and by 1000 BC the original proto-Ethiopian unity had become split into these various linguistic groups. The movement of peoples in these centuries forms a background to the conflicts and interactions of the various ethnic groupings which settled the Ethiopian mountains and plains in the historical period in which this ancient civilisation took shape.[1]

From the Semitic language group, several languages spoken in modern Ethiopia have evolved. These can be divided into a northern group of languages which includes Ge'ez (a language which is now only used in the church, as Latin is used in Western churches), Tigre and Tigrinya. The southern group includes Amharic, which has been the dominant language through much of Ethiopian history.

The arrival – or perhaps we should see this as the return – of groups of Semitic speakers from Arabia into the coastal regions of Ethiopia produced the rich cultural mix which is known as pre-Aksumite civilisation. There is archeological evidence for this civilisation in the writing, sculpture, massive architecture and possibly iron smelting, all of which appeared around the same time, showing influence from Arabia. The pre-Aksumite kingdom is described in inscriptions as *Da'amat*, or sometimes as *Da'mat*, and *Saba*. The combination of the two names, including Saba in Arabia, shows the relationships between the communities to the north and south of the Red Sea. Inscriptions are written in a language and script which is related to that of the south Arabian Sabaean and is the ancestor of modern Amharic and Tigrinya characters. Examples of pottery have also been found, and there are some examples of statuary, including a seated female figure dressed in pleated robes, and a throne decorated with carvings of ibex. The best-known monument of this pre-Aksumite culture is the great temple at Yeha, about 25 miles north-east of Aksum. This is a massive structure with walls still standing to a height of 13 m and which is dated to 700 BC.[2]

Pre-Aksumite civilisation arose from the convergence of two strands of what had been one human community of peoples, which had then become separated, and now came to occupy the same territory. At this stage of its history the people were connected not only with the interior of Africa, but also were part of a network of trading relationships connecting the ports along the coasts of the Red Sea. They were part of a maritime trading regional community with Semitic languages spoken and a culture shared.

FIGURE 2.1 The temple at Yeha was built around 700 BC. With walls 13 m in height, this is one of the great monuments to pre-Aksumite civilisation.

THE *KEBRÄ NÄGÄST* – A STORY OF ORIGINS

'We have to remember that the Ethiopian Orthodox Church is very old, and was founded many centuries before the birth of Christ.' This statement – made to me by a deacon working in the Patriarchate in Addis Ababa in the early days of my first visit to Ethiopia and repeated many times since – introduces the subject of the origins of Christianity in Ethiopia.

The comment shows that if we want to understand Christianity in Ethiopia we have to go back to an earlier time, and discover the relationships and connections which linked together the nations of the Middle East region from the beginning, and especially the religious traditions shared by Ethiopia and Israel. The Ethiopian Church is often spoken of as Judaic, a word which avoids the implication of shared beliefs but points to shared religious ideas and customs. A hotly debated question concerns the extent of influence from Judaism, the period when this happened, and the reasons for it.

The foundation narrative of Ethiopian Christianity is a book known as the *Kebrä Nägäst*, or the Glory, or Honour, of Kings. This is a visionary epic which sets before the people of Ethiopia their privileged position and their calling, and makes the claim that there is direct continuity between the Judaism of the Old Testament and the Christianity of modern Ethiopia. This is sometimes expressed by Ethiopians by saying that they became Jewish first at the time of Solomon and then Christian later through the preaching of the apostles.

The *Kebrä Nägäst* asserts that the people of Ethiopia are the chosen people of God. The historian Edward Ullendorff considered its importance for Ethiopians as equivalent to the Old Testament for Jews or the Qur'an for Muslims. It is 'the repository of Ethiopian national and religious feelings [...] perhaps the truest and most genuine expression of Abyssinian Christianity'.[3] It has also been compared to the *Aeneid* in Roman culture, which claims legitimacy for the regime of one country by looking back to the history of another.

The *Kebrä Nägäst* begins its story with the creation of the world and of the first human, Adam, and continues it up to the wars of the Ethiopian King Kaléb in the sixth century. A central section tells the story of Makeda, the queen of Ethiopia, who is identified with both the Queen of Sheba and the queen of the South (Matthew 12.42; Luke 11.31; 1 Kings 10).[4] She hears about King Solomon from a returning merchant and decides to visit him. On arrival, she is amazed at his wisdom and at the wonder of his house. In the biblical account she then returns home and we hear no more about her, but the *Kebrä Nägäst* tells us more. We discover that she is given a dinner by Solomon and then retires for the night. 'Swear', she says to Solomon, 'that you will not take me by force.' Solomon agrees that he will not do so, but on the condition that she, in her turn, swears that she will not take anything from him by force. She in turn agrees and they retire decorously but in the same chamber. Solomon instructs his servants to place a jug of cool water by her bedside and in due course she awakes thirsty since Solomon – in his wisdom – had served salty and spicy food at the meal. She looks carefully at him and sees that he is asleep and so quietly reaches out for the water. But he is dissembling and leaps up to catch her arm. Caught in the act of purloining the water she agrees that the oaths are void and they retire together with the result that a young boy is born. She calls the boy Bayna Lekhem, meaning 'son of the wise', which becomes, in the tradition, Menelek.[5]

Menelek returns with his mother to Ethiopia and when he becomes an adult he visits his father Solomon in Jerusalem. He receives favour in the sight of all and is there crowned king of Ethiopia and given the regnal name of David. As he prepares to return home to Ethiopia, one of his four companions has a dream in which the angel of the Lord appears to him and shows him that it is God's will for the Ark of the Covenant to go to Ethiopia with them. The companion goes to the temple with the angel leading him, the doors open before them and the Ark leaves the temple with them, while they leave in its place a suitably shaped object made out of planks of wood. As they return Menelek does not know what he is taking with him but the people of Jerusalem weep at the passing of God's glory. The Ark is the sign of God's presence which had led the people of Israel from Egypt to the land of Israel and now it leaves Israel and goes to Ethiopia.

Through this narrative the *Kebrä Nägäst* makes bold claims. It demonstrates, first, that the kings of Ethiopia are descended from the Old Testament royal line of David and Solomon, and, arising from that, that the Ark of the Covenant has passed to Ethiopia. These two divine interventions give a unique position to a new chosen people. This passing of divine favour from Israel to Ethiopia is further shown by the moral decline of Solomon in his later years with his marriage to numerous foreign women. At the end of the book, there is a series of interpretations of Old Testament passages which have a strongly anti-Jewish emphasis. These further show how Israel has fallen out of favour, and has been replaced by the new Israel in Africa. Ethiopia's place in the divine economy is described in more detail in a section of the book which narrates how Solomon had three sons. Menelek, the hero of the book, is the senior. Then there is Rehoboam, who succeeded Solomon on the throne of Israel. And there is a third son, Adramis, who married the daughter of Balthasar king of Constantinople. Since Menelek is the eldest, this shows that Ethiopia is pre-eminent over Constantinople, as well as Israel.[6]

The *Kebrä Nägäst* is a lengthy, rambling book, and there has been much discussion over its dating, its purpose and its sources. It encompasses a great sweep of history spanning many centuries, but the text as it is now can be attached to a specific period and set of events. The book ends with a colophon, or finishing touch, added to describe the circumstances of its production. It explains how the *Kebrä Nägäst* took its present form, and dates this redaction to the medieval period. It states that the text went through several versions, from Coptic to Arabic to Ge'ez, and was 'produced' in its final form by a scribe, Yeshaq, with the help of several named collaborators. It mentions the date of the '409th year of mercy'. There are several ways to understand the date of 409. It clearly cannot be 409 in the Ethiopian calendar, which would lead to an impossibly early date. It could refer to the year 409 in the Islamic calendar, which would be equivalent to the Western year 1018. However, there is another and more plausible suggestion that the years of mercy are dated from the Egyptian era of the martyrs, and this Egyptian calendar counts the years in cycles of 532 years, which is the Great Lunar Cycle. A new cycle began in 815. If this was used by the redactor, then the year 409 would take us to 1225, which coincides with the dates of the reign of King Lalibäla in Ethiopia.[7] This dating, even though unclear, enables us to conclude that the *Kebrä Nägäst,* in an Arabic recension, was copied in Ethiopia in the time of King Lalibäla, in the thirteenth century.

The events of this period of Ethiopian history provide a motive for the composition of the book. Ethiopia had been ruled by the Zagwe dynasty, but in 1270 a new line of kings, known as the Solomonic dynasty, came to power with the victory over the Zagwe by Yekuno Amlak.[8] They needed to affirm their claim to be legitimate successors to previous kings.

As well as giving a date, the colophon says that the book was produced at the initiative of prince Ya'ebikä 'Egzi. This prince came from Tigray in the north, and the traditions recounted in the *Kebrä Nägäst* belong in the north, with their emphasis on the city of Aksum and the legitimacy of the Solomonic dynasty. So it is suggested, on this dating, that the new king from the south, who has just asserted his military strength by defeating the Zagwe kings, used the book to claim a legitimacy which was derived from the old traditions of Tigray. It brought together the vibrant militarism of the south with the theological traditions of the north to set the new line of kings on a firm religious and political base.[9] It proved to be a powerful and seductive formula, and persisted until the fall of Haile Selassie 600 years later.

Some scholars have gone further, and argued that the *Kebrä Nägäst* was not only compiled but also composed in the thirteenth century, and so it is a theological fiction composed to provide justification for an opportunistic and usurping warlord.[10] They point to the fact that there is no manuscript evidence for the *Kebrä Nägäst* which dates from before the thirteenth century. This radical interpretation would further suggest that the connection between the Semitic world of the Old Testament and the later Ethiopian kingdom was also an idea devised in that same period, and that any resemblances to Judaism were introduced as part of that process.

This critical approach does not take account of the complex construction of the book and its use of many traditions. While the book itself may have been compiled and redacted in this period, it seems to include a series of sections that are most likely to have drawn on older traditions and to have depended on a variety of sources which come from various periods.

Examination of the structure of the book shows that it can be divided into three parts. First, there is the Queen of Sheba and Menelek narrative; then the later life of Solomon; and finally the collection of Christian, anti-Jewish prophecies.[11] This supports the conclusion that the *Kebrä Nägäst* is a work of several parts, and while the final version belongs in the thirteenth century, some material originated much earlier. The period of the sixth to the seventh centuries provides a plausible background to some of the material. The final chapter tells the story of King Kaléb, who reigned from *c.*500–34, and his son Gäbrä Mäsqäl, who defeated the Jewish king, Dhu Nawwas, in a campaign carried out in southern Arabia, and thus initiated a period of seventy years of Ethiopian rule in this region. If this section of the *Kebrä Nägäst* was written at the time of Kaléb's war, then the events of the time provide a context for the anti-Jewish polemic, since the Ethiopians, under a king who took the name Kaléb, a name reminiscent of the first of the children of Israel to enter the Promised Land, confronted a Jewish king who took the biblical name Yusuf or Joseph. It also makes sense of the story of the two sons of Solomon, with Menelek of Ethiopia taking precedence over Adramis of Constantinople. In this period, the Egyptians, or Copts, were being persecuted by the Byzantine emperors in Constantinople, since the Egyptians had rejected the decisions of the Council of Chalcedon (451), which was accepted by the Byzantines.[12] It is likely that they would have looked towards the expanding kingdom in Ethiopia as a source of support and encouragement. The superiority of the Ethiopian king over Constantinople is a theme found in other texts from the period.[13] Yet another indication of a sixth-century origin for at least this section is the surprising absence of any reference to the rise of Islam, which had a huge impact on Ethiopia in the period before the thirteenth century. It is hard to believe that a book written in the thirteenth century would not have made some reference to the momentous changes in the region brought about by the new faith of Islam. All this suggests that at least a large part of the *Kebrä Nägäst* was composed in the sixth century.

We can conclude that the *Kebrä Nägäst* was translated and collated in the period after the fall of the Zagwe, from a collection of material drawn from a variety of sources, mainly the Old Testament and interpretations and legends derived from it. There was a source document, which no longer survives, which derived from sixth-century Egypt, the existence of which is indicated, but not proved, by the claim of the colophon that the *Kebrä Nägäst* began its life in a Coptic version.

JEWISH INFLUENCE

Travellers to Ethiopia have often been struck by the Jewish character of the faith which they encountered. One of them was the seventeenth-century visitor Jeronimo Lobo who observed that 'it would not be easy to determine whether the Abyssinians are more Jews than Christians'.[14] Lobo and other travellers came from branches of the church which had distanced themselves from their Jewish roots.

The Acts of the Apostles describes how the church of the apostolic period expanded north and west into Asia Minor and Greece, and was forced to address the question of whether the new Greek converts were required to observe the laws of the Old Testament. The first recorded council, held at Jerusalem, addressed this problem and decided that only the minimal requirements to abstain from food sacrificed to idols and from fornication were to apply to converts (Acts 15.6–29).

But Ethiopians were not present at this council and knew nothing about the discussion and its resolutions. The Acts of the Apostles of the New Testament describe a missionary church, leaving its Israelite Hebrew origins behind and finding a new cultural identity in a Greek-speaking Mediterranean culture. As it extended westward it embraced a Latin legal and organisational approach, and then developed this through Renaissance, Reformation and Enlightenment. The *Kebrä Nägäst* takes a different approach. It affirms rather than rejects its continuity, and even identity, with the Old Testament religious tradition.

The presence of Judaic practices and traditions in Ethiopian religion takes many forms. Edward Ullendorff has collected a full and varied collection of customs, forms of worship, language and music which he offers as examples of the extent of Judaic influence. His list is extensive.

There is the *Kebrä Nägäst* itself with the story of the coming of the Ark to Ethiopia. The presence of the Ark of the Covenant in Ethiopia leads to the central place of the tabot, or representation of the Ark, in every church in Ethiopia. Arising from this presence of the tabot is the arrangement of the church around it in three spaces of declining levels of holiness radiating out of the central holy of holies where the Ark is placed. This threefold division of the building can be compared to the design of the Temple at Jerusalem. Within the liturgy prominence is given to the reading of Scripture, as it is in the synagogues of Judaism. Some prayers are based on the recitation of the names of God, and a sense of the power which comes from the use of the name, which show similarities to Jewish prayers. The clergy of the church include the order of *däbtära*, which has been compared to the position of the Levites in the Temple.[15] The musical styles used by the *däbtära* in worship may also be connected to the music of the Old Testament, and the rhythmical movements of Ethiopian hymnody invites comparison with scenes from the Old Testament such as the dancing before the Ark described in 2 Samuel 6.5, 14–15. It has even been suggested that the biblical acclamation Alleluia is equivalent to the ululation of women, with the high-pitched rhythmical melodic sound caused by drumming the tongue against the roof of the mouth, encountered across Africa. As well as these features of worship, there is the observance of legal provisions about diet, following the same division of animals into the clean which can be eaten and the unclean animals which are forbidden as in the law of the Old Testament – including the peculiarly Ethiopian prohibition on eating camel. Then there is the custom of circumcision on the eighth day. The Sabbath is also kept as a holy day, alongside Sunday the first day of the week, sometimes called the Sabbath of the Christians.[16]

This is a formidable list. While the Judaic origin of these is debated, the sheer extent and variety of the features identified by Ullendorff suggest that the church took shape in a culture which had many connections with the Judaism of the Old Testament. This suggests that they came from different sources and different times, and we do not need to conclude that there was a single period of cultural transfer. There are several identifiable points of contact when there were encounters between Ethiopia and Israel, and several possible routes along which these customs might have travelled. We need to identify the most likely route and the most likely period for this transmission.

There are two possible routes from Israel to Ethiopia along which cultural and literary traditions might be transmitted. They could have been transported either through Egypt along the Nile or through the maritime routes of the Red Sea. The land route goes through Egypt. We know that there was a close connection between Egypt and Israel. There are numerous references to this in the Bible from the slavery of the children of Israel in Egypt and Exodus into the Promised Land, up to the flight of the family of Jesus from the anger of King Herod. A community of Jews had settled in Egypt and these were responsible for the translation of the Old Testament into Greek, in the version known as the Septuagint. In the south of Egypt – and so closer to Ethiopia and more relevant to this discussion – is the evidence for the presence of Jews on the island of Elephantine on the Upper Nile from the seventh century BC. Perhaps some of these Jews might have carried on up the Nile and arrived in Ethiopia. It has even been speculated that these Jews might be the lost tribe of Dan who made their way to the south. The difficulty with this possible route is that the Nile between Egypt and Ethiopia is difficult to navigate and it is hard to see how these Jews could have made the journey.

The maritime route along the Red Sea is not only possible but likely. The modern Red Sea Israeli resort of Eilat was in use as a sea port by the time of King Solomon. It is recorded that Solomon built a fleet at Ezion-geber near Eloth, the modern Eilat, on the shore of the Red Sea, and that he imported large quantities of gold from Ophir, which is located in Arabia (1 Kings 9.26–8; see also 2 Kings 14.22; 16.6). Travels along the Red Sea are also described by later writers. The *Periplus of the Erythraean Sea* is a description of the region bordering the Red Sea and the Persian Gulf written by a merchant, probably from Egypt, in the first century AD. He describes a visit to Adulis and to Aksum. Later the writer Cosmas Indicopleustes – a name which means 'sailor to India' and is misleadingly used here since the author never actually got as far as India – visited Adulis about 520 and included a map of the Ethiopian coastline in his book. These accounts, from different historical periods, provide evidence for the use of the sea routes along the Red Sea at least from the time of King Solomon, around 1000 BC, and throughout the periods which have followed. They provide the context for the visit of the Queen of Sheba to Solomon described in the *Kebrä Nägäst*, as well as in the Old Testament. The routes connect Israel at the far northern tip, Arabia on the north coast and Ethiopia on the south.

There is no evidence for Jews settling in Arabia in Old Testament times, but many fled there after the destruction of the Temple by the Romans in AD 70. By 350 Jews had established communities, including the kingdom of Najran, in the south-eastern part of the Arabian peninsula, and this is close to Ethiopia. By the sixth century there were many contacts between the Christians of Ethiopia and the Jews of Najran. Some of this interaction had a destructive character as it took the form of Jewish persecution of Christians and then a war when Emperor Kaléb responded to Christian appeals for help by building a fleet and sending an army, which overcame the Jewish king Dhu Nawwas. After this, the Christian Aksum ruled over this part of Arabia for seventy years. War is a form of cultural interaction, and often communities at war develop methods of communication, trading and even conventions to enable hostilities to be conducted in a controlled manner.[17] Najran was a centre of Judaistic religion, and was one of only two kingdoms to accept Judaism as its state religion. The other was the kingdom of Khazaria in the Caucasus which converted to Jewish faith around 740.[18] The rarity of a state professing Judaism makes it more probable that cultural connections should be attributed to the presence of the Jewish state.

Within this system of communication and cultural exchange, scholars have tried to discover the most likely period for Jewish customs to have entered Ethiopia. The story of Solomon, the Queen of Sheba and her son Menelek is unlikely, since there is no independent evidence for this account. As we have noted, Ethiopian pre-Aksumite civilisation was formed by the immigration of Semitic groups from Arabia into northern Ethiopia. These included, at some point, Jews. Jews are likely to have arrived after AD 70 when the Temple in Jerusalem was destroyed. A group of Jews might have entered Ethiopia during the early years of the Aksumite kingdom as carriers of a Jewish culture, and left evidence of their influence in distinctive characteristics in the Ge'ez language. A later possible date for the entry of Judaic customs is the rise of the successors to the Zagwe, claiming Solomonic descent and so with an interest in affirming connections with Israel. This, as we have seen, is the period when the *Kebrä Nägäst* was written in its present form. These were periods when contact between Jews and Christians in Ethiopia can be demonstrated to have been active, and have been suggested as moments of cultural influence.

Judaic influence on Ethiopian Christianity is widely diffused and includes cultural traditions of clean and unclean foods, and circumcision; styles of worship and music; approaches to prayer; literary traditions especially the *Kebrä Nägäst* – and of course the importance of the Ark of the Covenant as defining the nature of Christianity. Such a diverse set of influences suggests that we should envisage a gradual process whereby traditions were disseminated along the Red Sea region, by sea and land. Communication existed at least as early as Solomon and probably earlier – and has continued since. The most probable explanation for the Judaic character of Ethiopian Christianity is a slow process of cultural influence and exchange from 1000 BC, with periods of close connection between the communities of Arabia and Ethiopia from AD 340 onwards, especially at the time of the Najran war. This connection was expressed in the writing and actions of King Zär'ä Ya'eqob in the fifteenth century.

The customs and practices which are considered to be Semitic were stronger in the north of the country, near the Red Sea coast, than they were in the south. This is not surprising considering the geographical proximity to the Semitic Middle East. Judaic customs are associated especially with the monastic house of Éwostatéwos (1273–1352) which adhered tenaciously to practices such as the observation of the Jewish Sabbath as a holy day as well as the Christian Sunday.

This group formed an alternative ecclesiastical community to that which developed in the south, and drew support from northern parts of the country, with monastic centres in various parts of Tigray. The legitimacy of this approach to Christianity was debated at the Council of Däbrä Metmaq, summoned in 1450 by emperor Zär'ä Ya'eqob, which accepted several Jewish practices, such as the observance of the Sabbath on Saturday as well as the first day of the week, Sunday. Among its centres of influence was a monastery in the region of Enfraz, which had a large population of Falasha.[19] Further evidence for the Judaic character of the Christianity of the north comes from the Stephanite communities, which flourished between 1400 and 1700, and followed Judaic traditions, including the observance of the Jewish Sabbath. The presence of Judaic practices in the north provides further encouragement to the conclusion that the Jewish nature of the church arises from a slow cultural accretion of customs rather than a propaganda programme fabricated by a medieval royal dynasty.

This was also the context of the much-discussed origins of the Falasha or Beta Israel. These Ethiopian Jews practised a form of Judaism which was faithful to the five books of the Torah, practised animal sacrifice and kept the Sabbath. But they also diverged from Judaism in various ways. They know nothing of later Jewish traditions in the Talmud and have a monastic tradition – two features which are definitely un-Jewish.

Some have tried to trace the origins of the Beta Israel back to roots in Israel. James Bruce, writing in the eighteenth century, described a tradition that they are descended from Menelek the son of Solomon and the Queen of Sheba. Others have suggested that they fled Israel after the destruction of the Temple by the Romans or were the lost tribe of Dan, or had come at some other period. More recent scholarship inclines to the view that the origins of the Beta Israel are to be found in Ethiopia itself. Their distinctive mix of beliefs and practices took shape between the fourteenth and sixteenth centuries. The chronicles of Amdä Seyon has a reference to people 'like Jews', and the name Falasha comes from a decree of King Yeshaq: 'He who is baptised in the Christian religion may inherit the land of his father, otherwise let him be a *fälasi*', or exile.[20]

An indication of the Christian origin of Falasha traditions is shown by the influence of monks. Monastic life arrived among the

Falasha in the late fourteenth century when a monk called Qozimos was forced out of his monastery of Wayna, because he had resolved to follow an ascetic discipline of avoiding the eating of cooked food. These forbidden cooked foods unfortunately included the eucharistic bread, because it was baked on a fire. Shocked by this, the archbishop Sälama instructed that Qozimos should be tied up and force-fed bread, meat and wine. Qozimos fled and found refuge among the Falasha, and here he copied the Old Testament for them. He was followed by another refugee monk, Sabra, who also set up a monastery. These monks used and adapted Christian texts. An influential work of Falasha literature, the *Te'ezazä Sänbät* or the Commandment of the Sabbath, is reputed to have been written by Abba Sabra and is drawn from various sources, some of which were Christian texts adapted by the substitution of the title 'God' for 'Jesus', and simplifying references to the 'sign of the cross' to the simpler and more anodyne 'sign'.[21]

These traditions suggest that the Falasha come from the same roots as Christians and shared in the same Semitic cultural traditions. Their identity was formed by monks, using local traditions of worship and placing ritual purity among other Judaic customs at the heart of worship. The growth of the Falasha community is a further indication that local traditions and customs are derived from a common Semitic culture which is encountered throughout the region. Christian monastic influence continued among the Falasha, and as late as the 1840s a monk from Quara, near Gondar, called Abba Waddaye worked among them to restore and build up their faith. Falasha monasteries finally faded out of existence after the great famine of 1888–92 caused by the spread of the rinderpest cattle disease. The reduced community could no longer afford to maintain the monasteries.

The Falasha have maintained their religious practices. Their existence became known to the international Jewish community through the work of Joseph Halévy who discovered, visited and raised awareness of the Judaism of this remote community in Ethiopia in 1867. This led to a surge of interest among Jews and the eventual recognition of the Beta Israel by the Israeli government in 1975 so that they could be considered to be Jews and have a right to settle in Israel under the Law of Return. There was a steady transfer of the Beta Israel to Israel, especially when Ethiopia was undergoing devastating famine. In Operation Solomon in 1991 El Al airlines gained special permission to fly on the Sabbath and arranged 34 flights in 36 hours in specially adapted planes and moved a total of 14,325 people to Israel. There are now only a few Falasha left in Ethiopia, with the census of 2006 providing a figure of just 3188 members of the community.

Later there would be some embarrassment about the Judaic aspects of Ethiopian Christianity. The emperor Claudius, Gälawdéwos, defended Ethiopia against European accusations of Judaising by claiming that these customs were cultural rather than religious, saying that circumcision was a local practice and that the avoidance of pork was purely a matter of taste. But these protestations come from a later age, and in response to criticism from Europeans, and cannot be regarded as evidence against a Judaic influence.[22]

The Semitic character of Ethiopian Christianity was further strengthened through the mission of early Christians who brought these forms of faith. From its foundation, Ethiopian Christianity flourished in a Semitic culture, in a land which was part of an inter-related network of communities sharing customs, forms of worship and approaches to faith. This led to continuity with pre-Christian customs and practices which were passed on from the Judaism of the Old Testament to the Christianity of the New. The Christian missionaries who came to Ethiopia built on what had gone before, but introduced something new. They needed a new vocabulary, a style of architecture which could accommodate the new forms of worship and a set of texts which could express the new faith. Here, too, the church drew on Semitic language and practice.

The Bible was translated from Greek into Ge'ez. The translators devised a vocabulary to express the good news of the new faith. Sometimes words were not available in the language currently in use and had to be borrowed from other languages. The loan-words show which languages were known by the translators and so where the main missionary initiatives came from.

Scholars have drafted lists of these new loan words. They include several words which convey essential Christian concepts. There is *haymonot*, or faith; *meswat*, or alms; *orit*, or law; *taot*, or idol; *qäsis*, or priest. The origins of these words have been explored to see if they show which branch of Semitic language was used, and so where the new Christian missions originated from. So for example the word *meswat* or alms is an Aramaic plural form of a Hebrew word for commandment, which was used in Midrashic literature to mean alms, and is unknown in Syriac. This could be seen as unmistakable evidence for Jewish – as opposed to a less specific Syriac or other Semitic – influence.[23] However, other words in the Semitic vocabulary of the Bible suggest a broader range of origins. Biblical words from Syrian sources come from several linguistic groups. The analysis of the new vocabulary, and other linguistic points such as the method of transcribing proper names, has shown influence from several sources. These include Syriac words and phrases, as well as Aramaic. It confirms that Ethiopian Christianity flourished in a Semitic setting, which drew on various languages and dialects for its Christian vocabulary.

AN AFRICAN WORLDVIEW

Up till now we have been exploring the Semitic influences. But there is a second cultural tradition. This is the mixture of indigenous Cushitic traditions of worship and belief which were deeply rooted in the area from prehistoric times and which pre-existed the contribution of the Semitic arrivals. Here we encounter a form of faith which had arisen from within Ethiopia.

We can discern hints of pre-Aksumite, pre-Christian beliefs. The serpent was an animal with strong religious significance. Several Ge'ez myths tell the story of the serpent-king Arwe who ruled for several centuries before the arrival of the Solomonic kings. He was a demonic figure who ate humans, and was killed by the human Angabo who became king in his place. Serpents retain a spiritual power and occur in many stories and practices. Abuna Arägawi climbed up a serpent as up a ladder to ascend to the summit of Däbrä Damo. But evidence is mainly oral and mythological and does not allow us to reconstruct the beliefs of people before the Aksumite Empire.

An early visitor to Ethiopia gives further description of traditional beliefs as he found them in the early seventeenth century: 'The Agaws of Gojjam are pagans and much given to fetishism. They adore a single creator of heaven, whom they call Doban, but have no idols. They also worship river springs, also some species of trees and groves, sacrificing to them and offering cows, milk and butter.'[24]

His observations can be confirmed from many parts of Ethiopia. The belief in the single creator of heaven is widely held. The high god is male and is associated with the sky, and this sky-association makes him distant and remote. His remoteness leaves space in the world around for other spiritual beings and divine qualities. Spirits are found in physical features, such as springs, hilltops and caves, and the spirits who inhabit these places need to be propitiated and negotiated with through gifts and ritual actions. As well as natural features of the landscape being important, ancestors also have to be recognised. They continue to be part of daily experience and influence those who are still alive.

This understanding of the natural world persists in attitudes still encountered in the villages of rural Ethiopia. Traditional forms of spirituality are striking when we seek to see the Ethiopian countryside through the eyes of its inhabitants. They are illustrated by experiences which I recorded in a journal entry made during a three-day visit to the Zege peninsula adjoining lake Tana in the company of anthropologist Tom Boylston:

> We walked around the wooded peninsula. It feels like a living place – where trees can't be cut down in case the spirit that lives in it is displeased, and if you trip over a stone it's good if it's the right foot but bad if it's the left, where if you eat in the sight of a rock hierax – *shshoko* – your food will be stolen, and where the *buda* spirit, known as the evil eye, threatens from all sides. People don't like walking at night because of the jinn or evil spirits. The lake especially is avoided after nightfall because it is full of jinn. Tom tells me that the fear of *buda* is the main anxiety people have. If a baby won't stop crying, even at night, the parents fear *buda* and might take the baby through narrow forest paths at 2 am to find treatment from the traditional doctor. We later visited the doctor's house, and it turned out that he was trained in modern medicine, as well as knowledge of herbs, and experience in dealing with spirits. He spent time with people and had great wisdom.

While this comes from a contemporary visit it points to a way of looking at the world which is rooted in a past which is distant and, we can suggest, pre-Christian.

Religious beliefs are rooted in the place that people inhabit and the ways they negotiate their relationships with the natural order. These constitute a way of looking at the world and negotiating a peaceful existence within it. Beliefs cannot be separated from the people who hold them and the place where they live. The observations of Alfred Kroeber, written in 1948 and in China, are also applicable to Ethiopia, and express the importance of a general worldview. He wrote of the 'tenacity of the attachment of cultural qualities to the soil [...] a stylistic set or faculty at once absorptive and resistive, that for thousands of years, however inventions might diffuse and culture elements circulate, succeed in keeping China something that can fairly be called Chinese'.[25] When I have discussed traditional faith with Ethiopian anthropologists and others in the course of field visits, they describe forms of faith which reach back before the time of Christianity and Islam, so that Christianity can be seen as a new arrival which has had to gain acceptance and make sense of these primal codes of belief.

Christians call God *egzi'abhér* which means Lord of the Earth. This choice of vocabulary detaches God from the sky and places him on the earth. Perhaps we can relate this placing of God on earth with the mission of early monks and evangelists in which they went into battle against the spirits and demonstrated the superior power of the Christian God. It is a model of mission which recognises and takes the existence of spirits seriously while claiming a greater and more effective power which can be relied on as an antidote and a liberator. The victory over spirits is a part of Christian mission preaching in the New Testament, for example Christ 'disarmed the rulers and authorities, and made a public example of them, triumphing over them' (Colossians 2.15). The Ethiopian experience of the pervasive presence of spiritual powers makes sense in this approach to faith.

There are many kinds of spirits, which influence lives in different ways. The classes of spirit most often encountered are the *buda* and *zar*. *Buda*, or the evil eye, is always evil and harmful. A *buda* spirit takes over a human body and acts through it to perform evil and destructive acts. A person possessed by this spirit becomes *buda* and is dangerous. He can cause illness, turn himself into a wild animal – usually a hyena – and suck the blood of victims. The sucking of blood can be sensed by the victim who realises that the evil eye is cast on him and feels as though blood is being drained from his body. Often skilled professions, such as the blacksmith or weaver, or groups such as the *falasha* or beta Israel, are suspected of being possessed by *buda*.

Zar are less dangerous, and can be seen as spiritual counterparts of humans. The origin of the *zar* is explained in a traditional story told in many places in East Africa.

> The first man and woman, Adam and Eve, had sixty children. One day God asked to see the children, and Eve was anxious in case God should take the children from her. So she showed thirty and hid thirty, hiding the most beautiful. As a punishment for this deception God decreed that the thirty that had been hidden would remain hidden, and they became the *zar*, who would from then on have the power to control their visible human siblings.

So *zar* are ever present, and have the power to enter into and possess people. They are not necessarily to be feared, but do need to be appeased and negotiated with.[26] They have power over human lives, relate to others, foretell the future and can intervene in politics and international problems. *Zar* are especially associated with women, and often appear in contexts of domestic strife or in marginalised groups. There are various rituals, dances and offerings of food which are practised in *zar* rituals, and are ways of building up better relations with the spirits.

It is possible that belief in both *buda* and *zar* evolved out of traditional pre-Christian beliefs. *Buda* could be the pagan gods who were opposed by the Christian missionaries and have taken on a new identity of opponents to Christians, and *zar* could have evolved out of respect shown to ancestors. However, the origin of cults and beliefs about spirit possession are obscure and little understood. Their presence in the life and practice of the church indicates an African way of understanding the world, which points to an approach to faith diffused across Africa, and which forms an essential dimension of Ethiopian faith.[27]

A MEETING PLACE OF CULTURES

The Semitic and Cushitic strands of the cultural tradition have been the main but not the only influences. The bearers of culture would have arrived in boats by sea or along land routes. Boats sailed along the Red Sea, and then travelled further to India. Land routes enabled trade to be carried out with goods from Asia reaching into Arabia and so to Ethiopia. Routes by both land and sea connected Ethiopia with places further east. There have been coins from the Ummayad and

Abbasid Islamic dynasties, from Kushan and regions of India excavated at the monastery of Däbrä Damo, although surprisingly only a single coin from Aksum in this hoard. There was a piece of metalwork found at Aksum, which could only have been welded in China.[28] The standing stelae are the great monuments of Aksumite civilisation and several possible influences on these have been discerned. Some have seen in them Egyptian styles of carving, or housebuilding customs in Arabia, and even the nine-storey pagodas of Bodhi Gaya in India.[29] The layout of Buddhist stupas in South India presents intriguing similarities with the arrangement of later circular churches in Ethiopia.[30] These influences from Asia should be seen in the context of extensive cultural contact which showed itself in many ways. One fascinating example is the story of Barlaam and Josaphat, a Christian version of the life of the Buddha who in this version lived in the Sinai desert rather than the forests of north India.[31] Ethiopia, with its access to sea routes connecting it with regions to the east, was drawn into this cultural exchange.

The extent of these cultural contacts and exchanges shows the range of influences on the church of Ethiopia. It challenges assumptions sometimes made by some Western observers that Ethiopia is isolated from the wider international community. One of the famous, or perhaps we should say infamous, comments about Ethiopia comes from Edward Gibbon: 'Encompassed on all sides by the enemies of their religion, the Aethiopians slept near a thousand years, forgetful of the world by whom they were forgotten.' This presents a Eurocentric sense of Ethiopia as distant and isolated. It suggests a cultural poverty in this distant land, with a people deprived of contacts with the civilising currents which created the enlightened world of Europe.

The place of Ethiopia in the Horn of Africa might have restricted contact with Western Europe but it enabled a wide range of contact with other areas, leading to a rich and varied culture. The Ethiopian Christian tradition is derived from many sources. Here we have identified a worldview derived from African sources, with its intuitive appreciation of a natural environment which has spiritual and personal as well as physical depths. To this was added the approach of Middle Eastern Semitic monotheism, which gave rise not only to Christianity but also to Judaism and Islam. Its position on the shores of the Red Sea also put Ethiopia in contact with South and East Asia in one direction and with the Mediterranean and Europe in the other. This conjunction of cultural influences and access to communication in different directions has given shape to Ethiopian culture and to its religion. The location of Ethiopia within Africa and on the shores of the Red Sea has opened it up to people, ideas, practices and imports from many directions.

Ethiopia was a cultural melting pot, bringing together streams from Western Europe, the Semitic Middle East and African understandings of the world, with influences from east and South Asia. Its location has enabled an incorporation of traditions from widely different places and peoples.

The people of Ethiopia have been able to learn from others and incorporate elements of the traditions of other peoples. Their approach has appeared syncretistic. A Roman Catholic missionary visitor, Fr Remedius Prutky, observed in 1752, 'They [the Ethiopian Church] have something in common with all people: baptism with Christians, Sabbath with Hebrews, a multitude of wives, circumcision and divorce with Turks, many superstitions with the Gentiles.'[32] A better way to describe this capacity of Ethiopia to absorb different cultural influences is the phrase, 'creative incorporation'.

> It is precisely a typical Ethiopian tendency to collect the data of foreign cultural and literary experience and transform them, sooner or later, to such an extent that even translations in Ethiopic are not always translations, in our sense of the term, but they frequently contain additions, supplementary material, [...] misrepresentations of the original, at other times [...] the insertion of new materials.[33]

The result is a tenaciously held native tradition, which could learn from foreign cultures, absorb attractive elements, reject what was alien or hostile and rework them into a distinctive Ethiopian style.

This creative incorporation is made possible by the location of Ethiopia at the meeting point of Asia and Africa, with access to East Asia and Europe. The streams of culture from different directions have produced a rich and individual form of Christianity. Instead of considering Ethiopia to be on the edge of a European world, we should recognise that it is at the centre of a wider world which includes Asia and Africa, as well as Europe.

CHAPTER 3

King and Abuna: The Formation of a Church

HISTORY: THE AKSUMITE STATE

The trading state of Aksum was known and respected as a centre of civilisation in the ancient world. The Persian prophet Mani recognised its greatness when he wrote, in the third century, 'There are four great kingdoms in the world. The first is the kingdom of Babylon and Persia; the second is the kingdom of the Romans; the third is the kingdom of the Aksumites; the fourth is the kingdom of Sileos.'[1] Mani's kingdoms are somewhat conveniently located at the points of the compass, with Babylon to the north, Rome to the west, Sileos, by which he probably meant China, to the east, and Aksum to the south. In his scheme, Aksum forms the southern axis of the known world.

Aksum had developed gradually to become prominent by the end of the first century AD. Its influence was based on economic activity, with its trade carried on sea routes used by the regional powers of first Egypt and then Rome. Ivory, and other goods, passed from the interior of Africa through Aksum and its sea port of Adulis and were exchanged for jewellery of gold and silver, iron and steel for the making of weapons, and luxury goods which arrived from as far away as India and China. At the height of its power in the fifth century, Aksum had expanded north to gain access to the sea ports of the Red Sea, south into the mountains to overcome the native Agaw, east into the Danakil to gain access to the incense trade and across the sea into Arabia to extend its control of the sea trade routes.

Excavation has revealed stone houses and temples, irrigation systems and bath houses, and coins minted from various metals. Aksum's greatest monuments are the standing stelae. These tall monoliths were set up to mark the tombs of the kings of Aksum before the formation of a Christian church in the fourth century. The carved faces of the columns represent many storied houses, and show characteristic features of Aksumite architecture, with recessed lines of stone, monkey-head beams and carved doorways. There are three stelae which are larger than the many other smaller stones. Of these, the largest is 30 m in height and over 500 tonnes in weight and is considered to be the largest single block of stone ever to have been cut for erection in the world. Unfortunately it now lies fallen and broken in the place where it should have stood, an accident which probably happened while it was being set up. Even broken and on the ground, it remains an impressive sight. Another stela fell and broke and was transported to Rome but was returned to Aksum in 2005, and now stands beside the remaining third stela which has remained in its original location since it was lifted into place – according to tradition by a team of elephants assisting a human labour force.

THE COPTIC CONNECTION

Christianity arrived early in Aksum. Traditions include Ethiopia among the countries which were included in the apostolic mission of New Testament times. A court official was baptised by the apostle Philip, but he came from Meroe to the north of Aksum; the apostle Matthew is said in several traditions to have preached and been martyred in Ethiopia, but these are late accounts and one of them demonstrates its unreliability by locating Ethiopia near the Caspian Sea; John Chrysostom says that Ethiopians were present at Jerusalem at the first Pentecost. While none of these claims can be relied on as historical evidence for the arrival of Christianity in Aksum, they arise out of the interconnected world of the Red Sea region, where merchants and others travelled freely and are likely to have come to Aksum. They would have included some Christians who stayed and settled, and communities of Christians, especially in the cosmopolitan centres along the sea coast, were present by 340.

Among the Christians who found their way to Ethiopia were two Syrian boys, Frumentius and Aedesius. Their story is told by the

FIGURE 3.1 The stelae at Aksum were built above tombs. The largest was 30 m in height and 500 tonnes in weight, but was probably broken in the course of erection. It is carved with the windows and beams of a many-storied building.

historian Rufinus Tyrannus of Tyre, who claims to have heard it from one of the brothers, Aedesius.[2]

Rufinus tells how the philosopher Meropius set out for India to seek wisdom taking with him the two boys – given the state of geographical knowledge at the time it is possible that his India was in fact Ethiopia. On the return journey the boat landed at a port on the African coast of the Red Sea to collect provisions and was boarded by a group of bloodthirsty local people who killed all the travellers in the ship, except for Frumentius and Aedesius, who were found quietly sitting under a tree reading books. Preserved by the 'mercy' of the barbarians they were taken to the king's court at Aksum where Aedesius became the king's cupbearer and Frumentius became his secretary and treasurer. As Frumentius grew up he began to seek out 'Roman' Christian merchants – he means Byzantine Greeks – and 'to give them great influence and to urge them to establish in various places churches where they might resort for prayer in the Roman manner'. He encouraged others, 'attracting them with his fervour and benefits, in every way promoting the seed of Christianity in the country'. Some years later, probably in 342, he went to Alexandria and explained the situation to the Archbishop Athanasius, suggesting that this was a valuable mission opportunity and also no doubt pointing out that it would enable Alexandria to promote its position and influence in a strategic region to the south. Athanasius replied to Frumentius, 'What other man shall we find in whom the Spirit of God is as in thee, who can accomplish these things?' He consecrated Frumentius as bishop for Aksum, and the new bishop returned. We read that 'countless numbers of barbarians were converted by him to the faith. From this time Christian peoples and churches have been created in the parts of India [again meaning Ethiopia] and the priesthood has begun.' Within the Ethiopian Church Frumentius is known as *Abba Sälama*, the Father of Peace;[3] or *Kassate Berhan*, the Bringer of Light.

This event marks the beginning of the Christian Church of Ethiopia. Rufinus' account is supported by coinage of the king Ezana marked with a sign of the cross, and a Greek inscription of the king in which he places his trust in 'the Father, and the Son, and the Holy Ghost', and 'Jesus Christ who has saved me'. Soon after the consecration of Frumentius, the Roman Emperor Constantius wrote to King Ezana warning him that a consecration by Athanasius of Alexandria, who did not adhere to the emperor's Arian form of Christianity, was not valid and suggesting a re-consecration by the respectably Arian archbishop, George of Cappadocia.[4] This array of evidence leaves no doubt as to the significance of these events. Ethiopia was among the first kingdoms to become Christian.

This process of church formation followed a different pattern from other areas. The earliest Christian communities grew in the cities of the Greek and Roman empires of the Mediterranean regions. They met in private houses, and sometimes suffered persecution, and it was only later that the emperor become Christian and the church became tolerated. This can be described as a bottom-up process. The Ethiopian experience was different. Here, the king was converted and an archbishop consecrated, and these organised and set up the church. So it can be described as top-down, not bottom-up. From this royal and episcopal initiative, Christian communities were set up.

The king and the archbishop – Ezana and Frumentius – worked together. This set up a pattern of shared leadership of the church which was to persist until 1974, when the monarchy was brought to a sudden and violent end. The roles and functions of both leaders changed and evolved over that long period, but the fact of their joint leadership remained. Both king and archbishop claimed an authority derived from outside the country, the king through his succession to Solomon and the kings of ancient Israel and the archbishop through his consecration by the patriarch of Alexandria. The relationship between these two sources of authority gave the church its place in Ethiopian society.

When Frumentius went to Alexandria to receive the consecration as archbishop, this began a tradition that archbishops of Ethiopia were chosen and consecrated in Egypt, that they were Egyptian by birth and that there should be only one archbishop. This had the result that Ethiopia could be considered to be a diocese of the Coptic Church, but an unusual diocese which soon became larger in size than the whole of the rest of its parent church.[5] The Ethiopian Church is, for this reason, sometimes called a Coptic Church, but since Copt is a form of *gibt*, the Arabic word for Egyptian, it is inaccurate to apply this word to Ethiopia.

The Metropolitan was called the *abuna*, or 'our father'. His situation changed through this long period of time but some features persisted and affected all holders of the office in varying degrees. Incidents from the careers of the abunas of various periods show both the consistent challenges facing successive abunas and also the development of the order and ministry of the church in Ethiopia – a way without parallel in other parts of the Christian world.

To begin with, the relationship between Egypt and Ethiopia made good sense. When Frumentius was consecrated there were political and economic, as well as cultural, connections. Egypt had strong trade links with the Aksumite kingdom; and the Byzantine emperors in Constantinople were concerned to maintain security in Arabia and the southern frontiers of the empire. The Patriarchate of Alexandria was the centre of church life in the region, and was well placed to provide leadership and support for the new church. The significance of Ethiopia is indicated by the use by chroniclers of the title of Patriarch of Alexandria, Ethiopia and Nubia to refer to the leader of the Egyptian church.[6] At this stage, the Church of Ethiopia was part of a North African church presided over by the Coptic Patriarch.

The situation changed in 640 when the armies of Islam conquered Egypt, and as a result the Coptic Patriarch became a subject of a Muslim state. This led to a shift in power. The head of the thriving church of the growing Christian kingdom of Ethiopia found himself dependent on the head of the smaller church of Egypt who was under the authority of a Muslim ruler. The Muslim rulers of Egypt could put pressure on the Coptic Patriarch of Alexandria to require the Ethiopian metropolitan to provide tolerance and benefits to the Islamic population of Ethiopia. The Christian abuna often found himself forced to be more sympathetic to the needs of Muslims than those of Christians.[7] Meanwhile the Christian churches of Nubia and other parts of modern Sudan went into a slow decline. Muslim merchants settled along the Nile, and the population was influenced by Arab language and Islamic faith, until the records of Christian existence in Nubia died out in the fourteenth century.[8] This further contributed to the break-up of the Alexandrian metropolitanate of north-east Africa, the isolation of Ethiopia and the growing influence of Islam.

Now that the relationship was becoming harder to maintain, an addition was made to the canons of the Council of Nicaea, which had met in 325 and remained the most authoritative and widely recognised of the church's ecumenical councils. This addition is known as canon 42, and was inserted into the canons of Nicaea about 700, from where it was introduced into Ethiopia, and was included in the *Fetha Nägäst* or law of kings.[9] It stated that Ethiopians did not have the power to choose their own patriarch, that he in turn did not have the power to consecrate other bishops and that none of these could be natives of Ethiopia. This had the result that all bishops had to be consecrated by the Patriarch of Alexandria who kept control of the ecclesiastical hierarchy firmly in Coptic hands. It gave legal support to a practice which was rapidly becoming anachronistic.

It was, at the very least, inconvenient. When the metropolitan of Ethiopia died and a replacement was required, a lengthy and arduous process began. The king sent a delegation to the patriarch in Egypt with generous gifts of gold to both the Coptic Patriarch and the Muslim ruler of Egypt with a request for a new abuna or metropolitan. The delegation was faced with a journey of 1500 miles through territory controlled by Muslim rulers and then had to negotiate with both the religious and state authorities in Egypt. Eventually a monk, usually from one of the larger monasteries, was selected, consecrated and set off on the long return journey to Ethiopia. The post was not popular, since the new abuna had to leave his home and move to a new country where he did not speak the language and did not know the customs. The candidate selected knew that he was faced with a demanding task and was often reluctant to assume the honour. The French consul in Cairo wrote, in 1700, that 'the Copts even the poor have so much horror for this country [Ethiopia] that they are obliged to chain whoever is selected to succeed the archbishop of Ethiopia when he dies'. He adds that the king of Ethiopia enclosed a gift for the Muslim pasha as well as the Coptic patriarch to ensure that political force is added to religious calling to ensure the dispatch of the new postholder.[10] We do not have records of the views of earlier abunas but their appointments were made under similar conditions and we can assume a similar reluctance.

Occasionally the system broke down, and this could lead to long periods when there was no abuna and people feared for the future of the church. The longest period when the church lacked the presence of an archbishop took place in the tenth century. In the early part of the century, the king of Ethiopia asked abuna Pétros to select his own successor as abuna from one of the two sons of the king. Pétros chose the younger, upon which two visiting Syrian monks challenged the legitimacy of the new abuna and promoted the cause of the elder son. The Patriarch of Alexandria, Cosmas III (923–34), refused to confirm the appointment of either, and so the king arranged for abuna Pétros' assistant to succeed him, but this choice was not acceptable to the patriarch either, and he insisted on making his own selection. The next four Coptic patriarchs in Cairo persisted in their refusal to allow the Ethiopian choice, and declined to send an abuna. Eventually Patriarch Philotheos (979–1003) consecrated abuna Daniel, thus bringing to an end an interregnum which had lasted over fifty years.[11]

There was another gap during the reign of the emperor Zär'ä Ya'eqob (1434–68). On this occasion the abuna had died some time before 1458 and the usual delegation to ask for a successor was not dispatched. In 1477 the emperor convened a council to consider breaking links with Egypt. It must have been an unruly affair. Four hundred monks from the nationalist 'house', or monastic order, of Éwostatéwos arrived determined to break the link, and they were opposed by three hundred monks from the rival house of Täklä Haymonot who wanted to maintain it.[12] The pro-Egypt group had the support of powerful figures in the royal circle and won the day. After the council finished, a request for a new abuna was sent to Egypt, with the required payment. The Coptic Patriarch gratefully responded with two, instead of one, abunas, Yeshaq II and Marqos, and also three episcopes and one qomos, who functioned as auxiliary bishops. This outburst of rebellious resistance was unusual.

Sometimes the Ethiopians explored the possibility of finding an archbishop from elsewhere, and sometimes another church tried to infiltrate a rival candidate. In 1237 Patriarch Ignatius of Antioch appointed a Syrian bishop called Thomas for Ethiopia. This had come about as a result of a dispute between the Patriarchs of Antioch and Alexandria. Patriarch Cyril II of Alexandria (1235–43) had sent a bishop to look after Copts living in Jerusalem, which was under the jurisdiction of Ignatius of Antioch (1222–53). In retaliation for this perceived usurpation, Ignatius sent his own bishop to Ethiopia. The Ethiopians did not accept Thomas, complaining that he did not know the language, which was an odd excuse since the Egyptian abunas were also ignorant of Ge'ez.

A notorious usurper was the Portuguese adventurer, João Bermudes. He had arrived in Ethiopia in 1520 with a group of Portuguese explorers and remained behind when the rest returned in 1526. He claimed to have been ordained priest and then patriarch by Abuna Marqos in 1535, travelled to Rome to promote his cause and then returned to Ethiopia in 1540 to enter into his ecclesiastical inheritance. This was not accepted by the Ethiopians. Later, in 1625, there was another appointment of a Catholic, Alfonso Mendes, made by the emperor Susenyos who had accepted the authority of Rome, but he was ejected from court along with other Catholics in 1632.[13]

These incidents led to disruption, but they were unusual. Their infrequency illustrates that, in spite of the huge difficulties in obtaining an abuna, both Egypt and Ethiopia valued the relationship and neither wanted to change it. The practice persisted until the mid-nineteenth century when change began with first an increase in the number of bishops and then the appointment of Ethiopians to these positions.

THE SACRAMENTAL ROLE OF THE ABUNA

The abuna had a prescribed place at the royal court. During the medieval period, when the Solomonic dynasty was at the height of its power, the king ruled from a mobile capital city formed out of numerous tents which moved around the kingdom. The arrangement of the tents reflected the exercise and distribution of power. The king's tent was at the centre of two circular enclosures. Also in the camp was the tent of the abuna and other heads of church administration. As well as a fixed place in the camp, the abuna had defined responsibilities.

His duties were sacramental. He presided at the coronation of the king and carried out ordinations of clergy. The ordaining of clergy was his most important task, and because of this exclusive right, the church could not carry on its life without him. In times when there was a long interregnum, there was anxiety for the future of the ministry of the church. So when an abuna was at last appointed and the opportunity for ordination arose, people took advantage in large numbers. The Portuguese traveller Francisco Alvares observed Abuna Marqos fulfilling his ministry in the fifteenth century. On an ordination day the abuna arrived at the place on a mule, where a white tent was pitched. He was greeted by between 5000 and 6000 candidates to whom he made a speech in Arabic warning them that no one with two wives could be ordained priest. The candidates then sat in rows for their reading ability to be tested, but they were only required to read two or three words, after which a mark made with a kind of white ink was stamped on their arm. Then the abuna sat on a chair in the tent and the candidates processed past him. He laid his hands on their head and said a few words. He then celebrated the *qedassé* and administered communion to them. Alvares states that these mass ordinations were carried out almost every day.[14]

The huge numbers of candidates reported by Alvares were part of a regular pattern which had the result that the church was generously supplied with a large body of clergy. Boys of ten or even younger became deacons. Families who farmed church land needed to ensure that the sons were ordained so as to ensure that they kept the use of the land in the family. There were no restrictions and no regulation on the numbers of candidates, or on their moral suitability or educational attainment.

Alvares gives further accounts of the ministry of clergy, and these show the large numbers of priests who were attached to the churches. He describes Emperor Lebnä Dengel (1508–40) transferring 200 clergy to his church at Mekane Selassie, and, on one occasion in 1521 when the emperor visited the church he was greeted by 20,000 priests and monks, or 30,000 according to some sources.[15] This established a pattern of maintaining large numbers of clergy, which has remained. It is estimated that today there are 500,000 clergy, serving a church of around 40 million members.[16]

Sometimes the abuna tried to carry out a more active leadership, teaching and evangelising the huge area of land in which he was the only bishop. But they were handicapped by the intractable limitations of their position. Abuna Ya'eqob, appointed in 1387, was determined to provide effective leadership and planned a programme of preaching and evangelisation. He commented, 'I have been thinking for a long time to establish the law of God but I am alone in this big country with no one to help in teaching the people who are numerous.'[17] To counter his isolation, abuna Ya'eqob worked alongside monastic leaders, Täklä Haymonot and Bäsalotä Mika'el. This led to a successful missionary expansion as the disciples of these monastic leaders travelled into pagan areas and set up new monastic communities. But there was a problem. The abuna became separated from the court, and instead was allied with the monastic clergy rather than the court clergy. Future metropolitans preferred to maintain good relations with the emperor, in preference to the popular leaders from the monasteries.

There was one essential consequence of the non-Ethiopian nationality of the abuna. He came from the church outside Ethiopia and so, by the simple fact of his nationality, was a representative of the worldwide Catholic and Orthodox Church. Through his own personal presence, he ensured a relationship with the wider church. He was appointed and consecrated by the Patriarch in Alexandria, and then later in Cairo. The Patriarch of Alexandria was one of the five senior bishops of the early church, a system known as pentarchy. Since he consecrated the Ethiopian abuna who in turn ordained the clergy, the Ethiopian Church was given an identity, a structure, a hierarchy and a recognised place within the universal Christian community. The Ethiopian Orthodox Church is today recognised as one of the five Orthodox Churches who did not accept the decisions of the Council of Chalcedon on the nature of Christ. Along with the churches of Egypt, Syria, Armenia and South India, it has been described as non-Chalcedonian or Monophysite, although the phrase pre-Chalcedonian is preferred to non-Chalcedonian, and Miaphysite is a more accurate description of its doctrinal position.[18] While medieval chroniclers would not have used this language, they took it for granted that they needed a bishop who was legitimately ordained by a bishop who stood in the tradition reaching back to the apostles and to Christ, and who would in turn ordain clergy in the church. The abuna was a personal connection with a wider church, and without him the authority of the church would have evaporated.

A CASE STUDY – ABUNA SÄLAMA

The trials and tribulations of an abuna are illustrated by the career of Abuna Sälama III, the 107th metropolitan of the church in Ethiopia. Sälama (1820–67) entered the Coptic seminary in Cairo, run by the British Church Mission Society, at the age of 14. Here he received a sound education, learning English and French as well as Arabic. Ge'ez and Amharic were not in the syllabus and so he had no knowledge of the languages of Ethiopia, but this was not seen as an obstacle to his selection to become abuna. He was just 21 years of age when he became archbishop.

The young man from Egypt arrived by boat in Massawa to preside over this huge church in a sprawling, inaccessible, mountainous land. On arrival he was mobbed by enthusiastic crowds, who escorted him in procession along his triumphal route in a relay of support handing him over to a new group on arrival at the next town. Such was the size and enthusiasm of the crowd that four men with whips cleared a path for him and large crowds followed after. He discovered that he was an important figure. The law stated that all who entered the king's presence were required to strip naked from the waist up, but the metropolitan, or abuna, wore rich clothing. Sälama is reported to have worn a robe of scarlet silk, yellow trousers, a white turban and a luxurious cloak of gold.[19] There were also opportunities for amassing a huge personal fortune. His predecessor, Qérelos, had a reputation for avarice and greed.

While not indulging in these excesses, Sälama lived well, and had large estates and could gain a huge income from exacting payment – in the currency of bars of salt – from those seeking ordination.[20]

The Ethiopia into which Sälama entered was a country where central authority was breaking down and was being fought over by rival warlords. He found himself passed from leader to leader. First, he was absorbed into the court of the dominant figure in northern Ethiopia, *dejazmach* Wabe Haylä Maryam, who was engaged in a struggle with *ras* Ali Alula. Wabe made the most of the presence of Sälama, and portrayed his rival as a Muslim. However, within three months, in February 1842, Wabe was defeated by Ali at a battle at Däbrä Tabor, and the young abuna was now pressed in to support Ali. He was escorted to the capital city of Gondar.

Once he arrived in Gondar he was thrust into the long-running doctrinal debate on the nature of Christ. He had already been placed in a compromising position before he arrived. The contemporary observer Dimotheos described the situation with which Sälama, like other abunas, was faced.

> No sooner would the new Coptic prelate set their feet to Tigray than the tricky inhabitants there eagerly announced to the provinces further to the interior that the new abuna belonged to their party. Soon the whole country would be agitated which put the prelate in trouble. The poor prelate arriving in Gondar would understand the blunder that he had made. But hardly having time, and feeling ashamed, he would not retract it. And this led to trouble.[21]

The protagonists in this period were two rival schools of thought. Sälama considered that the view of the *karra*, or sword group, with a stricter one-nature Christology, was closer to his own view, but an alternative view advocating a more Western approach, called the *sägga*, or grace, had powerful support.[22] The opposing sides clashed in noisy councils at Gondar. A century earlier James Bruce, who enjoyed shocking his readers with lurid description, had reported on a synod he witnessed. The participants were 'fanatics, false prophets, diviners, dreamers, living in perfect ignorance of what is passing at the present'. The support of the monks of the important monastery of Däbrä Libanos and also the support of Sahlä Selassé, the king of Shewa, who together were formidable opponents, was at stake. Sälama was resolute, and eventually excommunicated Sahlä Selassé.

As a result he was expelled from Gondar in 1846, and returned to Tigray in the north where he was welcomed again by his first patron, Wabe. He retired to the mountain-top monastery of Däbrä Damo.

It was eight years before the abuna was able to return to Gondar, again due to political changes. The new ruler was Kassa, who supported the *karra*, and so Sälama was once again welcomed at court. Immediately, the king summoned a council to Amba Cara, and Sälama found himself given a welcome but unaccustomed position as the teacher of orthodoxy, with Alexandrian christological teaching now officially accepted. A year later, on 11 February 1855, Sälama crowned Kassa as *negusä nägäst*, king of kings, Téwodros II.[23] This established his position, as the chief out of the various chieftains or kings, in the region. From then on the fortunes of Sälama were inextricably tied together with those of the king. He supported Téwodros as he brought centralised government and modern education to the kingdom of Ethiopia, but resisted him in his attempts to regulate the church by reducing tax exemptions, confiscating church property and limiting the number of clergy.

A further source of controversy was the presence of foreign missionaries. This was another challenging situation for the abuna. Both Protestant and Catholic missionaries had arrived in Ethiopia. Sälama, the pupil of CMS missionaries, sympathised with Protestants. He permitted them to receive communion in Orthodox churches – although the reverse was not allowed – and sympathised with their attempts to bring education and knowledge of the Bible to Ethiopia. Relations with Catholics were less cordial, mainly because they supported his opponents in the doctrinal controversies.

He died in the tragic events which ended Téwodros's reign. The king hoped for strong diplomatic ties with Great Britain, as a fellow Christian power, and when these were not forthcoming he imprisoned several of the foreign missionaries in the hope that this would persuade the British government to offer military support in campaigns against Islamic powers in exchange for the captives' release. By then, Abuna Sälama also found himself out of favour with the king and joined the missionaries in captivity where he died before the extraordinarily ambitious and costly military expedition led by General Napier could release him.

The career of Abuna Sälama took place in troubled times and towards the end of the long period of Egyptian authority over the church. It illustrates the peculiar position of the abuna, which also governed the lives of previous incumbents of the office. He was isolated in a country he did not know, remote from the support of fellow bishops and trapped by political intrigue he little understood and rivalry he was little able to influence, and obliged to take part in unfamiliar doctrinal controversies. He gained support from some and antagonism from others. The controversy he provoked in his life continued after his death, and is shown by varying estimates of his contribution by modern historians. For Donald Crummey he was 'an unremarkable man with an extremely difficult task', while Samuel Rubenson considered him to be one of the great figures of nineteenth-century Ethiopia.[24] The Catholic historian Ayele Tekla Haymonot, aware of the abuna's hostility to Catholic missionaries, took the view that he was 'among the most notorious metropolitans for his scandalous life and the intrigues that marked his government'.[25] The positions and sympathies of the observers affect their view of the subjects and personalities they describe.

Like other holders of this position, the views of people at the time were ambivalent. Sälama was not regarded as a source of holiness or sanctity. With the exception of the first abuna – Frumentius – none of the metropolitans is commemorated in the calendar of the Ethiopian Church. Perhaps it was because he was not expected to provide moral or doctrinal leadership that he could easily slip into an acquisitive and even scandalous lifestyle. Abuna Semon, who died in 1620, was accused of living in adultery with the wife of an Egyptian, and keeping a harem of Ethiopian girls, and had a reputation for drunkenness. While these accusations were made by political enemies, they indicate that the abuna's lifestyle and position at court made him vulnerable to attacks of this kind. They show both the benefits and the drawbacks of the position of the abuna.

The position of the abuna, as illustrated by the life of Sälama, proved to be useful, effective and durable. The tradition of a single, non-Ethiopian abuna persisted from the 340s when Frumentius was consecrated by Athanasius until 1881. It was in that year the number of bishops was increased from one to four. Then in 1929, Ethiopians were consecrated as archbishops, to work alongside the Coptic archbishop, and so for the first time there was an Ethiopian bishop in the Ethiopian Church. This indigenisation process was completed in 1951 when Gäbrä Giyorgis was consecrated as the first Ethiopian

Archbishop, taking the name Baselyos I. In the fifty years since Baselyos became Patriarch, the number of bishops has grown to over forty, and the church has been divided into more than fifty dioceses.[26]

A SACRAL KINGSHIP

Kebrä Nägäst means the glory of kings, and this title of the book makes clear what it is setting out to do – to glorify the kings of Ethiopia. It describes how the king of Ethiopia is descended from the kings of Israel and so is chosen by God to rule his people. It also shows how power is divided between the king and the priest. When the new David returns to Ethiopia, the firstborn of leading officials accompany him, including Azaryas, the eldest son of the High Priest. Azaryas's role is to ensure that the Ark can travel with the party, obeying the command of an angel to substitute the Ark with some planks of wood. In this journey the subordinate role of the priest is made clear. He is the priest who presides over and enables the worship of God. The ruler of the people is the king.

The Old Testament understanding of the divine nature of kingship was explored in various texts and traditions in different parts of the Christian world. The junior branch of the house of Solomon, following the description of the royal family already referred to, was the imperial line of Byzantium. Here too the kings derived their power from Old Testament sources. The mutual responsibilities of king and priest were described as of harmony or *symphonia*. The Emperor Justinian described *symphonia* in his Sixth Novella as

> the greatest blessings of mankind [...] and the gifts of God which have been granted us by the mercy on high are the priesthood and the imperial authority. The priesthood ministers to things divine; the imperial authority is set over and shows diligence in things human but both proceed from one and the same source and both adorn the life of man.

Later, in the fourteenth century, the theologian Nicholas Cabasilas pointed out that both king and priest are anointed with holy oil, and 'have the same intent and the same power'.[27] Passages such as these set out a social and political view of the nature of the church. Here, the church is not so much a community of believers but rather a department of state. It is part of the social fabric of society, and so under the rule of the king.

The sacred traditions of kingship were expressed in texts written in the medieval period. The king lived, not in a permanent settlement, but in a huge city of tents which settled in different parts of the kingdom, stayed until the firewood was used and the food consumed when it would move on. The camp varied in size as soldiers and others arrived and left depending on the season. It could have a diameter of several kilometres, and include 40,000 inhabitants.[28] The arrangement of the camp followed a fixed pattern, which was set out in the text *Ser'atä Mängest* or 'orders of power'. This text gives the rituals for setting up and dismantling the camp and the position of the different elements of it. The city of tents was set out according to carefully defined principles, with a double circle at its centre for the king and his court. The innermost part was reserved for the king and his personal servants. Around that was a second circular enclosure, with a fence marking out the compound, where the tents of the queens, usually three in number, the military leaders and the various church officials, including the abuna, were pitched. The king was at the centre of the camp, as he was at the centre of the state, appointed by God and with a sacred position.

The divine election of the king, and so his separateness from others, was demonstrated to all by the rituals of coronation, recorded at various points of the history of the kingdom. Royal chronicles describe the coronation of Särsä Dengel (1563–79) who was crowned at Aksum and was greeted by women chanting 'Be blessed O king of Israel', and was then asked who he was. He described his descent beginning with the reply, 'I am the son of David, son of Solomon, son of Ebna Hakim [or Menelek]', and continuing through more recent ancestors. He then cut a silken cord to enter the church as people proclaimed, 'truly truly, thou art the king of Zion, son of David, son of Solomon'.[29] He was then crowned and confirmed in his divinely appointed rule.

Within his tent at the centre of the innermost circle, the king sat behind a curtain and so could not be seen by his subjects. He communicated with them through a spokesman who kept his eyes lowered. If he rode outside people looked downwards so as not to see the king, and it was said that anyone who dared to raise his eyes was immediately executed. If a command of the king was addressed, then the recipient took off his clothes from the waist up and bowed down, placing his hands on the ground.

A fuller description of the awe-inspiring experience of an audience with the king comes from Francisco Alvares who visited King Lebnä Dengel in the early sixteenth century, in the final years of the great medieval Christian kingdom. He and his companions, he tells us, approached along a great avenue of arches, twenty on each side, covered alternately with red and white cotton cloths. Many people were gathered in rows, about 20,000 people in all, and four horses caparisoned and with diadems, and four lions. The king, however, they did not see. He remained in his tent, or perhaps seated on a high platform surrounded by canopies of cloth. It was his custom to show himself to his people only three times a year, at Christmas, Easter and Holy Cross Day. This concession of actually appearing was of recent origin since it was said that his grandfather never showed himself and in fact was dead for three years before the news leaked out. So now the king condescended to appear from time to time.

Eventually they were invited to set eyes on the king. It was after dark and when they had waited for three hours in the chilly night air they found many more people than before gathered around the tent. They passed though one set of curtains then another and then found themselves before a large platform with rich carpets. Around this were further curtains even richer than those before. When they were opened they saw the king, sitting on a platform of six steps. He had on his head a crown of gold and silver. There was a piece of blue taffeta cloth which covered his mouth and beard, which was from time to time lowered so that they could see all of his face. 'He was sitting in majesty as they paint God the Father on the wall [...] [I]n presence and state he looked like the great lord that he is'.[30]

This separation of the king from his subjects continued into the later Gondar period. James Bruce describes the arrangement of the court.

> [The king] sat constantly in a room of his palace, which communicated with the audience [chamber] by two folding doors [...] which were about three steps from the ground. These doors [...] were latticed with cross-bars of wood like a cage, and a thin curtain [...] was hung within it, so that, upon darkening the inner chamber, the King saw every person in the chamber while he himself was not seen at all.[31]

The power of the kings in this period was greatly diminished, yet the mystery and awe surrounding the figure of the king remained.

These features of kingship are also found in other states in the region, on both sides of the Red Sea. The divine status of the ruler is protected by a complex ritual system and a symbolic avoidance of contact. Western influences, especially when Jesuit missionaries were present, introduced different principles, but the divinely appointed status of the king persisted, as is shown by the account from Bruce. A much later example comes from the twentieth-century Caribbean when the figure of Haile Sellassie, with his titles showing divine choice, provided a focus for the aspirations of young Jamaicans forming the Rastafarian movement.[32]

The kingship descended within the chosen royal family. The succession was difficult to manage, since kings usually had several wives and many sons, and the principle of primogeniture was not necessarily followed. In 1508, for example, Alvares tells us that Lebnä Dengel was chosen by the abuna and queen, because they had 'all the great men and the treasure in their hands'. So, he commented, 'beside primogeniture, supporters, friendship and treasure enter into the question'.[33] A younger son might be seen as the more capable successor or might have more support from leading courtiers, or might be seen by powerful nobles to be less mature and so easier to manipulate. In order to reduce the risk of the emergence of rival claimants to the throne, prospective heirs were kept under close guard on a flat-topped amba, from where a suitable candidate could be selected when needed.

Descent within the family was valued and tenaciously adhered to. Even when the power of the king was in decline during the eighteenth century and later, the kings had little power but were maintained on the throne to preserve the Solomonic succession. Eventually power prevailed over descent. A bandit from the west of the country, Kassa Haylu, won a series of victories to overcome his rivals. He gained custody of abuna Sälama and was crowned king of kings, as emperor Téwodros II. He was the first of four great kings of the modern era who came from different families and different parts of the country. All were considered to be legitimate successors of a dynasty which reached back to Menelek and Solomon, even though they were not directly descended.[34]

The sacral nature of royal power had the result that kings were often ordained as priests. Many were brought up and educated in monasteries, learning alongside those who were ordained as priests.

It seems that some kings had also been made priests. Among these were three Zagwe kings, Yemrehännä Krestos, Lalibäla and Nä'akuto Lä'ab, and it was probably Yemrahännä Krestos who was observed by the Egyptian traveller Abu Makarim celebrating the Eucharist, or *qedassé*.[35] Many later kings were also priests. Even if not formally ordained priest, his royal power made him able to enter the holy of holies in the church, where, along with the priests and deacons, he took an active part in church liturgy. A later king, Iyäsu I the Great (1682–1706), visited Aksum on several occasions, on one of which he entered the holy of holies where the tabot, which was the Ark made by Moses, miraculously opened itself and instructed him how to rule the kingdom. The king could carry out priestly acts, and might carry the tabot in to the sanctuary.[36] Emperor Yohannes IV was among those who grew up in a monastery, and he intended at first to become a monk. He vowed never to take vengeance on his enemies or amass a personal fortune, and generally did behave in a more generous way than usual towards his enemies.[37]

The king chose the leading administrators and leaders of the church, and tents were allocated to them in prescribed positions in the royal camp. These were the leaders of the prominent monasteries. Their presence at court enabled the king to remain in contact and to communicate with the monasteries, which were scattered through the country. They have been described as a 'transmission belt between the royal power and the regional religious institutions, notably the monasteries, which exercised power locally'.[38] The abbot of Däbrä Libanos was the senior church official, called the *echägé*; with the abbot of Hayq, called *aqqabé sä'at*, as the second in command. The king had the power to dismiss them and replace them with others. The arrangement benefitted both the king who retained power over the church and the monasteries who received money and influence. It was believed that as a result of these benefactions the church owned a third of the land.[39]

Kings founded many churches. These churches became places which provided a focus for the power of the king. Often he set up his camp at one of the royal churches; he summoned church councils to meet at them; and when he died he was buried at one of them. Among the most celebrated was the Church of Däbrä Birhan Sellassie, or the Trinity of the Mountain of Light, founded by King Zär'ä Ya'eqob, and where he set up his camp for a period of fourteen years.

The town has kept the name of Däbrä Birhan, and it is an indication of the significance of these churches, at least to the kings, that a king who ruled two hundred years later chose the same name for his foundation of Däbrä Birhan Sellassie, in Gondar.[40]

The identity of church and state had the result that doctrinal division in the church led to disunity in the state. Doctrinal controversies often arose out of regional rivalry, and the opposing views were supported by rival monastic houses and nobles. So the only way to bring the kingdom to unity was for the king to enforce conformity on the warring factions. This was not easy, and could only be achieved by a strong king. Councils were summoned to resolve disagreements, but these were more like royal law courts in which opponents were punished than meetings of theologians debating points of doctrine.[41]

The importance of the king in resolving controversy is shown in his intervention in two major issues which divided the church. The Sabbatarian controversy divided the kingdom during the fourteenth and fifteenth centuries. The house of Éwostatéwos through its monasteries in the north observed the Jewish Sabbath as well as the Christian Sunday, while the house of Täklä Haymonot followed the teaching of Alexandria, as represented by the abuna, and opposed the keeping of the Sabbath. Zär'ä Ya'eqob (1434–68) legislated to establish the Christian faith. He recognised the tenacity and growth of the northern teaching of Éwostatéwos, and summoned a council to the new church of Däbrä Mitmaq in 1450. The king presided, overruled the bishops who were committed to the more usual position that Sunday only was a holy day, and decreed that the Sabbatarian teaching of the northern monks became the position of the church. This led to the end of a schism in the church and brought order to his kingdom. He also affirmed the central place of Mary in the life of the church, and commanded his subject to be tattooed on the forehead with the words 'belonging to the Father the Son and the Holy Spirit', along with other texts on the arms. His works of theology include the *Mäshaf Berhan* or Book of Light, and the *Mäshaf Milad* or the Book of the Birth of Jesus Christ.

Another long-running controversy concerned the nature of Christ, with three main regional parties struggling for dominance. The kings tirelessly summoned a series of councils through the seventeenth and eighteenth centuries, which supported varying positions depending on the sympathies of the king or the view of the dominant political power at the time. The weakness of the king through that period prevented a resolution of the conflict. In 1881 the Tigrayan Emperor Yohannes IV found himself strong enough to summon a council at Borru Meda. Under his leadership and authority, the Council declared that the doctrinal position of the northern area where Yohannes came from should be the official teaching of the church. The argument in support of this doctrine rested not on theological debate, but on the decision of the king. This council was influential in the foundation of the modern Ethiopian state, placing the Orthodox Christian faith as a central and defining characteristic.

It is often said that Yohannes relied on the *Kebrä Nägäst* as a justification for this set of policies, and that after General Napier had carried off texts of this work to London as part of the treasure procured during his rescue mission to save British missionaries from the emperor Téwodros in 1868, Yohannes wrote requesting the return, not of the wealth, crowns or sacred objects, but of the *Kebrä Nägäst.* He explained that he was making this request because the *Kebrä Nägäst* contained the regulations of the land and 'my people will not obey my orders without it'. These last words need to be treated with caution since they are not included in the Amharic version of this letter but only in the English translation. They were added, perhaps, to add emphasis to the request, and may well have been a fair representation of the view that was held by the king.[42]

Some aspects of Christian teaching proved less attractive to the kings. The biblical command to remain loyal to one wife was not seen as a requirement by the kings who followed the local practices of having several wives and concubines. Not only was polygamy an accepted local custom, but it was a part of the royal strategy to consolidate power, by connecting the king with leading families and local rulers through marriage. Five or six wives was seen as a sensible number of alliances to ensure the continuation of the dynasty. This polygamous practice led to tension with rigorists in the church, usually monks who were on occasion supported by the abuna. On these occasions the king eventually prevailed and dissident monks were forced to the southern areas of Ethiopia: the kings continued to marry several wives.

THE IDENTITY OF CHURCH AND STATE

The divine origin of kingship was expressed as recently as the constitution of 1955, formulated in the later years of Haile Selassie as an expression of his autocratic style of personal rule. During the early years of his reign the emperor had struggled to gain authority in the face of powerful nobles. As his reign continued, and especially after his return from exile after the defeat of the Italians in 1941, he became more confident in expressing the historical role and divine authorisation of the king. Article 2 of the Constitution states that the ruling dynasty is descended from Menelek I, son of Makeda and King Solomon. The king is the head of the church as well as the state, or rather state and church are indistinguishable. Earlier he had written in a letter to the Egyptian patriarch in 1945 in the course of negotiation for an Ethiopian abuna, that 'the church is like a sword and the government like an arm; therefore the sword cannot cut by itself without the use of the arm'.[43]

Within this kingdom, the abuna was the representative of the church. By his personal presence, he provided the relationship with the church beyond the borders of Ethiopia, and by his authority to ordain clergy, he provided a large class of religious ministers to carry out the worship of the church and to maintain the position as a source of spiritual power. Other forms of leadership were closed to him. He did not provide justice or hear law cases – that was the role of the king; nor did he administer the church – that task fell to the monastic leaders personally appointed by the king, especially the *echägé*; nor did he preside over councils or teach the faith – since he lacked the language and knowledge of the people. He had a clear but restricted role, and was excluded from the practical business of governing the church.

Church and state were contained within the same boundaries and were governed by the same power. The church in Ethiopia should not be described as a community of believers, but as a chosen people. These were ruled by a divinely appointed king, who was responsible for the well-being of his people through his personal government.

CHAPTER 4

Sacred Space and Sacred Time: An Approach to Worship

HISTORY: THE DECLINE OF AKSUM AND THE ZAGWE DYNASTY

The political and economic life of the region was transformed by the appearance of a new religion. When the prophet Muhammad died in Mecca, Arab armies were already beginning their rapid advance. They conquered Syria in 637, followed this up with victory over Egypt in 639, and then across much of the North African coast by 652. Alongside military victories on land, the Arab navy grew more powerful in the Red Sea, and disrupted the trading relations which had brought prosperity to the kingdom of Aksum. As a result trade at the port of Adulis declined, and with it the economic basis of the Aksumite kingdom. This led to changes in Aksum, as warfare and agriculture became the activities which bound the kingdom together. Political, economic and cultural influence shifted away from the north, and moved into new areas to the east and south.

This accelerated a trend of southward expansion within Ethiopia which was already in progress. In the previous century the seafarer Cosmas Indicopleustes had recorded that in the area around Aksum 'there are everywhere churches of the Christians, and bishops, martyrs, monks and recluses by whom the gospel of Christ is proclaimed [...] in Ethiopia and Axom and in all the country about it'.[1] His remark suggests that Christianity was already expanding into the mountains and becoming rooted among the farmers of the mountains of Tigray and the high plateau.

New political forces jockeyed for control of the Aksumite state. Several sources report a forty-year rule by a queen of great beauty and ruthlessness, and of the Jewish faith, Gudit or Jodit, who destroyed the church of Maryam Tsion at Aksum, as a result of which the Ark was removed for safekeeping to Zway in the south. She is said to have been queen of Bani al Hamwiyah, although it is not clear where this was located. She is remembered by later Christian writers as a destructive force which threatened the Christian faith.[2]

The eventual winners in the struggle for power in the vacuum left by the decline of Aksum was the new dynasty of the Zagwe. Unlike the kings of Aksum who spoke a Semitic language, the Zagwe were from one of the Cushitic ethnic groups, and spoke an Agaw language. They were a mountain people who came from the region to the south of the Tigrayan coastal plain, in the areas of Wag and Lasta. Their capital was a town called Adafa, although no trace of this settlement remains. From here they expanded their power base over a wide area, to Aksum in the north, Lake Tana in the west and into Amhara regions in the south.[3]

Reconstruction of the history of the dynasty is complicated by inconsistencies in the lists of kings. The different accounts provide lists of kings varying in number between five and eleven, and several kings are each said to have reigned for the suspiciously regular time span of exactly forty years. This variation in the king-lists allows for a period of Zagwe rule of anywhere between 133 and 333 years. The end date is undisputed since the defeat of the last Zagwe, Yitbarak, by the Shewan war lord Yekuno Amlak took place in 1270, but the beginning of the dynasty is uncertain. An early date is indicated by the date of the decline of Aksum, which would have left a power vacuum available to be filled by AD 900 at the latest. Other pieces of evidence point to a later date. An Egyptian chronicle for the year 1150 describes a usurping king of Ethiopia asking for a new abuna, which could be a reference to the start of the Zagwe dynasty, which would place the beginning of Zagwe power in the twelfth century. Taddesse Tamrat has proposed a list of seven kings, which has received general support from scholars. According to his list, the dynasty was founded by Marara, followed by Täntäwedem, Yemraha Krestos, Harbe, Lalibäla, Nä'akuto Lä'ab and Yitbarak.[4]

The Zagwe kings are – confusingly – remembered as both usurpers, who interrupted the line of Semitic kings descended from Menelek, but also as holy and devout, with some, including Lalibäla, commemorated as saints. This puzzling mixed message is best accounted for by the regional character of the traditions, with hagiographical traditions coming out of Lalibäla and surrounding regions, leading to the reverence given to the kings, while the circles around the next line of Solomonic kings dismissed their Zagwe predecessors as interlopers. Apologists for the Zagwe may be responsible for the tradition that they were also descended from Solomon but through the handmaid of the Queen of Sheba rather than the Queen herself.

KING LALIBÄLA AND THE NEW JERUSALEM

The great monuments left by the Zagwe are churches, especially the churches of the town of Lalibäla. These are recognised as a great achievement of Ethiopian civilisation and are now a UNESCO world heritage site. There are eleven churches, grouped in three clusters, all carved from rock, below ground level, connected by trenches and passages cut in the rock. The largest, Mehdane Alem, or Saviour of the World, is 30 m in length, while others are smaller. The church of Danagel, for example, measures only 9.5 by 8.5 m. The Portuguese traveller Alvares saw them in the fifteenth century and was amazed at the sight, and fears that his accounts will arouse incredulity. 'It wearied me to write more of these works because it seemed to me that they [my readers] will accuse me of untruth [...] [T]here is much more than I have already written and I have left it that they may not tax me with it being falsehood.'[5] While the uniqueness of the rock churches of Lalibäla have attracted and surprised visitors in the years which succeeded, they belong within a tradition of church construction, and a tradition of worship, which took a direction different from other parts of the Christian world.

Churches were constructed to serve the communities around. Their style and method of construction went through several stages. Both archeological remains and existing churches show an evolving tradition of church-building and of worship. We can distinguish four stages. Churches were, firstly, basilicas. Then, as the kingdom moved into the mountainous interior, rock-hewn and cave churches became the usual style of construction. These were increasingly replaced by the round church. A recent development is a return to the basilica style, as a result of influences from other parts of the Christian world.

The earliest churches of the Aksumite kingdom were basilicas. The most celebrated was the cathedral at Aksum, of which various reports have survived. It is said to have been a rectangular basilica with a large central nave with two aisles on each side, and was probably located on the site of the present church of Maryam Tsion, which dates from the seventeenth century. This older church was admired by Muslim refugees in the seventh century and visitors spoke of its beauty and of its wall paintings, and it was visited by Alvares in the fifteenth century.[6] Archeological research has uncovered remains of other basilica-style churches to the north of Aksum at Adulis and Matara. A rare surviving example of an Aksumite basilica is the monastic church of Däbrä Damo, on the top of a flat mountain east of Aksum, to which access is only possible by means of a rope hanging down a steep cliff face which allows the visitor to be pulled up by the monks. This church shows typical architectural features of Aksumite church-building, with alternate projections and recesses giving a striped appearance, with short horizontal beams binding the structure together and protruding to form 'monkey head' rounded shapes, and with carved ceilings with friezes and central panels. David Phillipson suggests a construction date for this church of some time between 600 and 700, based in part on similarity to some of the Aksumite tombs which are dated to that period, but others prefer a later date.[7]

The next stage of church-building took place at the time of the Zagwe. Several examples are found in the area around their capital, Arafa. The traditions of these churches associate them with the names of several of the Zagwe kings. Yemrha Krestos, who reigned in the period around 1175, constructed a church in a cave, which was constructed from stone and followed the architectural style of Aksum. Then Lalibäla, who ruled between 1200 and 1225, built the network of eleven churches carved into the rock of a settlement, which today retains his name. Lalibäla's nephew and successor Nä'akuto Lä'ab is recorded as building further churches, including – probably – the church of Asheten Maryam, higher up the mountain, and Gännäta Maryam. These churches were built in or around caves, either natural or man-made. Some, like the church of Yemrha Krestos, were built of stone and other materials, within an existing cave. Some were carved out of caves which were excavated and shaped to form churches. Some were built by first excavating the rock

FIGURE 4.1 Approaching the monastery of Däbrä Damo. Monasteries were often built on a flat-topped amba.

FIGURE 4.2 The church at Däbrä Damo is a late Aksumite basilica type church.

FIGURE 4.3 The exterior walls show the protruding cross beams, called monkey heads. These can also be seen on the stela in Figure 3.1.

to leave a large block of stone surrounded by a courtyard, which was then sculpted into a church, and of these the cruciform church of Giyorgis is a good example. Some had elements of different methods, for example Abba Libanos was carved within a cave so that the walls have been excavated and freed from surrounding rock while the top of the church has not been separated from the roof of the cave. The use of the cave provided permanence and indestructability so that, while many built churches were destroyed by enemy attack or by natural processes, rock churches have survived.

The use of the cave led to a new approach to the design of churches. At Aksum, as at other places, the church was central, visible, large and ornate. But at Lalibäla, instead of being visible, the churches were out of sight, below ground level; instead of there being one single church, there were eleven churches; instead of being a large place of worship, these were small and insufficient to accommodate the worshipping community. This change in church-building, from the church as a single prominent building constructed from various building materials, often in the centre of a town, to a

FIGURE 4.4 The church at Yemrha Krestos is a built church, but in a cave.

network of churches carved out of caves in rural areas, shows a change not only in the design of the church, but in the idea of what a church is for, and the nature of the worship carried out in it. The rock churches are a new and distinctive development in the history of the church which is shown at its clearest in the achievement of the Zagwe at Lalibäla.

To see how this new development took place we can begin with the life of Lalibäla. His story is told in a hagiographical life written several centuries after the events recorded.[8] The name Lalibäla means 'let the bees obey him' and this name was chosen because at his birth a swarm of bees surrounded him, a sign of his unique attractiveness to these insects who know all about what is sweet.[9] His brother was the king, Harbe, and both he and his sister hated their younger brother, and so she prepared a cup of poison for him. Lalibäla was a loving and generous man and so rather than drinking the refreshing cup himself, he gave it to his thirsty young deacon who drank from it and immediately died from the virulent poison, as did a passing dog which licked the dying man. Lalibäla, knowing his unworthiness and realising the cup was meant for him, took what was left after the demise of the deacon and the dog, finished it off and collapsed. However, instead of dying he was transported by an angel to the third heaven where he was shown ten fabulous churches carved out of a single rock. 'Each had its own style, colour and unique appearance. Some had narrow entrances and spacious interiors; others had large doors and slender interiors; their walls were long and high, and some were higher than others, and each had its own colour.'[10] After three days he returned to his body to find that preparations for his funeral were in hand. His friends were amazed at his unexpected return to his body.

In due course Lalibäla had a dream in which he was anointed king, and simultaneously his brother was instructed to hand over the throne in another dream. Harbe, the brother, now no longer consumed by hatred for Lalibäla, did this with joy, and Lalibäla, now renamed Gäbrä Mäsqäl or Servant of the Cross, began his reign. As he grew older his thoughts returned to his miraculous journey into the heavens and he began to construct churches as he had been shown. He assembled a great number of craftsmen for this great work of carving the churches out of the rock. These were joined in their work by angels. During the day both men and angels worked together and when night fell the angels continued the work while the men slept. So when the workmen woke in the morning, four times as much building had been done in the night as had been done in the preceding day. As a result the work continued quickly and the heavenly churches were faithfully reproduced.

Analysis of the churches of Lalibäla shows a mixture of styles and types of building. Because of this, David Phillipson thinks that the excavation of the churches was carried out over a long period, with the earliest parts of the complex made for secular use. He suggests a construction period starting in the seventh or eighth century, with the latest, Beta Giyorgis, excavated in the thirteenth or fourteenth centuries.[11] This does not rule out the initiative of king Lalibäla in creating this group of churches, but would attribute to the king the work of the adaptation and connection of a network of existing structures to form the complex of churches seen today, rather than the complete excavation. His reign more or less coincided with the fall of Jerusalem to Saladin in 1187, which made access to the holy city for pilgrims more difficult. The formation of the group of churches at Lalibäla may have been encouraged by a desire for a new pilgrimage centre at the heart of Ethiopia, which would become a new holy city of Zion.

His great project was not intended to be an exact copy of the holy city Jerusalem itself. It was not modelled on any specific location, like, say, the Madaba mosaic map in Jordan with its exact topographical detail representing the buildings of the holy city. Rather it was built to be a holy city, a new Jerusalem, revealed to the king, when he was carried in a death-and-resurrection experience into the highest heaven, and then followed up with a further miraculous visit to Jerusalem. Lalibäla set out to create a place where God's presence is found and where the worshipper and pilgrim can travel to enter the holy presence. In Lalibäla's new Jerusalem there is a river Jordan, a place of cleansing and repentance, which is an artificial valley dividing the groups of churches. The large church, Mehdane Alem, the Saviour of the World, stands in one of the clusters, and alongside it is the church of Maryam or Mary, since Mary, Jesus' mother, stands next to him.[12] They are surrounded by other churches which are connected to them. There is Golgotha where Jesus died, and churches dedicated to angels and virgins. After all the churches had been completed, St George, the great warrior who fights for the Ethiopians, realised that he had not been honoured with a church dedicated to him, and he appeared to Lalibäla in a dream to rebuke him for this oversight. On waking Lalibäla set out to create the most beautiful of all the churches, and the marks of the hooves of St George's horse can be seen in the passage which leads to the church as the saint approached to inspect it.

Pilgrims can travel to this new Jerusalem and find the fullness of their faith presented to them. Here, the space is given a new kind of meaning and is closely identified with the events commemorated. This identification of places with the events of the Bible was to be expressed in succeeding centuries and in other parts of Ethiopia by the choice of names of places. As the modern traveller goes to different parts of the country he encounters many places with biblical names. Near Däbrä Tabor, the Mount of Transfiguration, in South Gondar, is the monastery of Bethlehem which is approached through Ephratah. The Oromo town of Bishoftu became Däbrä Zäyt, the Mount of Olives, which is on the road to Nazret, the former Oromo Adamaa, to the east, while the town of Hosanna or Palm Sunday is in the opposite direction.

FIGURE 4.5 The largest church in the Lalibäla complex is the church of Mehdane Alem.

FIGURE 4.6 The cruciform church of St George is the most intricate in design.

FIGURE 4.7 The best examples of the carving and painting in the Lalibäla churches are in the church of Maryam.

ROCK CHURCHES

The churches of Lalibäla were known to European visitors, from Alvares onward. While they admired them, they were not aware that Lalibäla was only one example of a much wider style and practice. Not far away was another much larger cluster of rock churches, more extensive, more breathtaking in scale and achievement, and unknown to non-Ethiopians. These are the rock churches of north-east Tigray, where well over 150 churches are scattered over a rocky area of land north of the city of Makelle, and contain a number of villages which form the central point of groups of churches excavated in the countryside around – Atsbi, Wukro, Dugem, Megab, Hawzien and Abi Aday.

They have been places of worship for the local people for centuries but, extraordinarily, remained unknown and unvisited by people outside the communities of farmers and local people. There were just a few exceptions. In 1868 General Napier passed through Wukro with his expeditionary force on their way to the showdown with Emperor Téwodros at Maqdala. He visited a church cut into the rock. In the

FIGURE 4.8 The mountainous region of Tigray contains many rock churches. This is the region called Gheralta.

following century, in 1939, two Italian archeologists, Enza Parona and Antonio Mordini, described the church of Enda Maryam Weqro at Amba Sennayt, and suggested that they had heard of more rock-hewn churches. It was not until 1966, at the Conference of Ethiopian Studies, that the secretary of the Roman Catholic bishop of Adigrat, Father Täwaldä Medhin Josef, reported that he had been asking around the area and local people had told him of many more rock churches in the surrounding region, and that he concluded that there were many more of these churches. This suggestion initiated a series of expeditions in search of rock churches. Abba Täwaldä himself joined the Swiss photographer Georg Gerster and German scholar Roger Schneider for a series of explorations arranged by the Ethiopian Institute of Archeology. Later that year they visited thirty-six rock churches never before seen by non-Ethiopians, some of which were only a few minutes' walk from the main highway.

Another early researcher was David Buxton, an English entomologist whose main task was the control of mosquitoes but whose enthusiasm was the ancient churches of Tigray. He visited many of the churches and provided descriptions, architectural plans and photographs of features of their decoration. He described the different forms of construction, showing that most follow a basilica pattern, with some more primitive in style than others. Later a new cruciform or cross in a square style developed. In the cruciform style, the corners were removed from a square basilica structure to make the distinctive style seen at its most intricate at Giyorgis at Lalibäla. Buxton was struck by the continuity in the tradition, and the similarity between the rock churches and the built churches. He pointed out that the different construction methods shared common decorative features, derived from Aksumite styles of architecture, so that the architectural styles of the rock-hewn churches can be compared to the built churches of the Aksumite and subsequent periods. The same features, derived from Aksumite architecture, can be found in all churches of the period. In the case of the rock-hewn churches, these are carved imitations, and can be compared to the way that the stelae at Aksum are carved replicas of domestic architecture. From these conclusions, Buxton shows that the churches can be placed in different categories, according to architectural design, and can then be placed in a chronological sequence, according to the closeness of their style to Aksumite models. So from this he suggests that the churches of Tigray and Lalibäla were constructed in periods from the tenth to the fifteenth centuries.[13] In a more recent study, David Phillipson argues for an earlier dating. He considers that the earliest rock churches were excavated in the Aksumite period, perhaps as early as the sixth century. The phase of construction of rock churches in Tigray continued until AD 1000, when the power base of the kingdom shifted south to Lalibäla, which became the location for the next generation of rock churches. The next phase of Tigrayan churches came in the twelfth and thirteenth centuries with the reign of the Solomonic kings.[14] The researches of Buxton and Phillipson, among others, show a developing tradition of church-building within Ethiopia, originating in Aksum, and showing independence from foreign influence. The Lalibäla churches belong within this historical tradition.

We need to ask why this laborious method of construction was chosen. Some estimates suggest that 40,000 people would have been needed to carve the Lalibäla churches, and the life of Lalibäla provided the information that angels assisted in the work, which accounted for the achievement. Perhaps we should not exaggerate the size of the task. Rock churches are still being excavated. One church with a capacity of 100 cubic metres has recently been excavated by a priest, Fr Halefon Teka, in a village in Tigray called Mellehayzengi in his spare time over a period of twelve years.[15] The devoted work of Fr Halefon demonstrates the possibility of the task, but also shows the dedication and time needed. It leaves the question of why this method should have been chosen in preference to the earlier and more familiar styles of building with blocks of stone, wood or other available materials. It is easier to build a church than to carve it out of rock – yet the tradition of excavation in preference to construction became established in Ethiopia.

We can get a sense of why this development happened by visiting the churches, and especially through observing not only the church itself but its environment. The church of Adi Qosho Mehdane Alem is a good example. It is in Tigray 30 km north of the town of Wukro. The church is carved out of a cave in a rock face about 4 km east of the road. On the track approaching the church the visitor is shown the marks made in the rock by the horse ridden by Christ when he visited the place, then the cave is seen, sealed off by a stone wall. Once inside there is a large space, 13 m from west to east and 11 m from north to south, with four columns carved from the rock. There is a dome over the sanctuary and a carved Aksumite frieze. Outside there is a grove of trees, shading a spring of water. People come on the festivals of the church, visit the place and drink the holy water from the spring, called *sebel*. This church demonstrates both magnificent design and ambitious execution, but also a conjunction of physical features which suggests that the site was chosen carefully. The grove of trees and the spring of water suggest that it was a sacred place before the church was made.[16]

The church at Adi Qosho is located in a place of natural significance, with trees, a cave and water in a hilly site. This congruence of physical features shows us the reason for this choice of location. People came to these places to worship and to encounter the divine. Caves were the sites of churches because they were already recognised as holy. The process of church-building was an expression of the arrival of the new Christian faith, which retained the reverence in the place, but supplanted the spirits who had been

FIGURE 4.9 The church of Adi Qosho Mehdane Alem is built in the mountains and is surrounded by green trees.

seen as inhabiting the site. The lives of the monks give many examples of a missionary strategy which led them to come to a holy place, demonstrate the superior power of the Christian God and then build a church on the holy site.

This shows why there are many churches in rocky caves or tops of hills or near a stream or amidst groves of trees, or as at Adi Qosho in an environment with most of the four of these natural features. The caves were recognised as holy places because they enclose dark, mysterious depths – threatening and enticing, mysterious and inaccessible. Georg Gerster, who took part in an early survey of rock churches, recalls arriving at a church in Hawzien. The priest resolutely denied them access 'in their own interests' because an easily disturbed and dangerous snake inhabited the sanctuary of the church. They pointed out that they had a good first-aid kit with effective anti-snakebite serum. This of course was not the point, and they did not at that time gain admittance.[17] The snake was revered as divine, and the priest defended the holy place entrusted to him, recognising the significance and numinous quality of this place.

FIGURE 4.10 Alongside the church at Adi Qosho is a spring of holy water.

FIGURE 4.11 Many rock churches have magnificent carved interiors.

ROUND CHURCHES

The idea of the church as a sacred place went through a further stage of development with a new style of church-building which is found from the fifteenth century. The first reference to a round church is found in the reports of the Portuguese traveller Manuel de Almeida describing the church of the lady Mary at Amba Gishen as 'round, with two concentric rows of columns and a chapel in the centre'. This church was built in the reigns of Na'od (1495–1508) and Lebnä Dengel (1508–40).[18] After this, round churches became more common so that now it is a usual style of church found in Ethiopia.

The round church brings together the character of both the basilica and the cave. Like the Christian basilica, it has the three divisions of sanctuary, choir and nave. Like the cave church, it directs the worshipper towards the holiness and separateness enshrined in the church. But the round design leads to a change in the expression and relationship with that holiness in the church. In the cave, the holy is found in the darkness and depth at the end of the cave; while in the round church it is enclosed in a centre of concentric circles. Round churches were often located on the flat-topped ambas, which enabled other buildings, and so a community, to gather around them. The connection between the church and the mountain top is shown by the use of the word *däbr* for both monastery and mountain.

The familiar pattern of three divisions with the demarcation between sanctuary, choir and nave is retained, but in the round churches of Ethiopia the spaces are more sharply divided, so that instead of three divisions of one single space, they become three separate spaces, often forming different rooms. At the centre is the *mäqdäs*, or holy of holies, which is surrounded by a solid wall, with three doors leading into it – and into which only priests and deacons are permitted to enter.[19] Around the *mäqdäs* is the *qeddist*, or holy place, where those who receive communion stand, and this too is surrounded by a circular wall. Around the *qeddist* is yet another space in which the *däbtära* stand, which is called the *qené mahlet*. Sometimes the circle is adapted to become a rectangle, in which case the *mäqdäs* remains at the centre but is square, with walls often covered by paintings, and surrounded on all four sides by the *qeddist*.

In the round church, the holy place is still at the heart of the church but now it is in the centre of a circular structure rather than in the deepest end of a cave. In both cases the worshipper is in no doubt that she is in the presence of the holy. The circular design is found in domestic architecture, where a post is placed at the centre of the house and a circular roof and walls are built around it. This form of house, known as a *tukul*, is found in all parts of Ethiopia. But the closer parallel is the camp of the king, set out in circular form and containing at its centre the sacred presence of the king.[20]

The threefold design of the church has led to it being compared with the Jerusalem Temple.[21] The Temple was destroyed and rebuilt on two occasions, until the third Temple of Herod was finally destroyed by the Roman Emperor Titus in AD 70. The first Temple of Solomon has been progressively concealed under the relics of violent and climactic historical change, but its design can be reconstructed through the accounts of its building at two points in the Old Testament (1 Kings 6–8, with a parallel account in 2 Chronicles 2–4) and some occasional references which help us imagine what it was like.

The Temple in Jerusalem was a long building, rectangular in shape and surrounded by a large court. Its walls were plain and bare, with the

FIGURE 4.12 A typical round church. Ura Kidane Mehret is one of the monasteries on Lake Tana.

FIGURE 4.13 The church of Ura Kidane Mehret shows the triple design. The *mäqdäs* is behind the painted walls; the *qeddist* is the central space; while the *qené mahlet* is the exterior ambulatory.

roof higher in the middle. It was approached though one of the shorter ends, which was open. This was the vestibule – called in Hebrew *ulam*, which means 'in front'. From here the worshipper entered the large central section – the *hekal*, which can mean either 'palace' or 'temple'. Beyond that, probably reached by climbing a short flight of steps, was a square, windowless box-like shape around 30 feet in all directions.[22] This was the *debir* or Holy of Holies, where the Ark of the Covenant was placed. *Debir* might simply mean 'the back room' but it could also be derived from the verb root *dbr*, meaning speak. The second meaning is more evocative of the presence of God in the darkness from which words of power are spoken. The dimensions of the inner rooms are carefully calculated and given by the writers of the Old Testament, and from these it is clear that the inner measurements are smaller than the outer. This indicates that the three rooms are built within the outer structure with thick walls or possibly with partitions between the walls. They seem to be three separate rooms rather than one large space with screens or curtains dividing them.

Ethiopian round churches are more similar to this reconstruction of the Temple of Solomon than to the style of other churches across the Christian world. This similarity is not enough to prove that Ethiopian worship is modelled on the worship of the Old Testament Temple of Solomon, but it does point to a common culture and shared form of worship, which is derived from the Semitic historical and religious tradition, in which both Ethiopia and Israel participate, and for which the Old Testament is a significant source.

The round church forms the culmination of the development of the Ethiopian Church. The first churches were basilicas, usually placed in the centre of the town, as at Aksum, Adulis and Matara, or at a central point of the settlement as at Däbrä Damo. Later, churches were built in the holy places of the countryside to establish a Christian identity in the caves, mountains, trees and springs of traditional religion. With the new round layout, the church no longer has to be built in a holy place. The church itself has become the holy place. It can be – and often is – built on a hill, and is usually surrounded by trees, and sometimes has a holy spring nearby. But now the holy object is at the centre and inside the church. It can be built anywhere, and is the sacred centre of a community.

THE PRESENCE OF THE ARK OF THE COVENANT

The comparison with the Temple leads to the most important feature of the Ethiopian Church. The central *mäqdäs* is not an empty space enclosing a symbolic presence of God but contains the holy object, the tabot.

The tabot is an object of holiness, since it is the Ark of the Covenant which contains the presence of God. The *Kebrä Nägäst* describes the passage of the Ark from Jerusalem to Ethiopia. The original Ark is in the church of Maryam Tsion at Aksum, but there are copies or representations of the Ark in all churches, and these are known as the tabots. Hidden from the eyes of all but the clergy, and shrouded in mystery, it is the tabot which makes a church into a holy place. Since it is little seen or known, and the descriptions of it are not clearly defined, the language used to refer to it requires clarification.

The tabot is a rectangular board made of wood or stone, marked with crosses and sometimes the name of the saint to whom it is dedicated, blessed by the patriarch or bishop, and brought to the

FIGURE 4.14 The original Ark of the Covenant is kept in the treasure house at Aksum, but can only be seen the monk who guards it.

church. Since it is the tabot which makes the church holy, it follows that when it is removed on the biggest festivals such as Epiphany or *temqät*, or on the feast of the church, then the empty building is just that, an empty building and no longer a holy place. The tabot acquires the personality of the saint or the event which the church commemorates and locates. People speak of the tabot as though it is the saint himself or the event. Several layers of significance attach to the tabot – it is the holy object; it conveys the presence of the saint; it represents the Ark of the Covenant at Aksum.

The connection with the Ark of the Covenant of the Old Testament leads to a double reference. The book of Exodus describes the Ark as a casket or chest made of acacia wood, overlaid with gold, and with two golden cherubim above it. In it are placed the tablets of the Ten Commandments (Exodus 25.10–22). So it is both a chest or container, and also the tablets of the Law which are kept inside it. This dual meaning is reflected in the construction of the altars within the sanctuary of an Ethiopian church. The tabot is an altar plate made of hard wood or marble, which is placed on or in a chest or casket.

FIGURE 4.15 Each church has a representation of the Ark, called the tabot, which is brought out on festivals, wrapped in brocaded cloths and carried on the head of a priest.

The vocabulary used within Ethiopian Christianity includes both ideas, and so the word tabot can refer both to the tablets of the Ten Commandments and to the Ark or chest in which they are contained. The literal meaning of the word tabot is a box or container. Since it has this general meaning it can, by extension, refer to other chests or containers as well as the Ark of the Covenant, producing a rich set of images. The tabot can be the Ark in which Noah led the animals to save them from the great flood. It can also be compared to Mary who carried the Christ child within her, and so the tabot is feminine. The word is used first of the holy object at the centre of worship, and then evokes the memory of other tabots or containers as well as of the Ark of the Covenant.

Another word which can be used is *selle*, which means a tablet or board, and in its plural form of *sellat* refers to the tablets on which the Ten Commandments were inscribed. So in the church, tabot, or container, and *sellat*, or tablets, are equivalent, and both refer to the Ark of the Covenant which is the altar plate.

FIGURE 4.16 This large modern altar can contain the tabot inside.

The casket or container in which the plate is kept is called the *manbara tabot* or the seat or throne of the tabot. It is designed to hold the tabot which is placed on top of it for the *qeddasé*. It may have a space within it in which the tabot can be placed when not in use for liturgical purposes. We need to be clear that this is not an altar as is

FIGURE 4.17 This smaller style of altar is being shown by a monk at Yemrha Krestos.

known and used in other parts of the worldwide church. In Ethiopia the Eucharist is celebrated on a consecrated plate, which is placed on a container. If we compare the altar with household furniture, then it is a board which is kept in a cupboard, and not a table, as would be the case in the Western church.[23]

The connection between the tabot in an individual church, the Ark which resides at Aksum and the Ark of the Covenant which was taken from the Temple at Jerusalem has led to curiosity, speculation and a spate of fascination which reaches far beyond the Ethiopian Church.

The Ark has a central place in the history of the people of Israel as told in the Old Testament. It was made by Moses, following divine directions, to contain the tablets of the Ten Commandments. It then went before the children of Israel, leading them through the desert and watching over their victorious entry into the land of Israel. The Temple of Jerusalem was built to house it, and the entry of the Ark is described in graphic and splendid detail. But then it disappears from the written record. This is the last we hear of it in the Bible. Following its entry into the Temple, there is silence about what happened to it.

The sudden and unexplained disappearance has puzzled readers ever since. But the *Kebrä Nägäst* provides the answer both as to what happened next and to its present location. It tells us that it was brought to Aksum by Azaryas the son of the High Priest, who removed it from the Temple by a trick, but the Ark came willingly and the journey went at a miraculously fast pace as the Ark and its bearers hurried to reach the new chosen people.

Those outside the Ethiopian Church have had their curiosity provoked by the story of the tabot and want to know what it looks like and whether it might possibly be that Ark made by Moses. There are occasional reports from those who claim to have seen it. The first was an Armenian merchant, Tomas Tovmacean, who came to Gondar in 1764. He and his companion were insistent that the priests show them the tablets of the Ten Commandments which they said they had. Tovmacean describes what happened next.

> They took out a parcel wrapped in cloth, and began ceremoniously to unwrap it. There was a packet wrapped in another parcel of velvet and it was not until they had removed a hundred such wrappings that they at last took out a piece of stone, with a few incomplete letters on it, and kneeling they made the sign of the cross and kissed the stone, after which the object was again wrapped up.[24]

Another Armenian, a priest called Dimotheos Sapritchian, visited Aksum in 1869. He overcame the reluctance of the priests to allow this to be seen and was eventually shown

> a pinkish marble of the type found ordinarily in Egypt [...] quadrangular, 24 cm long by 22 cm wide, and only 3 cm thick. On the edges it was surrounded by engraved flowers about half an inch wide, in the centre was a second quadrangular line in the form of a fine chain [...] while the space between the two frames contained the Ten Commandments, five on one side and five on the other, written obliquely in the Turkish fashion.[25]

These are examples of Western curiosity about the Ark.[26]

Ethiopians start from a different point of view and so have a different approach. For them the Ark is a holy object and part of the tradition of faith. It is kept safe and secure, and as the foreign visitors discovered, it is not an object to be visited or investigated. A monk is appointed guardian of the Ark, who is entrusted with its care, who does not leave it, and as his death approaches passes on this sacred responsibility to a successor.

There was a rare encounter with the Ark at the time of Emperor Iyäsu I or the Great (1682–1706) at his coronation in Aksum. On a Monday, after receiving communion the day before, at the beginning of the fast of Nineveh, he enters the holy of holies. Then the priests bring the Ark to him. It is

> enclosed within a coffer with seven locks, each lock had its own key, whose form was in no way like the other [. . .] they brought the keys and the priests began to open each lock with its own key [. . .] they came to the seventh lock and they made great efforts to open it, but they did not succeed [. . .] they took it to the king and the lock opened of itself; all who saw this miracle were astonished and amazed [. . .] Then the king beheld and looked upon the Ark of Seyon and spoke to it face to face, as formerly Esdras saw and spoke to it. Then the Ark spoke and gave counsel to the king giving him wisdom and wise counsel to govern the earthly world and to inherit the heavenly world.[27]

The episode reminds the reader of the gift of wisdom to the Old Testament King Solomon and is a solemn moment in the life of the nation. The piety and uprightness of the king is emphasised, and it is rich with biblical language and imagery. There is no attempt to show what the Ark was like, but only that it is part of a mysterious experience of faith. It points to the presence of God at the heart of Orthodox worship and spirituality.

An understanding of the Ark which ties its meaning too closely with a single object made at a given time misses the richness and comprehensiveness of its significance. Zion and the Ark are signs of the presence of God here on earth, and so have a depth of meaning which is expressed in many episodes and events in the biblical history. Some extracts from the *Kebrä Nägäst* give a sense of the place of the Ark in the tradition of faith of the church:

> With regard to Zion the Ark of the Law of God, in the beginning (God) established heaven and He decided that she (Zion) should be the dwelling place of his glory. Having decided this, He made her come down to the earth, and He granted to Moses to make a likeness of her, and He said 'Make an Ark from wood which will not rot and overlay it with pure gold, and place inside her the Word of the Law which is the Covenant which I wrote with my own finger in order that they might

> keep my law [...]'. She was made by the mind of God and not by the hand of the craftsman of a man, but He himself made her as a dwelling place of his glory. It is spiritual and full of mercy, and it is heavenly and full of light, and it is a free thing and the dwelling place of the godhead, who dwells in heaven and who moves about on earth.

Even more evocative is this list of reasons for its significance:

> He makes righteous the one who worships in purity in the pure Ark of His law, because it is called 'mercy seat', and also it is called 'refuge' and it is called 'place of sacrifice' and it is called 'place of forgiveness of sin' and it is called 'gate of life' and it is called 'glorification' and it is called 'city of refuge' and it is called 'boat' and it is called 'anchor of salvation', it is called 'house of prayer' and it is called 'place of forgiveness of sin to one who prays in purity in it'. To those who enter into his dwelling and are held by the holy ark and who pray to him with all their hearts, He will hear them and He will save them from the day of their adversity, and He will do their will because He made the Holy Ark in the form of his throne.[28]

Both Zion and the Ark of the Covenant are signs of God's presence, which bring together a rich variety of biblical themes. These include the Ark of Noah, the Ark with the Ten Commandments and the manna which fed the children of Israel in the desert, and above all the womb of Mary which contained and gave birth to the Word of God. In churches, it becomes a place of meeting with God, and so is at the centre of the church building, and is the real content and meaning of the church. So when the pilgrim approaches the Ark, he does not encounter an ancient artefact, but the presence of God, as was with God from the beginning, as was given to Moses in the Ten Commandments, as dwelt in the womb of Mary, who is thus herself an Ark, and became flesh for our salvation.

LITURGY AND WORSHIP

The worship which takes place within these churches follows a rich and many-layered pattern. I made this diary note following one Sunday service, with worship in the night followed by the *qeddasé* or Eucharist at dawn, and include it here to show the impact that the worship of the church had on me as I became familiar with it. The church I was attending was a large church in Gondar, with students of theology, monks and nuns as well as priests and deacons.

I arrived at the church on Saturday evening soon after the sun had set and as darkness was falling. There was a warm welcome. We went first to the nun's house – a corrugated iron shack. In one corner she had built a fire and an *enjära* cooking pan was on it. She was making a kind of bread known as *sänbätkitta* which would be given out to everyone after the end of the service. She had mixed *tef*, corn and water, was pouring it on the plate, spreading it out with her hand and then covering it with a huge straw cover, and then removing the flat bread, and adding it to the pile of loaves she had already made. She gave us some to try. It was delicious, with that taste of fermented *enjära* and straight from the fire.

At about 7.45 pm we went into the church. The church students of *qené* and *aquaquam* were gathering in the *qené mahlet.*[29] The *aläqa* or head of the church, clergy and teachers sat against the west wall, and the students gathered around them, so that together they formed a square. Drums, prayer sticks and sistrums were distributed. There was a friendly argument and competition as each tried to force their neighbour to take the better made stick or instrument. I was given my set and tried to join in. The chants were prolonged and repetitive, each lasting for half an hour or more. The rhythms of the sistrums were unnatural and confusing and I had to work and watch hard to keep in time. Then suddenly and abruptly the chant stopped. After an hour or two there were some prayers and a short break. All the students knew what they were doing and there were no books used. The students were small in height, and so looked younger than they probably were, with faces which seemed both young and old. One student was crippled and moved awkwardly on all fours, a couple of others were blind and led by friends. The teachers were dressed in white for the worship. The *aläqa*, sat in the middle presiding and remained in his seat, scarcely moving all through the night. By 2 am the students were tired, some fell asleep where they stood leaning on their staff, others curled up in a corner for a while to rest. About 3 am the clergy moved to the reading desk on the north wall and sang the *kidan*, a service of preparation for the *qeddasé*. At 5 am all the students stood to sing the last song with enthusiasm and energy, and when it finished and the *qeddasé* began they left the church and returned to their huts, to rest while the *qeddasé* took place.

I stayed while the two priest and three deacons sang the liturgy. I watched as they came out in turn from the *mäqdäs* and chanted the five readings from the Bible; then as the priest washed his hands after the recitation of the creed, we all bowed to each other at the peace. The congregation in church consisted of about thirty people, some young children, who received communion, the priest shielding the holy bread from their sight with his hand as he placed it in their mouth.

> The worship had taken place on several levels. In the *mäqdäs*, concealed from the sight of the people outside – but audible through a loudspeaker – the holy action of the *qeddasé* are performed. In the *qeddist* – the prayers of the *kidan* and the *sä'atat* or hours, are sung by the clergy. In the *qené mahlet* the hymns were sung and acted out through the night. I knew that outside the people were standing, reading the psalter, or sitting, or maybe sleeping stretched out on the ground.
>
> Around 9 am the *qeddasé* finished, and I finally can go outside into the bright morning sun. I am stiff, aching and exhausted, but am amazed by the sight which greets me. The compound which had been almost empty when we entered the church the evening before is now crowded with people all wrapped in their white robes, shammas for the women and gabbis for the men. It is a sight of tranquillity and purity, with the serenity of the white, the shining light of the bright sun, the swaying of the green trees above, the thick long grass, with splashes of colour as the weaver birds dart from bush to bush. After a time of preaching, everyone sits down in rows and the deacons bring *sänbätkitta*, the thick dark soft bread made the day before, and distribute large pieces to everybody taking them from the huge straw baskets. People talk, laugh and eventually and reluctantly leave.
>
> On the way back home after well over twelve hours in church I stop at the first bar I pass for strong black coffee. I am exhausted.

The distinct and different roles of clergy and people are referred to by one modern commentator as 'indoor and outdoor'.[30] Indoor worship is the worship just described, carried out by the clergy, priests and deacons, in the *mäqdäs* and *qeddist*. The Eucharist is called *qeddasé*, and is celebrated by five clergy, two priests and three deacons. These are trained in the traditional liturgy schools of the church – called *qeddasé bet* – so that they can perform the complex eucharistic liturgy. This requires knowledge of the fourteen anaphora or eucharistic prayers, as well as a large body of eucharistic hymns.

Outdoor worship takes place in the *qené mahlet* and is the responsibility of the *däbtära*. *Mahlet* is the chanting of hymns, with rhythm provided by the movement of the prayer sticks or *maqomiya*, the shaking of *sistrum*, a kind of liturgical rattle, and the beating of drums. The hymns are part of the theological tradition of the church and are an essential part of its liturgy. *Mahlet* usually takes place before the *qeddasé*, and on major festivals continues through the night. It finishes at dawn, at which point the *qeddasé* begins. There may be further chanting of *mahlet* after the end of the Eucharist.

FIGURE 4.18 Church service. Orthodox congregations dress in white to go to church, often with a cross motif on the clothing.

FIGURE 4.19 *Mahlet*. The worship continues through the night on festivals.

FIGURE 4.20 After the service. Most people have stayed outside during the service and then listen to the preaching afterwards.

To this double form of indoor and outdoor worship should be added the worship of the people. The congregation usually stay outside in the church compound. Here they sit or stand, read and pray, listen to the sermon, or are just present in the holy place.

A possible approach to understanding and entering into this style of liturgy is through a reconstruction of Temple worship in the Old Testament. This has been studied by Margaret Barker, and presented in a series of studies, which, it must be noted, have not been accepted by all scholars. She suggests that the worship of the Jerusalem Temple is one of the sources of Christian worship, and she has sought to reconstruct the liturgy which took place. One of the main ritual actions was the great sacrifice when the high priest entered the holy of holies on the Day of Atonement carrying the blood of the sacrifice.

> The high priest, who was the Lord, entered 'heaven' carrying blood which represented the life of the Lord. It was sprinkled on the 'throne' or the ark and then brought out into the visible world to renew the eternal covenant and restore the creation. This ritual anticipated the day of the Lord.[31]

It was an action which expressed God's love in healing and renewing his creation. A second ritual action was the offering of the Bread of the Presence. This bread was prepared secretly and its shape and meaning were not disclosed. It was placed outside the holy of holies in the *hekal*, concealed from human gaze by covers, offered with incense and then consumed by the priest. This offering of holy bread may be an ancient form of worship which predated the blood sacrifices of the temple and which is hinted at in several biblical texts such as the bringing out of bread and wine by Melchizedek of Salem who 'was a priest of God Most High' and then offering it to Abraham (Genesis 14.18), or the elders of Israel being kept safe from God, and 'they beheld God and they ate and drank' (Exodus 24.11); or even the familiar verse of the psalm, 'you prepare a table before me in the face of my enemies' (Psalm 23.5). If the Day of Atonement liturgy refers to the longing for God to renew his covenant, then the offering of holy bread speaks of the relationship which is established through our participation in worship.

Both these great ritual liturgical acts have echoes and resemblances in the liturgy of the Ethiopian Church. Before the *qeddasé* starts, deacons make the bread and the wine according to a secret method in the Bethlehem, 'the house of bread', which is the small house in the compound reserved for this purpose. They carry this in a large basket covered with richly brocaded cloths, preceded by bells ringing, and go into the *mäqdäs* and place this on the *manbara tabot*. If the *manbara tabot* is small then the holy bread and wine are placed on top; or if larger, then inside. Inside the paten is placed a cloth, and the bread on the cloth. The wine is in the chalice which is covered with three veils, which sometimes are so long that they reach to the floor. The priests see and touch the holy elements, the deacons see but do not touch; the people who come to receive communion neither see nor touch since the communion is sheltered from their sight by the hand of the priest. Here we find both the making of the bread of the presence and the offering of it, and also the mysterious entry of the few chosen ones into the holy of holies to offer the sacrifice. Then the priests come out from the holy of holies carrying the holy bread and the blood of the sacrifice which is offered to the people gathered as a sign for the healing and life offered for the renewal of the creation by a generous God.

The different parts of worship show the multiple liturgical actions of the rituals, performed by a variety of different people, each with a defined role in the church. They are clearly shown in the example of the Sunday worship I attended at Gondar. The church where all this happens is more than a building. It is a holy place, and a sacred site. As well as the church building with its three divisions, the compound around is part of the church, and this also contains places for teaching, eating and sleeping, all of which form part of the church and are used for liturgical action. Liturgy is far more than set services, but extends outwards to embrace the life of the community.

THE CALENDAR

Worship takes place not only in a sacred space but also in sacred time. The worship of the church and the life of the faithful are regulated by a calendar which provides a cyclical rhythm. The calendar has different dimensions which together make up a textured and complex ritual of religious observance. There are several cycles of liturgical observation which are interlocking and simultaneous. These are, first, a seasonal pattern which provides a rhythm which reflects the changing weather and cycle of harvesting; then, second, a monthly set of holy days which affirm the continuing presence of saints and religious festivals within society; then, third, a number of big national celebrations which show the Christian allegiance of the state; then the fasts which give a personal identification of the worshipper with the events of the life of Christ. These combine to give a personal and communal rhythm of worship, and to place people within a sacred calendar of time as well as a sacred landscape of space.

The changing seasons provide a structure which governs the life of an agricultural community. As seasons change, so the prayers and hymns of the church change character according to the time of year. They mark the flow of time from the *masaw* or windy season, which lasts from October to December (26 Meskerem to 25 Tahsas); then *hagay* or the dry season from January to March (26 Tahsas to 25 Megabit); then *belg* or the sowing season from April to June (26 Megabit to 25 Sane); and then *keremt* or the rainy season from July to September (26 Sane to 25 Meskerem), after which the cycle is repeated. These seasons govern the rhythm of sowing and reaping in the agricultural year, and are reflected in the liturgy of the church, with hymns and prayers, fitting the patterns of weather and climate.

Alongside the growing and harvesting which gives food and life is a different pattern of liturgy which marks the place of the saints in presiding over and guiding daily living. Here too there are various cycles. Each year is dedicated to one of the evangelists, so there is a year of Matthew, then Mark, Luke and John. Within the year there is a monthly cycle of festivals of the saints. Each day of the month is dedicated to a saint or an event in the Bible. Among these, popular celebrations are on the fifth day of the month, which is Abo day, dedicated to the popular saint Gäbrä Mänfäs Qeddus, affectionately known as Abo; the seventh, which is Sellassé or Trinity day; the twenty-third, which is Giyorgis or St George day – and so on. People go to the church dedicated to that saint on its special feast day. So each month has a regular pattern with the saints entering into and guiding people's daily lives. One or two of these monthly celebrations will have special importance for the church, and on those days very large numbers attend the church celebrating the festival. Here sacred geography and sacred chronology interweave. The church is a space and the festival day is the time which is set aside for the saint. The gathering of people at that place on that day shows the presence of the saint in the life of the community.

The third level of liturgical celebration is the great national communal festivals. Soon after Ethiopian New Year, which is celebrated like Jewish New Year on 10 September according to the Western calendar, comes *mäsqäl* or the finding of the cross. On the eve of *mäsqäl*, bonfires of wooden branches are set up in pyramid shape, with a cross on top and with strings of yellow *mäsqäl* daisies, or *enkutatash*, woven into the wood. These are set up in the town centre or in private houses, and after singing, prayers and dancing, the bonfire is lit, and people wait to see whether the cross falls to the right – which is good – or the left – which is bad. The origins of the festival lie in a pre-Christian fire ceremony to mark the start of the year, when the rains finish and growth of crops begins.[32] It is observed in most parts of Ethiopia. In Christian areas, *mäsqäl* has been given a new significance. It recalls the journey of Helena, the mother of the Byzantine Emperor Constantine, to Jerusalem to look for the cross of Christ in the fourth century. She did not know where

FIGURE 4.21 The *mäsqäl* bonfire is lit at the celebrations at Gondar.

to look and so asked the advice of a hermit, Kyriakos. He told her to light a bonfire and to watch where the smoke drifted. The place where it touched the earth was where she should dig. There she found the crosses. So the bonfire becomes a sign of how the cross is discovered, and becomes part of a Christian feast. It also has national and political significance since it was the empress who found the cross, and so *mäsqäl* shows how the social order is built upon the discovery of the presence and protection of the cross. In periods when the emperor seldom showed himself, *mäsqäl* was a day on which he often made an appearance to be seen by the people, and so showing the significance of the finding of the cross for his government.[33] In civic celebrations people of all faiths gather, with local politicians and officials of the tourist office as guests of honour. Speeches are made describing how *mäsqäl* is for all Ethiopians, and the cross is at the heart of social life.

At *temqät*, or Epiphany, which is an even more popular festival, the tabots of the churches are taken to a source of water, which is then blessed, and people swim, wash and drink in the water. It is a time of purification and forgiveness for the whole community.

Both festivals have a political and social message and are celebrated publicly with more splendour than Christmas or Easter.

Several pilgrimage centres also have a national message. The church of Gabriel at Qullubi attracts many thousands of pilgrims on its two major annual festivals. It is a modern church, undistinguished architecturally but with a famous tabot of Gabriel which brought peace and victory in answer to prayer, and so is a protector of the Ethiopian people.

Another rhythm of worship is the movement between times of fasting and feasting. There are more fasts than feasts. The fasts are as follows:

- Every Friday – because Christ died on the cross on a Friday.
- And every Wednesday – because that was when the Jews met with Judas and offered to pay him money in order to betray Jesus.
- And the fast before Easter – *Abbi Tsom* – because Christ fasted for forty days and forty nights in the desert. The forty days becomes fifty-six after you add on the last week before Easter when we remember the events of Christ's passion and then add Sundays as well.
- And the fast of the Apostles – because the apostles fasted after receiving the Holy Spirit at Pentecost. This fast lasts for a variable length of time – between ten and forty days after Pentecost.
- And the Fast of Maryam – sixteen days before the feast of the Assumption or falling asleep of the Virgin Mary.
- And the fast of Christmas – another forty days.
- And finally the little fast of Nineveh – because the people of Nineveh fasted for three days after the prophet preached to them. This begins three weeks and three days before Lent and lasts for three days.

These fast days add up to a total of about 250 days. Only monks and those who are very devout fast on all of these days. Most Ethiopian Christians observe about 180 fast days in the year. On a fast day, she or he neither eats nor drinks until afternoon when the *qeddasé* finishes. It goes without saying that they do not smoke either – since smoking is gravely frowned on. People say that where Arius, the arch heretic, spat, there tobacco grew. On some days the fasting regime is more demanding.

Various reasons have been given as to why people fast. It could be seen as rooted in the preaching of Jesus in which the kingdom of heaven is spoken of as a great feast, and so if we set our hopes on sharing in this great heavenly feast, then earthly food becomes unimportant by comparison, and we abstain from it as a sign of our longing for the true food of heaven. Alternatively fasting might be a determined struggle to become a true human being as God intended, which is someone who is not dominated by the desires of the flesh, but whose mind and soul have mastery of the desires of the flesh. The control of eating and drinking then becomes a sign of the discipline which restores this balance to the body.

For Ethiopians there is another motivation for fasting. The fasts are not just random periods of time but are a dramatic re-enactment of the events of Scripture. By sharing with the rest of the church in the fasts, the believer shares in the great drama of Christ's redemption. He listens to the preaching of Jonah and shows repentance by fasting, she shows that she is following Christ into the wilderness by fasting, he shares in the longing of the apostles to receive the Holy Spirit by fasting. While many other Christians seek to identify themselves with Christ through eating, in the sharing in the Holy Communion, Ethiopians identify themselves with Christ by not eating. Believers attending church for the Eucharist, or *qeddasé*, usually do not enter into the church building but sit or stand outside in the church compound. The priests conduct the indoor worship, using Sergew Selassie's language, while the people stay outside, and do not usually receive the communion. Since people should approach holy things with reverence and caution, and avoid close contact, the observing of the fasts has become the main way that people identify with and participate in the life of Christ, and in the church community.

The worshipping life of the Ethiopian Christian is lived out within interlocking rhythms of fasting and feasting, of recognising the presence of the saints on their commemorations, of asking blessing on the harvest with the changing nature of hymnody, and of sharing in national holidays such as *mäsqäl* and *temqät* or visiting the great pilgrimage sites. All these observances are public and communal. They take place in the holy spaces which are found in both cities and rural areas. So an Ethiopian Christian's life takes place in a space and a time which is given form and structure by the Christian faith. The land belongs to the saints and to the mother of God, and this is shown by the dedication of strategic spaces to them. Time has a ritual quality so each day, month and year are lived in recognition of the presence of those same saints. Worship is communal not individualistic, holistic not spiritual, and includes everyone. People realise that they live in a climate of faith when the persons and events of the Christian faith give identity and meaning to their lives.

It is complicated. Faithful observance of the rules of the church requires help and guidance to negotiate accurately. As long ago as the fifteenth century, the emperor Zär'ä Ya'eqob enacted a law that all Christians were required to find a spiritual father, who looked after their spiritual well-being and who provided guidance over fasting regulations and participating in worship. This practice continues today, and Christians join a church by attaching themselves to a spiritual father. The father summons his spiritual children to meet together on a regular basis, arranges activities such as providing food for worshippers on festival days, and helps them to understand how and when they should worship.

A SACRED LANDSCAPE

There is a fourth style of church to be added to the previous three of basilica, cave and circle. Many modern churches have been influenced by Western church architecture. Here the threefold division remains but the arrangement is modified. The *qeddist* becomes the main part of the church and is similar to the nave of a Western cathedral. The *mäqdäs* is the sanctuary, still with a wall or curtain dividing it from the *qeddist*, but now at the east end. The *qené mahlet* is at the west end in a defined space, sometimes on a gallery with access by a staircase. At the *qeddasé*, many of the congregation stand in the *qeddist*, which has become the main body of the church. An example of this style is the cathedral of the Holy Trinity in Addis Ababa built by Emperor Haile Selassie in 1933. Large churches usually follow this Western-influenced style of building, such as the new churches at Aksum, Däbrä Libanos and many other places.

These various styles of church-building have contributed to the life and worship of the church in Ethiopia. There are examples of each style in the various parts of the country. Whichever form of church is built and worshipped in, the church belongs at the centre of the life of a Christian area. The importance of churches is demonstrated by

FIGURE 4.22 Modern churches have returned to the basilica style, like the large new cathedral in the Bole area of Addis Ababa.

FIGURE 4.23 The congregation are more likely to worship inside the building in a modern church.

the huge number of church buildings and the rate of construction. Church statistics show that the number of churches is growing fast. Figures issued by the Patriarchate in 1970, before the rule of the Derg, state that there were 12,596 churches in Ethiopia. By 2000 this number had increased to 32,230. The most recent estimates suggest that there are now 35,000 churches. Even allowing for a margin of error these figures show a huge revival of church-building. They also show how much churches matter to people.

The rock churches of Lalibäla are a great achievement of Ethiopian civilisation. I have argued that they are more than an architectural and cultural achievement. They are examples of a fresh direction in church-building, leading to a distinct style of worship. The tabot, at its centre, is a sign of the holy, or the presence of God. So a church ceases to be a meeting hall for a congregation of believers with an altar table on which the Eucharist, with its resonances of sacrificial meal, is offered. It becomes a holy site, with that holiness made present and real in an object. Worship is based on the presence of God in a specific place, rather than a gathering for worship of a community seeking forgiveness.

CHAPTER 5

Monks and Missionaries: The Growth of Popular Christianity

HISTORY: THE SOLOMONIC DYNASTY

The period following the defeat of the Zagwe in 1270 is considered to be the golden age of the Ethiopian Church. The kings who succeeded the Zagwe have come to be known as the Solomonic dynasty, and in their reigns the Christian kingdom was expanded, defined and consolidated.

The dynasty began with Yekuno Amlak (1270–80), ruler of the area of north Shewa, who defeated the last Zagwe king in 1270, and killed him inside a parish church. Later the kingdom was expanded and reached its greatest extent through the military conquests of Amdä Seyon (1314–44) who was the grandson of Yekuno Amlak and whose prowess is recorded in the earliest work of Amharic historical writing. He built his power on an economic base of trade in ivory, gold and slaves, and a feudal method of government granting land to his followers in return for service and soldiers. The church was united by Zär'ä Ya'eqob (1434–68) who was theologian and resolver of church controversies, and built up the national church. His authority over both the state and his direction of the church led to the form of nationalism which was both secular and religious. His successors Ba'eda Mariam (1468–78) and later Lebnä Dengel (1508–40) maintained the power of the state until the devastating series of attacks by the Muslim imam Ahmad ibn-Ibrahim al-Ghazi, always spoken of as Grañ the left-handed, in the early sixteenth century.

This line of kings claimed to be descended from Menelek I and described themselves as the Solomonic dynasty. This claim was explained in the *Kebrä Nägäst* in which the traditions of the north were employed in support of the claims of the new kings from the south, and which was written in its present form at this time. The tradition of Ethiopia's descent from ancient Israel was further affirmed towards the end of the period at the council of Däbrä Metmaq presided over by Zär'ä Ya'eqob, which decided that the Judaic approach to faith was to be followed by the whole church.

As this golden age of the church was drawing to a close and Islamic armies were about to launch their destructive attacks, an embassy arrived from Portugal in 1520 and stayed until 1526. The expedition's chaplain, Francisco Alvares, wrote an account of their visit which he published on his return to Portugal in 1540. It gives a vivid and meticulous account of the Christian kingdom at the height of its wealth, power and prestige, and is an invaluable record of a civilisation on the verge of impending destruction.[1]

The expansion of the kingdom was carried out by a collaboration of church and state. Before he began his series of battles which displaced the Zagwe, Yekuno Amlak made a commitment and agreement, known as a *kidan* or covenant, with the monastery of Estifanos on Lake Hayk to provide support for the church. As the state expanded, monastic holy men advanced alongside the armies, or sometimes in advance of them, settling in newly conquered regions and gathering communities of monks around them. The relationship between monasteries and court was sometimes stormy, if zealous monks challenged the kings to make their lifestyles conform to Christian teaching, especially in marriage practice. In spite of these periods of tension, the church and state shared both religious faith and political power to work together to build the Christian kingdom of Ethiopia. As a result of this collaboration, the monastic life spread through the kingdom. The large monasteries became centres of church life, with other monastic communities dependent on them. These networks became known as 'houses' and provided a framework for the life of the church.

THE NINE SAINTS AND THE BEGINNINGS OF MONASTIC LIFE

The origins of the monastic tradition in Ethiopia can be traced back to the fifth and sixth centuries with the arrival of the Nine Saints and the *Sadqan*. This is often referred to as the Second Evangelisation, following on from the First Evangelisation when Abuna Sälama brought Christianity to the royal court. This second stage of evangelisation was carried out by monks who settled in rural areas, made Ge'ez translations of various texts and carried the Christian faith across the northern part of the country.

Ethiopian church tradition describes how the Nine Saints came from different places on the Mediterranean seaboard, and settled in various places in the north of Ethiopia. The sources describe them as 'Roman' but this means only that they came from somewhere around the Mediterranean Sea. The places of origin and their Ethiopian destinations are recorded. Za Mika'el came from Rome, and became known as Arägawi, or the 'old man', and settled at Däbrä Damo. Päntälewon, also from Rome, and Liqanos, from Constantinople, settled on the outskirts of Aksum. Aftse, from somewhere in Asia Minor, established a Christian presence at the old pre-Aksumite temple at Yeha. Gärima, from Rome, and Guba, from Cilicia, went to Medara, near Adwa. Alef, from Caesarea, went north to Hallelujah; Yemata, probably from Egypt, went east to the rocky mountains of Geralta, where there are now many rock-hewn churches. A further saint, Sehma, is recorded in the traditions.[2]

Further traditions refer to other monks who were known as the *Sadqan*, or Righteous. These arrived at Aksum, and after staying there for a period, moved out into the country, especially into the areas to the east of Aksum – Baraknaha, Kadih and Hawzen. They lived in caves and ate grass. This detail of their diet suggests that they came from Syria, where living off the land was a familiar practice. The high-steppe plateaus of Syria are suited to the grazing of sheep and goats, and the local people rely on the edible plants which grow naturally as a source of food. Greek historians described a type of monk which they called *boskos* or grazer, who, they commented, lived off plants, like animals. The grazer life is often mentioned by writers from that area, such as John Moschus who was familiar with this source of nourishment.[3]

As a result of the arrival of monastic pioneers, a network of settlements was established across the north of the country, along the Marab river north of Aksum, and east and south into Tigray. The monks translated the Bible and other books into Ge'ez, provided education and gave an example of Christian living. As a result Christianity spread across the country, and became a popular movement. They often settled on the tops of hills, which became places of holiness and prayer, and many of which developed into important monasteries. As a result of their labours there was a network of monastic centres covering the main centres of settlement which looked towards Aksum.

Several suggestions have been made as to why the saints came to Ethiopia. An often repeated explanation is that they were Syrian refugees escaping from controversy and persecution during the religious controversy between Chalcedonians and Monophysites after the Council of Chalcedon (451).[4] The decisions of the council were controversial, especially in regions to the east of the Byzantine Empire, including Syria, and bitter conflict ensued. So this is a possible historical context for the arrival of a group of Syrian monks, fleeing from the Byzantine Emperor, seeking a refuge at a safe distance, and also bringing with them Monophysite teachings and books. This account explains the Syrian influence on Ethiopian Christianity and also accounts for the one-nature version of Christology which has remained a distinguishing mark of Ethiopian theology. But the hypothesis, while convenient, lacks evidence. The saints are said to have come from widely diverse parts of the Mediterranean, with a mixture of theological influences, and they were not all connected with Monophysite areas. If they had been Monophysites looking for safety they would not have needed to go as far as Ethiopia. There were plenty of vibrant Monophysite communities ready to provide a welcome to dissident monks across Egypt and Syria.[5]

Another possibility is that they were part of an evangelistic force encouraged by the Patriarch of Alexandria. The pagan kingdoms of present-day Sudan were converted to Christianity in the mid-sixth century. This helped to bring security to the southern border of the Byzantine Empire, which had been threatened by clashes with hostile intruders. On this view, the church in Aksum supported this expansionist strategy, and welcomed the Syrian ascetics who were being encouraged by the Emperor of Constantinople and the Patriarch of Alexandria so as to strengthen the church and hence empire in these volatile southern regions.[6]

The monks would not have responded to either possible pressure if there had not been a dynamic and restless character to the life of the early monks. From the beginnings in the third century, monastic life spread fast. Monks had left their homes and travelled to find remote places in which to carry out their ascetic struggles. The histories of the early monks describe a mobile and international monastic population. Monks who had arrived from a variety of homelands shared the lives of more local peasant recruits. Monks came as pilgrims to Jerusalem or elsewhere, as refugees from economic dislocation or barbarian invasion, or simply driven by curiosity and a desire to join in this movement. Within this fluid community, political pressures arising from persecution and conflict over christological debate could well have been a further pressure on some monks to move away from an unsympathetic or hostile ecclesiastical environment. The establishing of Ethiopian monastic life should be understood as part of a wider social and economic process which led to the international monastic movement.[7]

As a result of the work of the Syrian saints and the *Sadqan*, a broad band of territory along what is now the border between Ethiopia and Eritrea was evangelised by the monks. The communities maintained their life through the decline of the Aksumite Kingdom and the period of the Zagwe in Lalibäla.

ORAL TRADITION

These accounts of the beginning of monastic life have been subjected to a fundamental challenge by recent researchers. Speculation about this origin of monastic life is called into question by a critical assessment of the historical sources for the Nine Saints. The Lives which record the lives of the Nine Saints were written after the fourteenth century, 900 years after the events described. They contain many fantastic elements and historical inconsistences. Take, for example, the figure of Za Mika'el Arägawi. His life was written in the sixteenth century, and describes how Za Mika'el, or 'of Michael', popularly known as Arägawi, the Old Man, came from Rome, was a monk at the monastery of Pachomius who died in 348, came to Ethiopia, ascended the precipitous sides of the mountain of Däbrä Damo on the tail of a huge serpent who carried him to the top, and later consulted King Kaléb in the sixth century – when he would have been about 250 years old. Not surprisingly historians are sceptical, and question the reliability of these sources.[8] Other forms of historical evidence – royal chronicles, land grants and other contemporary chronicles – do not record their lives. So perhaps the lives were composed in the fourteenth century or after by monks in northern monasteries wanting to claim an early foundation date and a recognised authority in the face of new monastic houses growing up in southern areas. With such late and unreliable texts as evidence, many historians sometimes doubt even the existence of these seminal founders of Ethiopian monasticism, and certainly do not consider that the textual evidence can be trusted.

This brings us to an inescapable question when assessing the evidence for the growth of the church in Ethiopia. The evidence for the history of the church comes to us mainly through oral traditions. These contain a variety of kinds of material, and are passed on over long periods of time. The text has a long tradition of oral transmission behind it, and will continue to have an oral history after it is set in writing. An assessment of its historical value needs to take into account its place in that tradition. It's clear that a text written in the fourteenth century describing events which took place in the sixth century records a tradition which has been passed down by word of mouth over many centuries.

Studies of the way oral tradition is passed on in our own day can help us to recognise similar processes in historical periods. Kenneth Bailey studied how traditions are passed down through oral methods among Bedouin tribes in the Middle East. He distinguished three kinds of oral tradition. There is 'informal uncontrolled' which is best described as rumour. Then there is 'formal controlled'. This describes the passing on of a fixed text which is carefully memorised and regulated. The memorisation of the Qur'an is an example of this. In Ethiopia the *andamta* tradition of biblical interpretation is passed on by scholars, who gain the ability to memorise large amounts of material, to an extent hard for a Western observer to grasp.[9] A third form is 'informal controlled' which refers to a story passed down within a community, which is preserved but also expanded. There is a structure which is constant but then details and interpretation are added. These categories can help us grasp the variety and creativity of an oral tradition, which is lost when the act of writing fixes a fluid tradition and imposes a rigid and static quality. Bailey comments that 'the passing on of memorised tradition provided opportunity for explanation and discussion of its meaning which the cold lifeless book did not'.[10] Oral tradition ceases when it becomes fixed in written form.

The lives of the Nine Saints, and other hagiographical works, belong to this third category. They often follow a regular pattern. First, there is the life and achievements of the saint. Then comes the *kidan*, or covenant, with God, which arises out of the struggles of his life. God recognises his saintliness and assures forgiveness to those who pray or do good works in the name of the saint. This theme derives from Egyptian sources, of lives of martyrs. The third part is the record of miracles which he performs, many after his death. Finally comes the *mälk*, or hymns composed in his honour, often based on a list of the parts of his body, with a section relating to each of his limbs or faculties. These sections are different in character and origin. The actions of the life recount events which have a basis in history. Miracles performed after death come from later traditions which come from reflection on how the memory of the saint continues to be efficacious. *Mälk* are poetic compositions. However, behind all of these strands lie oral traditions which have different levels of historical reliability.

The scholar Carlo Conti Rossini has suggested an approach to reading the *gädlat*, or lives of the saints, which provides criteria for the assessment of their value as historical sources. He says, 'Their value as a contribution for the reconstruction of the political and ecclesiastical history of Ethiopia is inversely proportional to the distance, in time, between their compilation and the lifetime and of the saint whom they intend to celebrate.'[11] So if a writing comes from a period close to the life of the saint then it can be expected to contain reliable historical testimony, while if it is written long after the event then we should treat its historical reliability with caution.

But this is too simple. It does not recognise that a written text contains different kinds of material which originate from different periods, nor that oral tradition can pass on remembered material with great accuracy over long periods of time. Those who hold the tradition show great care in passing it on just as they had received it, as is shown by the statement of a priest from a different tradition, the Hinduism of South India.

> I am the sixty-third generation of temple priests in my family, and my son is the sixty-fourth. These traditions about our goddess have been handed down to us from the most ancient times. The same festivals, the same holidays, are celebrated just as they were at that time. Nothing not one detail has been changed.[12]

While variation may infiltrate the tradition, the intention to remain faithful and precisely accurate to the inherited tradition ensures that the historical record is valued and sustained.

In the same article Conti Rossini goes on to say 'the strong faith of Abyssinians has swallowed the most doubtful pseudepigraphic books as authentic, and they do not entertain any doubts at all about the most blatant magical texts. In his barbaric and uncritical superstitious spirit the Abyssinian will believe everything.'[13] The laudable desire for sound historical criticism of texts can still lead to an excessively sceptical approach which does not recognise the rigour and reliability of orally transmitted traditions, and risks missing the richness and diversity of the tradition, and overlooking its roots in history.

Tradition contains a mixture of elements.

> An oral tradition, an inscription, and a charter are all messages. Messages are information that has been interpreted in the mind of one or more persons, contemporary to the events or situation in question, and has to be interpreted again through the mind of the person who receives them, in the last analysis the historian who uses them.[14]

The stories of monastic saints have been built up by their followers over a long period of time, stories and pieces of information, later traditions, local legend and stories from different traditions have accumulated. A written text is a snap shot of a tradition at a given time of its development.

The reconstruction of the lives of the monastic saints of Ethiopia relies on this accumulation of tradition. Some parts may lack historical accuracy. Chronological information is often inaccurate in oral tradition and this extends to the written works which rely on these.[15] Other parts of the story are more likely to be reliable. Among the events of the – admittedly late – lives of the Nine Saints which belong to the historical core is the arrival from a distant land, the settling in a given location, the arrival of disciples and the death of the monk, leading to the establishing of the monastic community. These would have been remembered by the community on the anniversary of the death, as was the custom in monasteries across the Christian world, and would form the basis of the oral tradition, to which other stories and miracles were added, and which was eventually recorded in writing some centuries later. A recognition of the dynamic structure and growth of oral tradition enables us to seek the core of historical evidence contained within the later written traditions.

The narratives of the Nine Saints belong within a period of history when monks were travelling and setting up new communities around the Christian world; when there were historical circumstances, including religious conflict which led to the dispersion of some communities, to account for the arrival of monks in Ethiopia; and when Christianity was growing in the region around Aksum. The arrival of some monks from around the Mediterranean is a likely explanation for the evangelisation of rural north Ethiopia, and is described and handed down in the tradition of the Nine Saints.

THE GROWTH OF MONASTERIES IN THE MEDIEVAL PERIOD

We know little about the monasteries in the centuries following their foundation until the reigns of the Solomonic kings. We can assume that ascetics continued to be attracted to the sites established by the founding monks. The Life of Gärima, one of the Nine Saints, is told in a homily of Yohannes, a bishop of Aksum, composed in the fifteenth century, which indicates that his memory and the tradition of his monastery had been preserved through several centuries and was still remembered in the church.[16] Däbrä Damo remained a centre of religious life throughout the period, and provided training and monastic formation for the generation of monks who led the later monastic expansion. The present monastery church was built in this early period. Its size and the quality of its building materials indicate a thriving community worshipping in this traditional monastic site.

It was to this monastery of Däbrä Damo, on its flat-topped plateau in the mountains of Tigray, that a young man in his thirties, Iyäsus Mo'a, or 'Jesus conquers', arrived in around 1241. He was introduced to the demanding disciplines of the ascetic life by the elder Yohanni who clothed him with the monastic habit 'of the angels'. From there, Iyäsus Mo'a went south to Lake Hayk (*hayk* is in fact the Amharic word for 'lake' so it just means 'the lake') where there were already twin churches, Estifanos on an island in the lake and Däbrä Eghzi'abhér on the hill above, both built in 870, according to the tradition preserved in the monasteries. Iyäsus Mo'a settled on the island, became abbot and opened a school. Among the pupils at his school was the future king who would defeat the last of the Zagwe and found a restored Solomonic dynasty, Yekuno Amlak. The association between abbot and future king was to bear fruit in a lasting relationship between the monastery and the royal court. The abbot was given the title *aqqabe sä'at,* or keeper of the hours – a title first given to the abbot of Däbrä Libanos of Samazana – and he became a leading official in the court.[17] Iyäsus Mo'a remained abbot until his death in 1292.

Hayk became a recognised centre, and others came to learn. Among them was a young priest from Shewa called Täklä Haymonot. Like Iyäsus Mo'a, he started to follow the monastic way of life when he was in his thirties. He settled first at Hayk and then moved to Däbrä Damo, where Iyäsus Mo'a's old teacher, Yohanni, was still living. The reputation of Täklä Haymonot spread and a circle of followers formed around him. These in due course settled in various communities around the north.[18] Täklä Haymonot then returned to Lake Hayk and from there back to his home in Shewa, where he settled at Däbrä Asbo.

His life contains rich and colourful traditions. He engaged in a lengthy conflict with the pagan king Motälomé, who abducted his mother, who was then miraculously rescued by the archangel Michael, restored to her husband and then gave birth to the saint, who in later years converted the wicked king to Christianity. While staying at Däbrä Damo he was being lowered down the mountain when the rope broke and while he was falling to the ground six wings were given to him to enable him to escape a certain death. At the end of his life he prayed in a cave with eight sharpened stakes placed in the ground and pointing at this body to prevent him falling into sleep. Here he prayed standing on one leg for seven years until it dropped off, and then prayed for a further seven years standing on the other. His icon is a familiar sight in churches, showing him in monk's clothing with six wings and standing on one leg, often with the other dismembered leg supported by two small wings, presumably so that it will be available to complete his resurrection body.

He lived in a cave, which was divided in two by a curtain of straw, with half of it set aside as a place of worship and half as living quarters for himself and his fifteen disciples. He stayed in this place for twenty-nine years and died in 1313.[19] The group of disciples in the cave developed into a more formalised monastic community and changed the name to Däbrä Libanos. This development is connected with the bringing of the body of the saint for re-burial in 1370, and a closer relationship with the royal court.[20] Däbrä Libanos became the most important monastery in Ethiopia, and its abbot was given the title *echägé*, lived at court and was the senior ecclesiastical official, after the abuna.

The foundation of the community coincided with a period of military activity and territorial growth. The reign of King Amdä Seyon (1314–44) was a period of vigorous and successful military campaigning, which extended the kingdom to new areas. Often monks accompanied the advancing armies and established monasteries, with military protection to ensure its safety and prosperity. This evangelistic advance, which accompanied the military offensive, was supported by the new abuna Ya'eqob. He was motivated by a longing to evangelise the new areas coming under Christian rule, and bring the Christian faith to this extensive territory. He collaborated with the monks of Däbrä Asbo, and encouraged them to set out on a mission to bring the Christian faith to the area around the monastery. This combination of military advance, the initiative of the abuna and the zeal of the monks led to the extension of Christianity through large parts of central Ethiopia, in the region of Shewa. Twelve of the followers of Täklä Haymonot are associated with this growth. Filpos had succeeded Täklä Haymonot, and remained as abbot of Däbrä Asbo. Yohannes, Qawestos, Tadewos and Matyas went south-east; Anorewos the younger and Märqorewos went north-east; Iyosyas went south; Gäbrä Krestos, Yosef, Anoréwos the elder and Adhäni went west. Between them they extended the church's life to a wide area reaching out 150 miles in all directions from Däbrä Asbo. There were further waves of expansion in other parts of Ethiopia.

The missionary strategy of the monks is described in the records of their lives. They set out to do battle with the spirits which resided on various natural features of the landscape. A typical pattern was that on arrival at a new location the monk went to the place where the spirits were, which was often a tree or the top of a mountain. The spirit was driven out by the spiritual power of the monk and the holy place became the church or the monastery. The Christian faith brought by the monks was a stronger form of spiritual power which overcame the power of pagan magicians. The powers of the spirits are not imaginary or false – it's simply that the power of the saint is stronger. When the spirit is driven out of the place then the saint moves in and it becomes a church. Here faith in Christ is not presented as an offer of forgiveness of sins, or conversion to faith in Christ, or the call to a new life. It's the arrival of a new source of spiritual power, coming from God, which can overcome evil, manage an environment which is populated by spiritual beings, and which sustains the community and persons in it. This approach to faith has been described as gaining adherents rather than making converts. It rests on showing that its brand of power works, and so it makes sense to follow the practices and customs of the church in preference to those of magic and other forms of religion because the church is more effective.

The missionary method is shown by the activities of Täklä Haymonot in the region of Katata. This narrative is placed at the start of his missionary journeys and demonstrates a pattern repeated throughout the evangelisation process. The hagiographer tells how the saint came to the area and found that there was a sacred tree which the local people worshipped. After a dialogue with the devil inhabiting the tree, Täklä Haymonot casts it out, to the indignant protests of the devil, which says it has already been expelled from Israel by the power of Christ and now it has to be on the move again. The tree is uprooted and flies through the air as a demonstration of the saint's power, killing twenty-one people as its roots drift over the place. These are brought back to life by the prayers of Täklä Haymonot, along with another 4004 bodies of people already buried and enduring the pains of hell. All are baptised, and the dead return gratefully to their rest in the cemetery, no longer tormented. Meanwhile the governor of the region is infuriated at the loss of revenue from the worshippers of the tree. He arrives as the tree is being cut down so that it can be used to build the new church. He is furious, at which point a large splinter flies into his eye from the tree-cutting. The holy man heals him and he joins in the church construction. Priests are summoned from Täklä Haymonot's own monastery to serve in the church. The holy man fasts, prays, preaches and then after three years moves on to Damot, his next mission field.[21]

While some elements of the story might seem far-fetched and legendary, it demonstrates the mission methods of the monks. There is the focus on holy places, here a tree but elsewhere hilltops, streams or caves; then the power of the saint shown to be stronger than the power of the spirits; the initial hostility of the local rulers; the building of a new church in the place where the former shrine was; and the setting up of a new monastic community. It is in the context of this mission strategy that the rock and other churches were built. The old pagan holy places became the new church community, and these were in natural settings with features traditionally seen as significant. Churches in caves, surrounded by trees, are testimonies to the victory of the Christian missionaries in their titanic struggle with the spirits.

Through this process of expansion the natural sacred sites were claimed by the monks. The camps of the king and of the armies were mobile, and moved around the country. The monasteries, on the other hand, became fixed centres, located in the significant sacred sites of the region. They became centres of social life, providing education, a safe place to store books and treasures, centres of economic activity and resolution of conflict. The formation of monasteries made the establishment of the kingdom possible.

Monastic expansion took place alongside the military activities of the king. Church and state shared in this growth and worked together. But relations with the king were not always cordial. Disagreement arose over the polygamous marriage customs at court. Monastic leaders, especially Bäsalotä Mikael, attacked these practices as contrary to the gospel, and were supported by the abuna Ya'eqob. The moral outrage of the monks was directed against Amdä Seyon and his successor Säyfä Ar'ad. The king reacted by punishing his opponents, beating and exiling them.[22] Far from impeding the activities of the monastic evangelists, the conflict with the court accelerated the process. Exile had the unintended consequence of driving the monks beyond the frontiers of the kingdom into uncharted territory. The exiled monks were sent first to areas to the north and then to the south, and then taken to more distant and hostile areas as places of banishment. The monks became the advance guard of the armies.

Some were sent to the region around lake Zway. 'Those who lived there were Muslim and they did not know Christ. They were murderers and the king sent his enemies to them so that they might take his revenge for him.'[23] But the monks persevered, eventually converted local people and founded monasteries in these hostile regions. Two of these monastic exiles, Filpos, the former abbot of Däbrä Asbo, and Anoréwos, founded a community at Lake Zway, which became a centre of education and evangelisation. Some of the younger monks moved further away, beyond the places they were sent to, and extended monastic life further. By the end of the fourteenth century the church had expanded into the southern area of Sidamo through the missionary work of the monks.

There were parallel developments of monasticism in the north of the country. This arose out of the life of the monk Éwostatéwos (*c.*1273–1352), whose communities followed a style of faith which was opposed to the teaching and practice of Alexandria. Éwostatéwos was a monk in Sar'ae in the north of Ethiopia, who attracted a community of students and disciples. His teaching aroused controversy and he left Ethiopia and set out on a life of wandering which took him from Egypt, to Jerusalem, to Cyprus and then to Armenia where he died. A group of his followers had travelled with him and on his death they returned to Ethiopia to join one of his disciples, Absadi, who had remained in Ethiopia during Éwostatéwos's self-imposed exile. Together they set up a monastic community at Däbrä Maryam in Qohayin, and from there extended their influence across the northern part of Ethiopia to form the 'house' of Éwostatéwos, which became the dominant style of Christianity in the north. It was based in three monasteries in the north of Ethiopia – Däbrä Maryam, Däbrä Bizen and Däbrä Yita, each of which presided over several smaller houses.

The roots of the style of life of the house of Éwostatéwos lie in the Semitic form of Christianity which was characteristic of the north. They kept the Sabbath as well as Sunday, practised circumcision as well as baptism, and followed other Judaic practices. They considered that this was a pure form of Christianity uncorrupted by the practices imported from Alexandria. Since they rejected the teaching of the abuna, they did not send candidates to him for ordination as priests. Their monasteries were led by lay members of the community, and their clergy consisted of priests who had joined them from other parts of the church and who had already been ordained. These priests who had defected from the abuna's church celebrated the liturgy. This approach was summarised by Zär'ä Ya'eqob:

> The disciples of [Éwostatéwos] observed the Sabbath, Saturday and Sunday, but they did not enter in the residence of the king nor in the

> house of the metropolitans. And they did not receive the Holy Orders because the observance of the Sabbath was not in force in the kingdom, and the Sabbath was abolished in the realm of the patriarchs of Alexandria.[24]

The movement grew as it became identified with the northern style of faith. In 1399 a council led by the abuna Bärtälomewos demanded that Filpos, the abbot of Debra Bizen and so a leader of the Ewostatians, deny the Sabbath and when he refused he was imprisoned on the island at Hayk for four years. On his release he travelled back north, and made a triumphal procession back to his monastery in Tigray. Later King Dawit proclaimed the toleration of the Sabbath, and in 1455 at the council of Däbrä Metmaq the views of the Sabbath party were supported by King Zär'ä Ya'eqob. So the views of the house of Éwostatéwos prevailed and the Ethiopian Church has celebrated the liturgy on both Saturday and Sunday.

Another monastic group which flourished in this period was the Stephanites. Estifanos was born at the end of the fourteenth century. He settled in the area around the Takazze river in Tigray, and developed a strict style of monastic life. He was a fierce critic of any sign of laxity and opposed too much veneration of the cross and some of the new festivals of Mary. He also opposed the power of the king, rejecting royal supremacy over the church. Some Evangelical groups have claimed him – anachronistically – as an early example of a Protestant approach to church life. Not surprisingly in light of his political views, Estifanos was imprisoned and died in 1444. Like the Ewostatians they were faced with the question of how to find priests to maintain a sacramental life, since they were alienated from the court and hence the abuna. Estifanos's successor, Abäkärazun, tried to resolve this dilemma by sending a group of twelve to Jerusalem for ordination, and some were ordained by the Armenian Patriarch. Stephanite monasteries continued these practices, looking to the monastery of Gunde Gunda, until 1700. Their persistence is a further sign of the decentralised nature of the church. Networks of monastic brotherhoods, looking to a founder and a mother house, claimed the allegiance of the faithful.

The controversy between the 'houses' of Éwostatéwos and Täklä Haymonot, and the presence of other groups of monks of which the Stephanites are one example, shows us how the church took shape. It was built up as monks settled in new areas. The communities remained loyal to the original community from which they came, and which was descended from a founder from whom dependent houses recognised an allegiance and a descent. These new houses retained their connections with the mother house and so the great 'houses' developed. They developed a distinct identity, gained support within the surrounding region, and affirmed their own traditions of faith and practice. The relationships between them, and sometimes the conflicts which divided them, shaped the historical development of church and state in medieval Ethiopia.

THE MONASTIC HOUSES AND THEIR PLACE IN THE CHURCH

The new monastery remained in close contact with the mother house. The connections between houses were formed and maintained through the personal relationships which bound the monks to those who had gone before them. Care was taken to establish a genealogy which traces the monastic ancestors back to the beginning. The hagiographer of Täklä Haymonot records a list which connects the saint with a succession of monks who had lived on Däbrä Damo, back to the founder abba Arägawi, then back through the monks of Egypt to abba Antony, who had been incorporated into the monastic life by the archangel Michael himself.[25] The formation of a monastic 'house' took place through recognising descent through fathers in monastic life, rather than following a rule or being organised into an institution.

The new monk was included among the descendants of the father by being given his monastic clothing. When the prospective monk was received by the teacher, he was given the distinctive garments which were the signs of his profession as a monk. There were four articles of clothing. There was, first, the *qamis*, which is the cloak or blanket, usually white or yellow, with the yellow indicating the status of a pilgrim. This is the gabbi or shamma which is still the normal clothing for going to church. Then, second, the monk wore the *qinat*, a leather belt, worn over the *qamis* or round the neck. Then, he wore the *qob*, or round monk's hat. Then, finally, he would receive the *askema*. The *askema*, equivalent to the Greek schema, is a scapula which hangs over the front and back of a monk's body, and is marked by twelve crosses. It is usually given at a later stage than the other garments and shows a high level of monastic attainment. As he was given these clothes by the master, the disciple was incorporated into the house which looked to the master for leadership and guidance. They established a personal bond of allegiance.

The importance of the process of clothing for the formation of community is shown by an argument between the monks of Hayk and the monks of Däbrä Libanos about which was more important. The lives of Iyäsus Mo'a and Täklä Haymonot provide two different versions of which of the two clothed the other. Some accounts describe both Iyäsus Mo'a and Täklä Haymonot going to learn from abba Yohanni at Däbrä Damo and receiving their monastic clothes from him on different occasions, after they had showed their worthiness and before continuing their mission. But the monks of Däbrä Libanos go on to claim that Täklä Haymonot received the clothes from Yohanni and then bestowed them on Iyäsus Mo'a, which had the result that Täklä Haymonot has precedence over Iyäsus Mo'a in the hierarchy of monastic life. This claim can be traced to the growing importance of the monasteries of Täklä Haymonot from the end of the fourteenth century, with the series of events including the re-burial of the body of Täklä Haymonot at Däbrä Asbo, the giving of the new name of Däbrä Libanos and the appointment of the abbot as *echägé*, leading to a prominent place in the royal camp.[26]

These two conflicting accounts show that the personal relationship of teacher and disciple set up and formed the monastic tradition. The number of communities gradually extended as disciples set out for new places, but they remained part of the mother house, and looked back to the example of the leader who began the investiture process. They were conscious that they were part of the 'house' of Täklä Haymonot, or the 'house' of Éwostatéwos. The clothing procedures were, at first, informal, and only later followed a regular process with set prayers, so rather than referring to this as investiture with monastic habit, we should speak of a more informal process of the giving of clothes to a new monk, which could be done in different ways at different times at the discretion of the teacher.

ROYAL CHURCHES

The evangelisation of the newly conquered areas was not carried out only by monks. The kings shared in this task through the building and endowment of churches. Some of the largest and most famous churches were royal foundations. A total of thirty-four royal churches are recorded by the chroniclers and there were certainly others. The practice began with the founding of one church, Gännäta Maryam, by the first of the Solomonic kings, Yekuno Amlak. The frosty relations between monks and kings which arose out of the dispute over royal marriage practices did not allow this to continue, but many churches were founded during the fifteenth and sixteenth centuries. Zär'ä Ya'eqob built nine churches, and his son Bä'edä Maryam built a further four.

These churches became centres of the life of the kingdom. Often the royal camp was located in the vicinity; church councils were held at them; and kings and abunas were buried in them. Land and revenues were assigned to the church, and the buildings were in fine-dressed stone. Visitors record large numbers of clergy, and *däbtära* attached to these churches. Some of the famous religious centres of the kingdom, such as Däbrä Birhan, Atronsa Maryam and Tädbaba Maryam, were royal foundations.[27]

They had the valuable function of connecting the religious power of the monasteries to the secular power of the king. In many cases monks were invited to serve in the new foundation and so they became part of the monastic house. Most were attached to the dominant house of Täklä Haymonot, but one church, Martula Maryam, was given to the northern house of Éwostatéwos. This gave the Ewostatians a foothold in Gojjam, which was to become a power base in later controversies. Royal churches continued to provide centres of church life, and many were to be founded by the later kings at Gondar.[28]

A LAND OF MONASTERIES

In 1520 the Portuguese traveller Francisco Alvares travelled around Ethiopia and provided a meticulous report of the lively and extensive church which he found. He describes a land in which monasteries were centres of faith. These had been established in all parts of the Christian kingdom. Then, as now, the largest number were in the north, in Eritrea and Tigray, with the dominant tradition of teaching being that of Éwostatéwos. Then there were the monasteries founded from Däbrä Asbo/Libanos, in the central region of Shewa and the surrounding country. This was the 'house of Täklä Haymonot'. The monasteries dependent on Däbrä Hayq had declined in importance with the royal preference for the house of Täklä Haymonot. Another important centre was the large centre of the eremetic life at Waldebba, in the west of the country near the Sudanese border, founded by the ascetic Daniel. This has a present-day membership of several hundred monks, who live grouped around four churches, in an area so broad that it takes four days to walk from one end of the monastery to the other. The houses of both Täklä Haymonot and Éwostatéwos have their own churches at Waldebba. Another well-known site is Zuquala, a volcanic mountain with a monastery founded by the popular saint Gäbrä Manfus Qiddus (servant of the Holy Spirit), affectionately known as Abo, a second-generation disciple of Täklä Haymonot whose Life was written long after his death and which reports him to be an Egyptian who lived six hundred years.[29]

Since the abuna had little involvement in the life of the church outside the court, the monastic traditions formed the style of church life across Ethiopia. A network of monasteries had spread across the country, providing centres for the local communities. They were connected through shared descent from the founder, and a regional base in the areas where the mother house was located. In other parts of the worldwide church, organisation was provided by the bishop presiding over his diocese. Here, in Ethiopia, the church was formed from networks of monastic communities, established in recognised holy places, with strong regional power bases, often affirming strongly held doctrinal positions. While royal churches formed wealthy centres of church life, it was the monasteries which held the church together and formed it into a national community.

CHAPTER 6

Islam and Christianity: How Two Faiths Coexisted

HISTORY: THE INVASIONS OF GRAÑ

The holy city of Harar has eighty mosques and numerous tombs of holy men. It is considered to be one of the four holy cities of Islam.[1] Islamic tradition recounts a night journey to heaven made by the prophet Muhammad. As he travelled he saw a hill shining with light, which, an angel informed him, was to be the Mountain of Saints, and this was the site of the future city of Harar. An alternative and more historical account attributes its foundation to the arrival of Shaykh Abadir Umar ar-Rida with 405 saints from Mecca in 1216. They settled in Harar and carried out military campaigns against Portuguese arrivals. The chronicles of King Amdä Seyon describe his campaigns against Harar in 1332, and the scale of the campaign shows that by then it was an important city.[2]

Harar had become the capital of the sultanate of Adal when Sultan Abr Bekr Muhammad took over power in 1520. After Abu Bekr had ruled for five years, he was killed by a popular young and ambitious imam, Ahmad ibn Ibrahim el Ghazi, nicknamed Gurey by the Somalis and Grañ by the Ethiopians, both meaning left-handed. Grañ resolved to bring about a reform of the declining and reputedly debauched and anarchic city. He began by withholding the tribute levied by the Christian Emperor Lebnä Dengel (1508–40) and then defeated the expedition sent by the emperor to punish him. He recruited an army of Somalis, supported by Ottoman Turks who brought firearms with

FIGURE 6.1 At Harar there are many tombs of holy men. Veneration of holy men is a distinctive part of Ethiopian Islam.

them, and set out to fight the Christians. His campaign lasted fourteen years, from 1529 to 1543, in the course of which Christian Ethiopia was devastated. Churches were looted and destroyed; manuscripts were burned; priests and monks were killed. At this point the two worlds of the Muslim lowlands and Christian highlands clashed violently, with devastating results for the Christian church.

Relief came to the beleaguered Christian remnant through a band of 400 Portuguese adventurers. They were led by Christovão da Gama, one of the sons of the explorer Vasco da Gama, and came to help the new King Gälawdéwos (1540–59). Their first engagement with Grañ's forces was at the peak of a precipitous amba. Christovão's men stormed it, beating back the defenders and losing eight men in the process. Then they faced Grañ himself. The two generals traded insults. Grañ sent a letter to da Gama enclosing a monk's robe – to show that he expected the Portuguese to fight like a quiet and meek religious; and in reply Christovão enclosed a looking glass and a pair of eyebrow tweezers – to indicate his expectation that he would encounter an effeminate and vain opponent. A series of engagements in the inaccessible mountains of central Ethiopia followed in which the 400 Portuguese led by the tough, determined and reckless young Christovão, fought vastly superior forces. Both generals lost their lives. Christovão was the first to die. He was separated from the main body of the Portuguese and was captured. His hair and beard were slowly extracted with the same tweezers he had humorously enclosed to Grañ, before being beheaded and then buried next to a dead dog. A spring of healing water sprang from the ground in the place where da Gama's blood fell, and a tree uprooted itself and stood on its head to mark the unnatural and horrifying events which had taken place. Grañ's end happened less dramatically in a later battle. He was hit by a stray Portuguese bullet, his terrified horse galloped away, and a young Ethiopian cut off his head and brought it to Gälawdéwos, who had by this time arrived to take part in the battles. Gälawdéwos had promised his sister as a bride to anyone who killed Grañ and the young Ethiopian hoped he might gain this prize until subsequent enquiry revealed that the Muslim general had been dead when discovered.[3] The death of Grañ was a decisive moment, and the ascendancy of the Christian forces in the highlands was restored.

EARLY TRADITIONS

This period of violent conflict lasted less than twenty years. It is a rare example of open confrontation between the two faiths. A longer-term view of relations between these two great monotheistic faiths tells a story of various forms of coexistence. Christians and Muslims have shared the same living space throughout their common history. They have had to find ways to live together.

Islam spread fast. Within the lifetime of the prophet, the divided Arab tribes of the peninsula had been united, and under Abu Bakr, the successor of Muhammad, military expansion began. The new faith of Islam had spread with extraordinary speed across the northern parts of Africa, into Spain; across the Middle East, including Alexandria and Jerusalem; into Persia and as far as India; and even, eventually, in 1450, besieged and conquered Constantinople, the capital city of the Christian east, which then became a Muslim city. Yet – apart from the short interlude under Grañ which we described earlier – Ethiopia alone in this broad sweep of territory continued to be ruled by Christian kings. It was, to use the famous image of Menelek II, 'a Christian island in a Muslim sea'. It was the only nation in the wider region to have retained independence from Islamic government.

Ethiopia and Arabia are close neighbours, with a distance of just twenty miles separating their borders at the closest point of the Bab el Mandab, at the mouth of the Red Sea. While they are geographically close, the two lands are separated by a body of water. In modern societies, seas are boundaries, setting up a barrier against invasion by hostile intruders. But in the ancient world, the sea was a means of communication, since it is usually much easier to travel on the sea by boat than it is to negotiate a land route, often over difficult terrain and inhabited by bandits. The Red Sea, or Erythrean Sea as it was known at this time (from which the modern state of Eritrea derives its name), was easily navigated and enabled movement between its two coasts.

Viewed from the perspective of twenty-first-century Western Europe, there is a sharp contrast between the Christian and Muslim faith traditions, which has led to an expectation of separation and conflict. But from an Ethiopian viewpoint, within the Horn of Africa bordering the Red Sea, Christians and Muslims share a geography, a history and, to some extent, a culture. This common experience and cultural relationship has led to contrasting themes of peaceful coexistence and tolerance, on the one hand, and rivalry and conflict, on the other. Both these have been part of the shared experience from the beginning. The pattern of later relationships was set up in the early period of their history, and was influenced by the early history of Christianity and Islam, where two faiths intertwined in a shared history.

Christianity was brought to the Arabian peninsula by Faymiyun, a Christian who was sold as a slave to a merchant at Najran. He discovered that the Arabs worshipped a palm tree and used to hang clothing and jewels on the tree as an offering. Faymiyun prayed, the palm tree was blown down by a mighty wind and the people became Christian. His influence did not last long. Before long this Christian faith was rejected by local people, and so, the Islamic source comments, 'they suffered the misfortunes which befell their co-religionists in every land'.[4]

The Christian kingdom of Aksum invaded and ruled the southern parts of Arabia, called Najran, which covered the area of modern Yemen, in the early sixth century. The Christians of Najran had appealed for help because they were being persecuted by the local Jewish ruler. A force led by Asbeha, king of Aksum, crossed over into Arabia in 524 and conquered the region, and appointed a regent, called Abraha al Ashram. Abraha built a church – called in some sources al-Qullais or *ekklesia* – in Sana'a, which he planned would become an alternative pilgrimage site to the Ka'aba or black stone at Mecca.[5] According to the chronicler Ishaq, he launched a military campaign against Mecca in 570, which included the involvement of an elephant called Mahmud. On arrival the elephant knelt before the black stone and a flock of birds carried stones in their beaks and claws which they dropped on the invading Christian army, which as a result withdrew.[6] Abraha returned to Sana'a where he died, his heart bursting out of his body. This attack is recorded in the Qur'an, and Abraha has become a mythical figure of evil in Islamic tradition. This attack lives on in the minds of Muslims and fears remain that a 'long legged' invader will come out of Ethiopia to attack Mecca once more.[7] This early conflict resulted in withdrawal and stand-off.

Soon after that disaster struck the kingdom of Najran. Its agriculture relied on irrigation provided by the Marib dam, which had been constructed in the eighth century BC but had suffered from lack of maintenance and regular breaches. Water penetrated again in the late sixth century and repairs were not undertaken, and the dam ceased to function.[8] This had far-reaching consequences, as the civilisation of the southern part of the peninsula declined, leaving space for the dramatic rise of a vibrant new religious movement based on Mecca to the north, initiated by a merchant called Muhammad.

The events of the early history of Islam spilled over from Arabia into Ethiopia. During the lifetime of the prophet, the early followers of Muhammad were persecuted by the Quraish in Mecca, and forced to flee in 615. The flight became known as the *hijra*. The prophet suggested Ethiopia as a place of safe refuge 'for the [Christian] king will not tolerate injustice and it is a friendly country'. Eighty-two, or possibly eighty-three, Muslims went to Ethiopia where they were welcomed by King Najashi. They reported that 'the Negus gave us a kind reception. We safely practised our religion and worshipped God and suffered no wrong in word or deed.' The Quraish asked for them to be extradited back to Mecca and on receiving this request the king decided that he needed to find out more about them, and their faith. They explained what they believed and read sections of the Qur'an to the king. The life of Muhammad tells us that 'the Negus wept until his beard was wet and the bishops wept until their scrolls were wet, when they heard what was read to them. The king said "of a truth, this and what Jesus brought have come from the same niche."'[9] The Muslims summarised their belief about Jesus in these words: 'we say about him that which our prophet brought, saying he is the slave of God, and his apostle, and his spirit, and his sword which he cast into Mary the blessed virgin'.[10]

Some of these Muslim visitors became Christian, and so were the first converts away from Islam to another faith. One of them was Ubaid Allah ibn Jahsh. We are told

> he remained in doubt until he became a Muslim, then he emigrated to Abyssinia, with his wife, Umm Habiba, who was a Muslim. But after he married her he became a Christian [...] [H]e used to pass by the companions of the prophet and say to them 'we now see clearly, but you are still blinking' [...] [T]he word he used is applied to a puppy when it tries to open its eyes to see.[11]

Writing in 1923, Sir William Muir reflected that 'if an Arab asylum had not at last offered itself at Medina, the Prophet might haply himself have emigrated to Abyssinia, and Mohammedanism dwindled, like Montanism, into an ephemeral Christian heresy'.[12]

Later, when Islamic armies began their rapid advance over the Middle East, they did not invade Ethiopia. 'Leave the Abyssinians alone', Muhammad told them, 'so long as they do not take the offensive'. Islamic lawyers have described Ethiopia as *dar al-hiyad* or land of neutrality, and when the armies of Islam set out on the wars of jihad, they did not attack the Christian kingdom of Ethiopia. A verse of the Qur'an says, 'you will find the Christians the nearest in affection to you'.[13] So Ethiopia provides an example of Islam and Christianity coexisting peacefully – an example valued by both Muslims and Christians.

Some traditions offer an alternative end to this early episode, changing the story of mutual respect and support into a story of conflict and betrayal. These versions report that in 628 Muhammad wrote to seven kings of the region asking them to accept Islam, including his old friend the Najashi Ashama. The Najashi was the only one of the recipients to respond positively and to accept Islam. But his subjects remained Christian. Soon after, there was a rebellion against the Negus by rival claimants to the throne, in which the king was killed. His death is sometimes attributed to treacherous Christians who betrayed and possibly killed the good Islamic king. When he heard this news the prophet Muhammad 'prayed over him and begged that his sins might be forgiven'.[14] So this episode leads to a different conclusion. Since the king was converted, Ethiopia has become part of *dar al Islam* – the land of Islam, and furthermore the first country to be included within Islam, after Arabia. It has become the duty of all Muslims to reclaim Ethiopia and bring it back to its rightful place within Islam.[15]

These early meetings took place before the lines of division between the faiths became hardened and clear. So they can be used to support various positions. The negus was 'a semi-legendary king who gradually turned out to be employable for a variety of religious and political purposes'.[16] There are records of Muslims who became Christian, and Christians who became Muslim. The early history of the relationships between Christianity and Islam shows both how the faiths supported each other and also how Ethiopia became the first Islamic country outside Arabia. The closeness also led to conflict and competition for territory and power.

These alternative narratives can be described as paradigms for relations between the faiths. Members of both faiths were usually able to live harmoniously together, but from time to time conflicts broke out between groups within the faiths which could be violent and destructive.

THE NATURE OF ETHIOPIAN ISLAM

Muhammad's injunction to avoid war against Christian Ethiopia – unless they started it – was observed. Islam moved into Ethiopia using more peaceable methods. As well as holy men and scholars who settled in various parts of Ethiopia, Muslims were recognised as traders and merchants. The main exports of Ethiopia were ivory, incense and above all slaves, and Muslim merchants managed the sale and transportation of these desirable commodities. A chain of Muslim states were set up to the east of the Christian kingdom, in the flat desert areas. Ifat was founded in the tenth century, followed by Shewa, Dawaro, Arababni, Hadiyya, Sarha, Bale and Dara. From the fifteenth century the largest of these states was Adal, of which

Harar was the capital and from which the attacks of Grañ set out. Both faith communities settled in the Horn of Africa, with the result that the land was divided. The Christian kingdom controlled the mountain plateau, which Muslim states developed in the lower-level regions. The two swathes of territory ran north to the south, with the escarpment which delineated the extent of the plateau lying between them.

Muslims moved in to the Christian kingdom in the highlands as well as developing their own states to the east. The missions of the Christian monks and missionaries were directed to the pagan inhabitants of the land, and the stories of saints are filled with accounts of the struggles of the monks with the spirits and devils of the places they settled. Their action against these pagan spirits left a space in society which Muslim merchants were able to occupy. They also proved to be useful as diplomats, assisting the Christian kings in their relationships with Muslim rulers. When an abuna died Muslims joined the delegation to Egypt to negotiate with the Muslim rulers for the dispatch of a new abuna. Their involvement in this process had the further consequence that the abuna, a Christian bishop, was put under pressure to protect and support Muslim communities in Ethiopia.

Muslims continued to provide commercial activity to the kingdom, and so had a recognised niche in society, which continued after the period of warfare with the imam Grañ. James Bruce estimated that there were 3000 Muslim households in Gondar in the seventeenth century. In 1668, Emperor Yohannes I (1667–82) decreed that Muslims should live in a special part of town, called Islam Bet, in the valley beneath the ridge on which the royal palace was situated.[17] The commercial and diplomatic contribution of Muslims to the Christian state gave them a social role and so allowed them to find a place in Christian society.

The form of Islam which grew in Ethiopia was able to absorb local traditions. The tombs of holy men became centres of devotion and pilgrimage. Many pilgrimage centres sprang up over the country. The most popular Muslim pilgrimage site is the tomb of Shaykh Husayn in Anaagina in Bale. Shaykh Husayn probably lived in the thirteenth century and may have taken part in the evangelisation of the Bale region. This shaky historical evidence has been supplemented by a rich tradition describing miracles and signs worked by the Shaykh. His cult grew in the eighteenth century, and the practice of pilgrimage to his tomb evolved out of an older Oromo custom of pilgrimage to visit the *abbaa mudaa* or religious head who was located in this area of Bale. Large numbers come to the shrine on two occasions in the year, one of which is in the same month as the hajj to Mecca. There are similarities between the customs of Shaykh Husayn and the hajj to Mecca, such as kissing a black stone, and these helped to make the tomb of Shaykh Husayn into a local substitute for the great pilgrimage to Mecca. This, and similar shrines, form a focus for religious devotion which include others as well as Muslims, and have contributed to a shared and inclusive religious practice.

The respect for holy teachers, and the practice of visiting their tombs, was one of the reasons for the attraction of the Sufi brotherhoods, which arrived in Ethiopia from the sixteenth but expanded in the nineteenth century. The *qadiri* order was the first to arrive from Yemen and spread first to Harar and then to other areas. The main Sufi orders have followers in Ethiopia. Ethiopian Muslims were more sympathetic to the Sufi revival of the nineteenth century than they were to more radical forms of Islam, such as Wahhabism or Mahdism. The influence of Sufism contributed to the tradition of peaceful coexistence.

ISLAM IN MODERN ETHIOPIA

During the nineteenth and twentieth centuries the Christian kingdom of Ethiopia trebled in size to include the areas which had previously been ruled by Islamic emirs. This led to new patterns of coexistence and regional variation.

Emperor Yohannes IV (1872–89) gained control of Welo, and adopted a policy of enforced conversion of Muslims to Christianity. This was attributed by some to religious fanaticism. The English General Charles Gordon wrote to his sister that 'Yohannes, oddly enough, is like myself a religious fanatic. He has a mission and will fulfil it, and that mission is to Christianise all Mussulmans.'[18] Others saw in this policy as a sign of the moderation of a humane leader, who had once had an ambition to live as a monk. Whereas his predecessor Téwodros II often treated his conquered adversaries with vicious brutality, mutilating many opponents by cutting off their hands and feet, Yohannes simply asked them to support his unifying national religious ideology. The synod of Borru Meda in 1878, as well as forcing a resolution of the long-running christological controversy, decreed that everyone should join the national church.[19] Muslims were given three years to do this. They were ordered to build churches, pay tithes to the Orthodox clergy, and any official who declined to be baptised was forced to leave office. The chief, Muhammad Ali became the *ras* Mikael, and was guided by Emperor Yohannes himself who became his godfather.

Soon after the death of Yohannes, a Muslim shaykh Zakaryas, from Begemder, had a series of visions which propelled him into a movement of reform of the Qur'an and a ministry of preaching. As he approached the end of his life, he adopted the Christian faith and was baptised into the Orthodox Church in 1910, at the age of 65. Three thousand of his followers followed his example, a number which grew to a reported 10,000 by 1916. When attacked by conservative Muslims he defended himself by referring to texts from the Qur'an and the Bible. His selection of authoritative teaching, called the 'Fixed and Permanent Selection', included passages from the Qur'an; the Old Testament, especially the Psalms and the prophets; and the New Testament, especially the Gospels. He interpreted many passages of the Qur'an to Jesus rather than the prophet Muhammad. His success shows the possibility and attraction of recognising that both the Bible and the Qur'an are authoritative.[20]

A flexible syncretism is often associated with those living in Welo, where an unintended consequence of Yohannes's policy of forced conversions was an ease of moving between faiths. Many Muslims were baptised to comply with Yohannes's law, but then went to the mosque to ask for the effects of baptism to be removed by the imam. Anecdotal evidence suggests that this has shaped a continuing open approach in the region. I have been told by local people that it is common to move between faiths. Often this comes about after a dream. The angel Gabriel – or, if it concerns a Muslim, it is of course Jibril – appears to tell the dreamer to change his faith. On rising he tells his wife and they go to the church – or mosque – to carry out the instruction. I was also told of a church in an area of Welo with few Christians. The local imam arranged for some of his young men to become deacons so that they could maintain this holy place, which was valued by Muslims as well as Christians.[21]

The practice continues. The former principal of the Mekane Yesus seminary in Addis Ababa conducted research into the attitudes of

Muslim converts to Christianity. He reports that of the 252 Christians who had been converted from Islam whom he interviewed, 19.4 per cent continue to pray in the Muslim way, 29.8 per cent continue to read the Qur'an and 18.7 per cent keep the fast of Ramadan. Contemporary observers report the presence of Jesus worshippers in mosques, although it was unclear to me whether this practice arose out of a desire to maintain acceptance of both faiths or as a mission strategy by Christian evangelists to infiltrate the mosques.[22]

In other regions the Islamic rulers continued in power, and were not subjected to the same level of control. Muhammad ibn Da'ud (1861–1934) became king of the south-west region around Jimma when he was fifteen years old, and was known as Abba Jiffar II. When Menelek's armies advanced south, he submitted without a struggle, and was allowed to retain his kingdom. He was learned and devout. His capital of Jimma became a centre of learning with many schools and centres of scholarship – as well as being a centre of the slave trade. It was not until 1933, shortly before his death, that his power was removed and the state of Jimma became fully absorbed into the kingdom of Ethiopia. The slave market was closed, but the schools continued traditions of learning and ensured Muslim identity.

Later Jimma was to become the site of the most notorious example of interfaith violence in recent years. In March 2011, seventy churches were burned, one Christian was killed and several thousand fled from their homes after a copy of the Qur'an was believed to have been desecrated, around the town of Abendabo, in the region of Jimma. This incident is a rare example of religious conflict, and suggests that Jimma's stronger Islamic identity enabled fundamentalist groups to gain support.

The pattern of relationship has varied from region to region and from period to period. There has been political rivalry and social competition, with phases of violent conflict. At the local level adherents of the two faiths share holy places, pilgrimages and festivals. The shared claim to the same land has produced a form of Islam which, like so much else in Ethiopia, has taken a different shape from other parts of the Islamic world.

Muslims form an integral part of modern Ethiopian society. Most recent census figures show that Muslims compose around a third of the population, but some estimates claim a larger number, including surveys carried out during the Italian occupation which suggest that

Muslims formed almost half of the population, with 2,250,000 adherents compared to 2,625,000 Christians.[23] Many Muslims, and other commentators, think that around 45 per cent, rather than a third, of the population is Muslim.

Since the declaration of freedom of religion in 1991, the Islamic community has taken a greater part in Ethiopian society. The traditional commercial activity has continued, and this has led to a growing influence in the economic life of the nation. One informant told me that many Muslims fled the country during the time of the Derg. They came from the merchant class, and worked as market traders. When abroad they diversified their business interests and returned as owners of electronics businesses.

The richest man in Ethiopia is a Muslim, Shaykh Muhammad al-Ahmudi. He was born in 1944 (or 1945) in Dessie in Welo province, to a Muslim mother from Ethiopia and a Saudi Arabian father. His wealth was estimated to be $10.8 billion in 2015, and he plans to invest over $3.4 billion in agriculture and industry over the next five years. His interests include the oil industry and he set up the first steel production plant in Ethiopia. He also owns the largest gold mine and is the country's only gold exporter.[24] He has funded the building of many mosques, among them the mosque over the tomb of King al Najashi who first welcomed the followers of the prophet on their arrival in 615. Another of his constructions is the mosque which he arranged to be built is in the village of Mai Agam in Tigray, a Muslim village in a Christian region. A visitor reports being told that there are thirty-seven Muslim families in the village, but the mosque is large enough to accommodate 2000 worshippers. This village is the birth place of the mother of Shaykh Muhammad al-Ahmudi.[25]

A sign of this increased economic influence is the number of new mosques being built across the country. The rate of building is such that any estimate of the extent of this programme is immediately out of date. It has been estimated that there were thirty mosques in Addis Ababa in 2000, and this number had increased to over 100 by 2004. New mosques are a visual indication of a prosperous and confident community becoming more assertive within modern Ethiopian society.

The two possibilities of coexistence or conflict continue to be open to Muslims. Extremism has entered from Saudi Arabia, referred to as Salafism. Salafist ideas, requiring strict observance of Qur'anic rules and rejecting many popular Sufi practices, were brought to Ethiopia from 1940 by students returning from Arabia. At first limited in appeal, easier communication with the wider Muslim world accelerated the growth of various radical groups. These are found in several parts of the country, including Harar, Jimma and Addis Ababa. The large Aweliyya School and Mission Centre was founded in Addis Ababa in the 1960s with funding from the World Muslim League, based in Saudi Arabia. The site includes an orphanage and training centre as well as a school, and it has become a base from which Salafist approaches have been disseminated. It has helped to shape a sense of identity and morality among Muslims finding their way in a changing society. Only a few smaller groups such as Takfir wal Hijra have extended their activities into radical political opposition, refusing to pay taxes or carry identity cards.[26]

The alternative approach of coexistence is associated with a movement known as al-Ahbash or Ethiopian. Its origins go back to the 1940s and a teacher called Shaykh Abdallah ibn Yusuf al-Harari (1910–2008) who was a leading figure in Harar, and was involved in controversy with extreme groups in the city. It is unclear what happened in this conflict, but the shaykh was described as *shaykh al fitna* or the sheikh of strife, and left Ethiopia in 1948.

He settled in Beirut, where he became a leading figure in the Association of Islamic Philanthropical Projects, which became the organising force in the al-Ahbash, or Ethiopian, movement. Al-Ahbash derives its name from the traditions of the early settlement of the followers of Muhammad at the first hijra, and argues for tolerance, rejection of violence, acceptance of non-Muslim authorities and greater emancipation for women. It has clashed strongly with some Muslim groups and has been associated with the governments of Syria and Lebanon, and so is seen by Muslims as controversial and divisive.

It arrived in Ethiopia in 2011 when it sent fifteen representatives to a conference in Harar, organised by the Supreme Council of Islamic Affairs, or the Majlis, with support from the government. Since then it has become part of the life of Islam in Ethiopia, and receives government support.[27] The Majlis has continued its programme of education in constitutional obligations by providing certified preachers for mosques, which is seen by many as state interference in religious affairs. In 2011 the Majlis banned the Islamic Relief

Organisation, which was providing financial support, and dismissed teachers of the Aweliyya School who were suspected of extremism. This led to indignation and protest by Muslims at this perceived state influence, which continued through 2012, and has still not been resolved.

Alongside the encouragement of moderate forms of Islam at home, the Ethiopian government has opposed fundamentalist groups abroad. On 29 December 2006 the Ethiopian army entered Mogadishu, in neighbouring Somalia, and occupied the city for the following two years. This occupation of the capital of a Muslim country by a non-Muslim power aroused outrage among many Islamic groups. Within the rapidly changing political composition of the Middle Eastern and North African regions, Ethiopia continues to maintain a multi-faith state. The traditions of coexistence which have been an element of the religious traditions of Ethiopia have so far prevented the large-scale violence and division which has led to the disintegration of other societies in the region.

CHAPTER 7

Catholic Missions and Christological Debate: Exploring Doctrine

HISTORY: RECONSTRUCTION AFTER GRAÑ

The defeat of Grañ was the result of the military success of the Ethiopian armies under Emperor Gälawdéwos who adopted a hit-and-run strategy, using their familiarity with the mountainous terrain to make sudden assaults on the Muslim armies, and was also the result of the support of the small but well-armed and motivated Portuguese soldiers under Christovão da Gama. But the forces of Grañ were far from home, with supply lines stretched and resources diminishing. They were overstretched and the attacks were already losing momentum. However, while the Islamic forces were repulsed the Christian kingdom was also exhausted. The glories of the medieval Christian kingdom could not be restored.

At the time that the Muslims were conquered, another group of invaders was arriving, this time from the south, and their attacks were more prolonged, more effective and led to lasting change in the racial composition of Ethiopia.

The expansion of the Galla peoples is considered to be one of the great movements of peoples in history. The Galla, or Oromo as they are more correctly called, came from the area between the Bale Mountains and the Rift Valley lakes in the south of Ethiopia.[1] They had developed a democratic social organisation based on the *gadaa* system, a complex arrangement which varies between various groups of Oromo.[2] The *gadaa* is based on age, and locates each Oromo as a member of an age-set which has defined responsibilities in society. The social roles change after each eight-year period as the man grows older. The fourth eight-year period, when the young man is around twenty-four years old, is that of warrior, and the members of that group should show their acceptance of this role by carrying out warlike activities against their neighbours. This social requirement to wage war on a regular basis has been suggested as a reason for the cyclical wave of attacks which began around 1520, reached Harar in 1567, and continued until the Oromo had settled over most of modern-day Ethiopia and much of Kenya. But the thesis of *gadaa*-based expansion does not explain why the group remained contained within its Bale homeland in the years before 1520. Another possible explanation is population growth, but, here too, it is unclear why the Oromo population suddenly began to grow after 1520.

The Oromo are from a non-Semitic racial group which is distinguished from both Christians and Muslims, who came from a Semitic origin. The Oromo brought a different social, religious and political culture, and this brought greater diversity in the north. Their arrival led to a period of instability and turbulence, but eventually the Oromo settled and accommodated their way of life to that of their more organised hosts. As one historian comments, 'the story of the various accommodations between the Galla and the other peoples of Greater Ethiopia is the story of the making of modern Ethiopian society'.[3]

To these invaders who had an impact on Ethiopia can be added yet another group who were present for a limited period but also bequeathed a lasting legacy. The Portuguese arrived as invited guests but grew into unwelcome intruders, who were eventually forcibly ejected. They came from a continent which was becoming more aware of the existence and opportunities of the wider world, and within it the country of Ethiopia. As well as providing lucrative opportunities for trade, it was also a fertile ground for religious evangelism. It was especially attractive to the new religious order of the Society of Jesus, or Jesuits, founded by Ignatius Loyola in 1534 as a part of a renewed and empowered movement of reform within Roman Catholicism.[4] The Jesuit order had spread quickly and established a base for its eastern operations at Goa, on the coast of

India. From here Francis Xavier had gone to Japan and exclaimed on landing in 1549, with the joyous optimism of the period, 'this people is the delight of my heart'.[5] China was a later target with several failed attempts to enter before Mateo Ricci penetrated China and was welcomed by the emperor in Peking in 1602. The Ethiopian adventure was also carried out by Jesuits and lasted for the seventy-nine years under consideration here, from 1555 to 1634.

At first the Portuguese were welcomed. They brought military hardware, commercial expertise and new technologies, especially in building. But alongside these came new religious ideas and approaches.

Emperor Gälawdéwos (1540–59) welcomed Jesuits to court, and engaged in a lively religious debate. He wrote a *Confession of Faith,* setting out the beliefs of Ethiopian Christianity for the education of Catholic arrivals. Särsä Dengel (1563–97) strengthened the army by recruiting troops which he placed under his own command. Susenyos (1607–32) tried to make creative use of the new situation to establish his state. He had been brought up among Oromo and had married an Oromo wife. He invited Oromo to settle in the border areas and so to become integrated into the new Ethiopian state. At the same time he tried to renew the church through the influence of Jesuit missionaries, and made a personal submission to the pope, thus becoming Roman Catholic. This new basis for a state turned out to be ephemeral, and disintegrated in anti-Catholic revolts and civil war. He abdicated in 1632.

TWO MISSIONARIES

The Christianity of Europe had retained occasional contacts with the Christianity of Africa, especially through their shared concern for the city of Jerusalem. Letters written from Jerusalem to Rome about 380 say that there were Ethiopian pilgrims, although these might have come from Nubia since the Ethiopia of that time covered a wide area. There is evidence for Ethiopian communities from the fourteenth century with two chapels in the Holy Sepulchre and a monastery on Mount Zion. By 1530 the monastery of Deir es Sultan had been set up on at the roof level of the Holy Sepulchre.[6] The life of the Ethiopians in Jerusalem was disrupted not only by the reverberations of the Grañ assaults back home, but also by the Ottoman conquest of Jerusalem. Ethiopian monks left the holy city and some went west to settle in

Rome where they brought knowledge of the Christian tradition of Ethiopia. This added to the occasional contacts which had already been taking place. The Ethiopian king had written to the Council of Florence in 1438, and this had led to a commission to discuss relations between the churches, which had issued a bull of union in 1442, Cantate Domino.

Interest in Ethiopia had been further stimulated by rumours of a fabulous Christian kingdom in Ethiopia ruled by a king who was also a priest, Prester John, who was reputed to be a descendant of one of the wise men who visited the Christ Child. Christian Europe had first heard of Prester John in a letter which had arrived around 1160. It described the fabulous kingdom which dominated the three Indias and which was located next to the earthly paradise, which contained the Fountain of Youth (which enabled the great Prester John to remain on the throne for many hundreds of years). There were seven kings, sixty-two dukes and 365 counts who served Prester John at table, and fabulous animals, including the unicorn, which was tricked by the lion who hid behind a tree so that, when the unicorn charged, its horn became embedded in the tree so that the lion could overcome and consume it. The letter explained how it was a kingdom with no flattery, lying or strife, and how the ruler would not accept the title of king or duke, but because of his great humility was known simply as prester or priest. This document was popular and was widely read. It was available in many languages and enthralled its readers with its wonderful tales of far-off places.[7]

Curiosity about this great ruler grew into excitement when Jacques de Vitry, Bishop of Acre in the Holy Land, reported in 1221 that Prester John, or possibly his son or grandson, was on the march and had conquered Persia, and was on the way to support the beleaguered Christian enclaves in the Holy Land. 'A new and mighty protector of Christianity has arisen. He is King David of India, who has taken the field of battle against the unbelievers at the head of an army of unparalleled size.' The bishop was partly right – there was a mighty warrior, and he had defeated the Muslims of Persia. But he was the mighty Genghis Khan, leading the Mongol hordes. The Mongols had swept in to central Asia from the east, where they had been influenced by both Buddhism and Christianity, which at that time had spread as far as China. Genghis Khan himself had been under the protection of the Christian Kerait chieftain Toghrul and married a Christian wife. Later Mongol rulers – including Kublai Khan – became Christian and Muslims feared for their future. By the end of the century, however, Christian influence on the Mongol court was in decline and Islam was taking its place. The hoped-for salvation from the great eastern priest king never came. The protector turned out to be yet another persecutor. So it became clear that Asia was not the place to look to in the search for the great Prester John.

At this point the Prester John hunters decided that his kingdom must be in Africa, in Ethiopia to be more precise, and so their attention was redirected. Alvares and his men, like others at the time, had been fascinated by the Prester John stories and decided to refer to the King of Ethiopia as Prester John. He called his book 'truthful information about the countries of Prester John of the Indies'. When the envoys of the Ethiopian King Zär'a Ya'eqob had come to the Council of Florence in 1441, they discovered that their king was described by Europeans as Prester John and protested that while their king had several names both personal and traditional, Prester John was not one of them. This did not matter, however. As far as Europe was concerned – Prester John was the King of Ethiopia. It was not until the seventeenth century when the German scholar Hiob Ludolf showed that there was no connection between this wonderful story and the kingdom of Ethiopia that the name was reluctantly abandoned.

The awareness of the existence of the Christian kingdom in the mountains of the Horn of Africa, with the titillating stories of Prester John, is the background to the Jesuit period of Ethiopian church history.

The mission to Ethiopia was carried out by a small number of dedicated missionaries. Two came in 1555, then five more in 1557 and smaller numbers thereafter. Getting there was dangerous and difficult due to the arduous terrain and the more arduous necessity of somehow penetrating to the interior through a coastal hinterland controlled by Turks or Turkish supporters. Once there they were often confined to a Portuguese village on a hill not far from Aksum in the north which they named Fremona, after the great Frumentius the apostle of the Ethiopians, and in conditions which amounted to house arrest; or they might be invited to live with the emperor as he travelled around the country on his various military operations, which also had a character of confinement about it.

Two figures stand out among the Jesuit missionaries: Pero Paez, who lived in Ethiopia from 1601 until his death in 1622, and Alfonso

Mendes, from 1624 to 1634. During the time of Pero Paez two successive emperors decided to become Catholic, and during the time of Alfonso Mendes all Jesuits were expelled from the country and not permitted to return. Paez and Mendes set about their task in apparently sharply differing ways.[8]

Pero Paez was born near Madrid in 1564. At the age of eighteen he became a member of the Society of Jesus. Like many young novices he was stirred by the example of those who travelled to distant lands and died as martyrs to the faith, and so wrote to his superiors humbly requesting permission to be sent on the missions. He thought that Japan would be a suitably challenging destination. Clearly he impressed his superiors because the next year he set off on the first leg of this journey to Goa in India. But instead of continuing further east he was asked to go instead to Ethiopia.

His first attempt was unsuccessful. He and another priest left in early 1589 and tried to travel by sea and then by land across Arabia. He went through places never previously visited by Europeans, and reached Sana'a in what is now north Yemen. Here they were arrested, spent five years in prison, were put up for sale in a slave market and when no one would buy them – perhaps because they were in such poor condition after their confinement – were passed on to the owner of a fleet of galleys where they were chained to the oars of the boats. Paez remembered that time:

> It was never cleaned and the dirt was unbelievable. Throughout the night we were forced to remain sitting up. If we were overcome by sleep we covered our face, but the lice forced us to get up and kept torturing us until morning. Our food was a handful of seeds like millet and nothing more. We lived like this for two and a half months.

Then came a spell in the quarries for a further year. Eventually money was paid for their release and they returned to Goa in November 1596. They had left Goa seven and a half years previously and now they were back where they started.

Paez tried again five years later, this time using a more subtle approach. He had taken the precaution of learning fluent Arabic, and managed to persuade a merchant to take him to Massawa. He wore the clothing of local people, and told them he was an Armenian on his way to Jerusalem and that he had a friend who had died and he wanted to collect some of his possessions from the interior. He was given every assistance and courtesy on this mission and ten days later found himself giving thanks for a safe arrival at the Jesuit church at Fremona. His arrival took place thirteen years after he first set out from Goa in 1589.

This story of the long and arduous process which Pero Paez undertook shows vividly the extreme difficulties and hardships of the missionary's life. These were men of extraordinary dedication and resourcefulness and it is not surprising that Paez won the admiration and affection of the court when he arrived at the cluster of tents at the invitation of the then emperor, Zä Dengel (1603–4), in 1604, and where he stayed for most of the next eighteen years. We are told that he was tall with a reddish face and a lively mind, and was 'so affable in his manner that he captivated the hearts of all who had any dealings with him', and that he made himself the servant and slave of all. The emperor commented that 'whenever I set eyes on him, I look on the face of an angel.'

Paez became a close friend and adviser of Zä Dengel's successor, Susenyos (1607–32). He was an educator, an adviser, a diplomat, a builder, a theologian, a reformer. His approach to the Ethiopian Church has been described as 'concealed opposition', since he seemed so open and accepting of Ethiopian culture and custom, while working towards eventual conversion.[9] When Emperor Susenyos decided to become Catholic in 1624, Paez did his best to dissuade him from this course. He did this for pragmatic reasons, realising that a public declaration would inflame anti-Catholic feeling. It may be that he hoped for a renewal of faith and practice, but not necessarily an outward conformity. Behind Paez's relationships with emperors and others was his fascination and respect for Ethiopian customs and literature. He collected translations of texts and observations of what he saw in his *Historia da Etiopia*, which he completed in 1621. This influenced later writers, but was not published until the twentieth century.

Paez was succeeded by Alfonso Mendes who arrived in Ethiopia in 1625 with the title of Patriarch. He was the choice of King Philip of Spain and did not have the support of either Pope Urban VIII nor the General of the Jesuit order. Mendes requested that the pope present him with vestments from his private chapel so that he could celebrate the liturgy in style among 'an uncultivated people'. He also asked that two assistant bishops should be appointed to provide assistance.

He then set out to Ethiopia to meet his flock. He made careful preparations for his meeting with Susenyos. When he drew near he dismounted and put on ecclesiastical dress and allowed all those present to kiss his hand. A little further on he entered a tent and put on a cope and white mitre, mounted a new horse clothed in white damask, and proceeded with a canopy held over him. As he approached, Susenyos came to meet him and embraced him. He then addressed the people. Mendes himself reports the content of his speech. In his version it comes to 30,000 words and would have taken most of the day to deliver. It moves at a majestic pace through the history of the church, demonstrating the authority and leadership of Rome. It must have been incomprehensible to most of the listeners. He finished by saying that previous attempts to restore unity with Rome had failed but promised to his hearers, 'That day I shall re-erect the tottering house of David, make good the gaps in it, restore its ruins and rebuild it as it was in the days of old.' He immediately demonstrated how he intended to do this by making a solemn proclamation. No priest was to celebrate mass in the country without a document issued by himself; all clergy were to be reordained; the faithful rebaptised and the Roman calendar to be adopted. Susenyos, who had made a declaration of loyalty to Rome two years previously, was asked to repeat this in front of the court.

About the same time as Mendes arrived, large numbers of locusts also arrived, and caused devastation over much of the land. It was clear to local people that it was no accident that these two arrivals were simultaneous. In vain the Jesuits pointed out that there had been locusts in Ethiopia before their arrival. The Ethiopians found the connection clear enough, and patiently pointed out to the Jesuits that wherever they went – so the Ethiopian priests said – they were followed by a cloud of locusts demonstrating that they were cursed. This explained why people seemed so frightened of them however much they tried to do good works, a fact which had puzzled the Jesuits.

The sharply contrasting approaches by, and reactions to, the work of these two missionaries obscures the unity of purpose between them. The Jesuit mission in Ethiopia encountered a people who had been Christian for many centuries, while in other mission areas such as Japan the Christian faith was unknown. The Jesuits developed an approach which they called 'reduction', translating the Spanish *reduccion*. This was based on the need for harmony and order in the lives of individual persons and in society, to replace the confusion and disorder which prevails without the discipline of Christian formation. They worked towards this end following a three-stage approach. The first was to understand. The Jesuits applied themselves to this through study of the language and culture. They produced a series of writings which have become the main sources of knowledge of the Ethiopia of this period, including the accounts of Francisco Alvares, Pero Paez, Jeronimo Lobo and Manuel de Almeida. This was followed by deconstruction of corrupt or heretical features, in which the Christianity of Ethiopia was examined and engaged with to show where correction and reform were needed. Then came the third stage of introducing Roman Catholic forms of worship and teaching. Both Paez and Mendes were committed to the same end, but contributed to different and successive stages, with Paez providing study and debate and Mendes following with a programme of active reform.[10]

Jesuit missionaries were received at court and were supported by both Zä Dengel and then Susenyos. This led to an extension of their mission across the country, with success in setting up centres of mission, making growing numbers of converts and building good relationships with some monasteries. Their identification with the king was also a factor in their downfall. Not only did Susenyos favour a Catholic form of faith but set out to gain firm control over the nobility. This provoked resistance and rebellion, which led to the downfall of Susenyos, and alongside him, his Jesuit allies.[11]

The Jesuits were expelled from court in 1632 and from the country in 1634.

CHRISTOLOGY: THE DEBATE BEGINS

The day after Paez arrived at the court of Zä Dengel and had set up at his camp at Wayna Dega, weary after a long journey, he was summoned by the emperor and found himself surrounded by monks and others and asked about the merits of the Roman version of Christianity in comparison with the Ethiopian. Then two Catholic children were brought in and asked to recite the catechism and an instruction manual was produced and aroused much interest. On the following day a tent was set up and Paez said mass and preached in the presence of the emperor. Thus began a long and ongoing debate in the course of which Catholic teaching was meticulously examined.

These debates fascinated the court and the assembled clergy of Ethiopia. Paez wrote later, 'All you could see at the Emperor's court were squadrons of monks and with them wandering wherever they pleased was a crowd of nuns all resolved to die for their old faith.'

The conversations and debates which started at Wayna Daga on that day in 1604 continued after the Jesuits departed, and did not reach a formal resolution until 1878 at the Council of Borru Meda, and have continued to arouse controversy. The subject of the debate was the person of Christ, and the differences of understanding which had been expressed at the Council of Chalcedon several centuries previously.

For Orthodox Churches in communion with Constantinople, the Council of Chalcedon of 451 had defined orthodox belief in the person of Christ. At Chalcedon, a suburb of the city of Constantinople, bishops had met to discuss the correct definition of who Christ was, and to resolve disputes which had arisen. Among the heretical views they debated, and rejected, was the belief that Christ had a single divine nature, which had put on human attributes, a view known as Monophysite, or single-nature, in Greek. This view had developed especially in Egypt and Syria. The bishops at Chalcedon used Greek language and philosophical ideas to produce their definition. They proclaimed that Christ is one person (*prosopon*) and one substance (*hypostasis*), but in two natures (*en duo physeis*), 'without confusion, without change, without division and without separation'. Further refinements were added by later councils at Constantinople (in 553 and 680–1) and Nicaea (787). These conciliar decisions were accepted by churches who were dependent on both Constantinople and Rome. Paez argued for this Catholic approach, which affirmed that Christ had both a divine and a human nature, which subsisted in one person.

His Ethiopian conversation partners expressed their faith differently. They had not taken part in the Christological Councils, partly because of their geographical isolation from the rest of the church. No Ethiopian representative attended the Council of Chalcedon, and its decisions were not communicated to them.[12] Instead their authority in matters of faith came from Alexandria, and were based on a number of texts which were written before the Council of Chalcedon. The collection is known as the *Qérelos*, or writings of Cyril of Alexandria (376–444). The writings included the *Prosphonetikos* 'on right faith', the dialogue 'that Christ is one' and homilies from the Council of Ephesus. In them the church of Ethiopia found the formula which became a slogan, which is that Christ is 'one incarnate nature of God the Word' (*mia physis tou theou logou sesarkomene*). This was enough – a clear statement of faith in the one Christ who was both divine and human. These writings of Cyril came from the period before the debate at Chalcedon took place and so presented an understanding of the person of Christ which had not been modified and refined through the debate at Chalcedon and other councils.

The position of the Church of Ethiopia and others who reject the decision of Chalcedon are sometimes referred to as non-Chalcedonian or Monophysite. Neither of these terms is helpful, and are not used by the churches themselves. It is better to say pre-Chalcedonian than non-Chalcedonian, since this recognises that the basis of the faith was thinking and writing which represented an understanding earlier than Chalcedon, and were not necessarily opposed to it.

The term miaphysite is preferred to monophysite since it has a different emphasis. The word monophysite is derived from two Greek words, *monos* or single, and *physis* or nature. Ethiopians, and others who reject the language of Chalcedon, reject this title. Monos, they point out, means 'one' in the sense of single or alone, even solitary. But there is an alternative word, *mia*, which is the numeral one – as opposed to two or more. So Ethiopian theologians prefer to say Miaphysite. This shows that Christ has one nature, as opposed to two (or more) but allows them to affirm that this is a nature which is composite, drawn from both divine and human sources. So they affirm a 'one nature' Christology, but not a 'single nature' Christology. Ethiopian theologians are determined to rule out any suggestion of duality in Christ – or any suggestion that he had a double existence with his human nature being tired or hungry or angry, and his divine nature healing the sick or raising the dead. There is one Christ who is God the Word, a human being, acting for our salvation. 'We speak of one nature after the union. We hold *mia physis*, a composite nature, one united nature.'[13] This is seen as vital to a right understanding of faith.

The *Qérelos*, with its 'pre-Chalcedonian' approach, became an authoritative definition of faith, and was memorised, discussed and transmitted. In discussing the theological traditions of Ethiopia, the historian Adrian Hastings makes this comment: 'The Christianity of

Ethiopia [was] a continual redigestion across centuries of a very limited range of texts, a process carried out with no more than minimal contact with the rest of the church.'[14] By the time that Paez arrived at Wayna Daga, further texts were becoming available. A further collection of writings had been translated during the sixteenth century, the *Haymonotä Abäw*, or Faith of the Fathers. This was a collection of texts on the Trinity and on Christ, translated from Arabic, and was derived from a wider range of sources than the *Qérelos*. Paez demonstrated how much there was in common between this traditional Ethiopian book and the Roman teaching of the Jesuits, especially on the person of Christ. He also used the books produced by Jesuits, Maldonado and Geronimo Nadal, and people found that these explanations of passages of Scripture were preferable to Ethiopian texts.

So two approaches to Christian theology met. On one side was the Western Catholic teaching, which described Christ as having two natures, divine and human, which subsisted in one person of Christ. On the other was the traditional Ethiopian teaching which affirmed the one nature of Christ, who was the word of God made flesh. The two doctrinal positions, which arose out of different languages and cultures, then led to the formation of three understandings of the Ethiopian version of christological teaching. These then became entrenched in different regional groupings, and so gained a political character. The three christological schools have influenced the history of the Ethiopian Church since then.

CHRISTOLOGY: THE THREE SCHOOLS

Paez was an influential figure who impressed those who met him with his scholarship, openness to Ethiopian culture and his devout way of life. The monks were challenged to set out their own views. Their task was to maintain an Alexandrian one-nature Christology which gave a satisfactory account of the texts presented by the missionaries.

The christological debate in Ethiopia had a principle theme – Christ himself. The name Christ is equivalent to the Hebrew Messiah and means anointed. Ethiopian Christology brought together two previously divergent streams of tradition. The Jewish strand of Ethiopian Christianity emphasised that Jesus is the Christ, the Messiah, chosen by God and anointed. Alongside this approach was the Greek philosophical approach, taught in Alexandria, which stated unequivocally that Christ is the one incarnate Son of God. The question was how these two apparently contradictory traditions could be integrated. If Christ is the Son of God, then what meaning can it have to speak of his being anointed? What can the anointing mean and what can this action bestow on him which he did not already have? What difference can it make to him, and what can it add to him which was not there before?

For the Jesuits, with their Western two-nature Christology, the answer was clear. The man Jesus, in his human nature, was chosen and anointed by God. One of the texts was Acts 10.38: 'God anointed Jesus of Nazareth with the Holy Spirit and with power.' But for Ethiopians this was not an option. They asked that if Jesus' nature is that he is already God, how can he be anointed by the Holy Spirit?

There were three answers given to this mysterious conundrum. These were given by the three groups into which the Ethiopian theologians are divided, which are called *qebat, karra* and *sägga.*[15]

One answer was given by the *qebat* school. *Qebat* means unction, and so the Qebat party are often called the Unctionists. They were also called *hulett ledet* or two births. The 'birth' here, it should be pointed out, was important because it was a way of describing the different sources or origins of Christ's being. If you could not speak of two natures after the union, then you might possibly be able to speak of two births, or two points of origin, when the one Christ came into being. So the one Christ has two births. The first is from the Father before all ages and the second is from the Virgin Mary at a point in time. The unction took place when Christ was in the womb of the Virgin when the Holy Spirit brought about the union of God and Man into one nature and this was the anointing. All references to anointing must be referred to the union of the Word and the man. There was no anointing apart from that. This view was summarised in the slogan, 'The Father the anointer, the Son the anointed and the Holy Spirit the unction or ointment.' It was also said that Christ became 'by unction a natural Son'.

Other Ethiopian scholars argued for a simple approach which did not give a place to the action of the Spirit. This group was called *Karra,* or knife, and was also known as Unionists. They preferred to call themselves *tawehedo* or made one. This is the strict 'one nature' party. Several explanations have been given for the intimidating title of *karra* or knife. Either it was because their ferocious arguments cut away opposing positions, or because they cut away the Holy Spirit out of the truth of the Incarnation, or because the Son of God passed through Mary's womb as a sword passes through a scabbard, without making contact with it. According to this view, the divinity of the Son of God becomes united with the humanity in the womb of Mary. There is an anointing but it consists only in the uniting of the divine and the human. In response to the question as to who is the anointer, anointed and ointment, the answer which the *karra* gave is that it is the Son who is all these three. The slogan which summarised their position was 'the Son himself is the anointer, the anointed and the unction' (*wold lalihu qebay, täqebay, qeb*). There is no place for either the Father or the Holy Spirit in the union according to their view. Rather the Son entered the womb of the virgin and thus the union with humanity took place. It is a radical and simple statement of the one-nature view of Christ. At first this group was influential but was superseded by a more sophisticated version which recognised that the anointing is an action associated with the Holy Spirit. The *karra* supporters then retired to the north of the country, to Tigray and North Welo. An opportunity for return came when a new emperor from their region, Yohannes IV, was crowned and summoned the final synod of this long-running debate at Borru Meda. Their teaching eventually became the official view of the church.

The third group was the *sägga* or grace school. They were also called the *sägga lijj* or son by grace, and *sost ledet* or three births. Like the *karra* they used the term *tawehedo* to describe themselves. The term three births indicates their approach to the problem. The first birth was from God the Father from all eternity, the second birth was from Mary and was accomplished in the union in the womb. But there was a third birth which was distinct from these and took place when the Spirit anointed Jesus either in the womb or, according to some theologians, at the baptism. This gives a place to the Holy Spirit and recognises the anointing as a distinct action.

It has often been concluded from this that the group had adopted a christological position which is close to the two-nature Christology of Chalcedon, with its teaching that Jesus was anointed by the spirit at baptism. It has also been suggested that it has gone further and become a form of adoptionism, which is a heretical approach which considers that Christ's divine power was bestowed on him by the Spirit, and so he can be seen as simply an inspired man, similar in kind to prophets or kings although to a higher degree. An example of this view is the comment of Donald Crummey that the *sägga* was a two-nature Christology and 'may well have moved beyond Chalcedon'.[16]

This understanding of the *sägga* view is repeated by most writers on this period, but has been challenged by some Ethiopian theologians. These argue that the anointing by the Spirit did not take place at the baptism of Jesus but before his birth, while still in the womb of Mary. This changes the meaning of the anointing from being a moment when Jesus is given special authority and power at a point in his life, to a way of understanding the mysterious union which was accomplished within the womb of Mary. This view suggests that the *sägga*, far from being a Western-style adoptionism, is instead a further development of the traditional Ethiopian one-nature approach and so is a more refined version of the *karra*. While there is some variation of approach and interpretation within the *sägga* school, the texts show that there is clear continuity and consistency with the *tawehedo* tradition.[17]

On this understanding, teachers had come to see that the *karra* view was open to the charge of being too simple, and a rejection of any kind of anointing did not do justice to the relevant scriptural texts. So some of the adherents of the *karra* started to teach the reality of the anointing by the Spirit but saw it as separate from the union. They considered that the anointing took place in the womb, when the Word became flesh, and the divine became human. The choice of this moment for the anointing is important. It happens when Christ becomes man, and since he becomes man for our sake, then the anointing is for our sake too. It was an anointing of the united divine-human person which is a part of the salvation offered to the human race. It does nothing to change the one divine-human nature of Christ, but instead initiates the story of salvation by making Christ into the second Adam and becoming a new kind of human being restoring the condition of man before the Fall.[18] Their catchphrase was 'by the union [Christ in his humanity] was ennobled and by the unction he became a Son by grace' (*bätawähedo lij käbära bäqebat yäsägga*). There is a distinction between the union which makes Christ a Son by nature, and unction which makes him a Son by grace. The second sonship is functional, and inaugurates and empowers the work of the Messiah, for the salvation of humanity.

Like the other views, the *sägga lijj* was a clearly one-nature Christology, affirming the position of Alexandria. Like others, it rejected any suggestion that Christ had two natures or that his humanity was in some way adopted to become God as an action of the bestowing of grace.

The third birth makes Christ into a new kind of human being. It brings into being a renewed humanity which is radically different from the old fallen humanity, and is a transformation by the Holy Spirit of the old humanity to enable it to become a new form of humanity, or rather a restoration of the perfect humanity as Adam had before the Fall. So, as a result of the third birth, Christ can be spoken of as a new Adam. It belongs in the category of soteriology rather than theology – explaining how Christ achieves salvation for us rather than who he is in himself.

A salvation which is the gift of a new kind of humanity resonated in a church with a strong monastic and ascetic tradition of spirituality. The ideal of a perfect humanity was attractive and evocative for the monk, who was following the ascetic path. It provided a context for the disciplines of the monastic life, and set out the goal towards which they were moving. The monastic context of this spirituality are illustrated in a passage from a medieval text, the *Mäzgäba Haymonot* or Treasure of Faith. The author is discussing the various bodily functions of Christ, aspects of his one divine-human nature. Obviously Christ ate – because the Bible tells us that he did, consuming for example a piece of boiled fish after the Resurrection. But he cannot, surely, undergo what is decorously called the 'emptying of the stomach' or urination, since this is a part of our fallen humanity which is subjected to physical weakness and necessity. Similarly Mary did not have a monthly period after the birth of Christ.

> Thus when Christ put on the flesh of Adam, it was pure flesh before the first sin, because the Holy Spirit purified our Lady Mary when Gabriel said to her 'the Holy Spirit will come upon you'. Therefore Christ had no emptying of the body or urine like us. When he had hunger he had it not out of necessity but out of free will; and when he had thirst, then not out of necessity but out of free will.

The ideal of the monk is to follow a strict ascetic life, avoiding food, drink, pleasure and possessions, as well as sexual enjoyment, as much as possible so as to live a pure angelic life, governed by the spiritual relationship with God rather than by the needs of the body. According to this understanding, the three-birth idea is not a heretical adoptionist idea but is a powerful statement of what human nature can be and an encouragement to the monk to continue in his agonising and relentless fasting.[19]

Behind all three schools of Christology lay the shared premise of faith that there is one single person of Christ with a single nature. This was the Alexandrian teaching which they all shared, and from which they opposed the Chalcedonian teaching of the Jesuits. This raises the question of why the conflict was so long-lasting and so bitter.

THE EVENTUAL TRIUMPH OF THE *TAWEHEDO*

Since the three schools shared the same starting point, which was opposed to the two-nature Christology of the Jesuits, it might have been expected that once the Jesuits had been expelled peace would return to the church. But this did not prove to be the case. Instead the conflict dragged on and became increasingly violent and entrenched. Each approach was associated with a different monastic house and then with a different region. The *qebat* was taught by the monks of the house of Éwostatéwos, whose power base was in the Gojjam region. The *karra* was rooted in the north, and was taught in Tigray and the north of Welo. The *sägga* was the position of the monks of Täklä Haymonot, whose monasteries were spread through Shewa, Begemder and south Welo. The house of Täklä Haymonot also set up a house in Azozo, a few miles south of the capital at Gondar, which proved to be a valuable base from which to advocate their views at the court. The views were not confined to their areas of strength, but spread across the country, dividing communities and monasteries. The monastery of Waldebba was in the north-west of the country and so in an area supporting the *karra* or *sägga* viewpoint. It was a large community of around a thousand monks and spread over a wide area. It was divided between two separate groups – the Beta Minas which followed the *qebat* view, and the Beta Tama which was *sägga*. They worshipped separately and did not participate at each other's Eucharist.[20] These divisions were repeated throughout the country.

The *sägga* and the *qebat* were both represented in Gondar and struggled to gain the ascendancy. The *qebat* gained ground during the early eighteenth century. During the reign of Dawit III (1716–21), who favoured the *qebat*, the *sägga* group decided to approach the abuna and went to the house of the abuna Kerstodolu, and persuaded him to support them. While they were rejoicing at this success, disaster struck and there was a dramatic reversal of fortunes. A detachment of the palace guard arrived and massacred one hundred abbots of the Täklä Haymonot monasteries, and so this led to a further period of *qebat* ascendancy. After 1770 the kingdom descended into disorder. The three christological views retreated to their regions of strength, and since the princes of the regions held the power, and central authority was weak, reconciliation proved hard to achieve. The migration of the parties into their own region also had the outcome that a mixture of religious ideas and opinions became hardened into a rigid political programme, with doctrinal statements used as political slogans and badges of identity of different opinions. The emperors convened a series of synods to resolve the divisions, but these became less frequent as the kings became weaker. The period from 1769 to 1855 is referred to as the *zämänä mäsafent*, or the era of the princes or judges. The title is drawn from the time of the judges in the Old Testament when everyone did what was right in his own eyes.

Resolution had to await the arrival of a king strong enough to unite the country, and with it the church. This process began with the accession of Téwodros II (1855–68) who summoned a council at Amba Cara in 1854. He was supported by the abuna Sälama and affirmed the simple *tawehedo* teaching of the *karra*. This was repeated by his successor. Kassa, the ras of Tigray, had been crowned with the name Yohannes IV (1871–89) and summoned a synod to Borru Meda (1878). The abuna was not present at this council and the king made a declaration. He decided in favour of the teaching he was familiar with, which also happened to be the least well supported of the three – the *karra*. This has remained the official teaching of the church.

The Christology of the church is seen as the doctrine which identifies its beliefs. The Ethiopian Church affirms Christ is a divine person, with its nature, which was joined in the womb of Mary to a human person, with its complete nature, and that after Christ is born there is a single person with its nature, which is composed out of the two natures. Along with others who share this faith, they agree that

Christ can be spoken of as 'from two natures', but they oppose the phrase used at the Council of Chalcedon of 'in two natures'.

The title of the church is the Ethiopian Orthodox Tawehedo Church. The word *tawehedo* has been attached to the formal title of the church over the last twenty years to make this point clearly. *Tawehedo* is the gerund or past form of the verb *tawähädä* – meaning 'be united'. It can be used in various contexts, such as the amalgamation of two commercial companies, the mixture of two liquids or even the digestion of food. It points to a central doctrine that Christ is one, united and composite in nature and person. It is more than an article of faith – it's a badge of identity and a distinguishing mark, which defines the church and distinguishes it from other intruding and proselytising Christian church communities.

WESTERN AND ETHIOPIAN THINKING CONTRASTED

There has been a further chapter in this long-running conflict. It was once again a Roman Catholic who sparked off this new phase of the controversy. Ayele Tekla Haymonot published his doctoral thesis in 1956, which argued that the teachings of the Ethiopian Orthodox and Roman Catholic understandings shared the same faith in the nature of Christ and were really the same, so that differences between them were due to misunderstandings of language; and also due to the influence of the Coptic church. This led to a series of studies by Ethiopian Orthodox theologians refuting Dr Ayele's argument and demonstrating that the Ethiopian Church holds firmly to the '*tawehedo*' or 'miaphysite' understanding of Christ. The traditional understanding has been set out in a further series of Ethiopian doctrinal statements and contributions to ecumenical dialogues.[21]

The work of Ayele Tekla Haymonot claims that the differences between the Roman Catholic Chalcedonian position and the Ethiopian one-nature position are verbal rather than substantial. The problem was that neither side fully understood what the other was saying, and so did not grasp that they shared the same fundamental faith. He suggests that the disagreements arose from language, rather than faith.

The controversy demonstrates the gulf between the two sides which arose from the differences in language, in the development of the tradition and in the ability to appreciate what the other was saying. Differences in language, worldview and ways of thinking of the two sides led to misunderstanding and conflict. On this reading, even if the Ethiopians had been present at the Council of Chalcedon they might have had difficulty grasping and expressing the language and ideas being expressed. Other nations also had difficulties with language too. The Armenians also rejected the approach of Chalcedon. One reason for their response was the difficulty over the language used. The Armenian equivalent for the Greek 'nature' was derived from an Iranian root which also meant 'foundation' or 'origin' and so, for them, to speak of two natures led to an impossible duality.[22]

An approach to the understanding of cultural difference is provided by the work of Iain McGilchrist, who is both a consultant psychiatrist and a lecturer in English literature. These two disciplines have helped him to grasp the relationship between the workings of our brains, our perception of the world around and the culture we create. He shows how different stages of human civilisation have resulted in different ways of perceiving and processing experiences. These findings suggest that the difficulty of reaching a common understanding might be rooted in radically different ways of thinking, which show themselves in how language is structured and expressed. This in turn affects how ideas and experiences of God are expressed.

The European traditions of Christian theology were expressed in the writings of Greek and Latin theologians. McGilchrist shows that Greek is a phonemic language, and so is constructed out of letters, which are formed into words, which are then used to express ideas. This approach to language allows a clarity of meaning and a lack of ambiguity, and is well suited to the expression of rational argument. The use of the definite article originated in Greek and this had an impact on how experience could be expressed, and enabled abstract thought. Consider the word 'beautiful', which is an adjective and refers to a quality found in a person or object. If a definite article is added then it becomes 'the beautiful', and so acquires an existence independently of the object it is found in, and becomes an intellectual reality. This in turn leads to the claim that the intellectual idea of beauty is more real than the beauty found in objects, and becomes the subject of philosophical debate. So Plato could write in

The Republic that even the stars in the sky are less real than the intellectual concepts behind them. 'The stars that decorate the sky are far inferior to the true relative velocities, in pure numbers and perfect figures, which are perceptible to reason and thought but are not visible to the eye.'[23] If abstract and intellectual concepts are recognised as real and as the basis of experience, then a different kind of enquiry into the nature of Christ becomes possible. His being – or *ousia* – enters into the discussion. The relations of human nature and divine nature within the person of Christ are the subject of definition at Chalcedon and at other councils.

To the phonemic Greek we can contrast the syllabic Ethiopic. Here, characters are syllables rather than letters. A language which has a basis of syllables has a greater flexibility, fluidity and expressiveness which takes a different form from a phonemic language, and it enables shifts in word-meaning, allowing a variety of meaning. The syllable-characters can be pointed and understood in different ways, and so lead to inferences and implications which give Amharic its richness and complexity. This is demonstrated in the poetic form of *qené*, which will be discussed in the next chapter. There are no definite or indefinite articles, so while it is possible to say beautiful – *wub*, or beauty, *wubit* – it is not possible to say 'the beautiful', as can be said with greater emphasis in Greek.[24]

Ethiopian theological language has a concrete and non-abstract character. This is shown by the consideration of meanings of words that were used in the theological discussions. In the *Qérelos* the word for nature is *hellawé*, or existence. To this further words were added. There is *akal*, which means person, and *bahrey*, which can be translated as nature.

The word *bahrey* or nature provides a starting point for this discussion of the language used, and to show the concrete and non-abstract quality of the terms. It has an interesting history. The first meaning of *bahrey* is pearl. At first it was *gawhar bahrey*, literally 'gem of the sea' but the word *gawhar* or gem was lost to leave just *bahrey*, derived from *baher*, or sea. The pearl is an image much used in Semitic poetry to refer to the human soul. Ephrem the Syrian (*c*.306–73) wrote a series of five poems on the pearl. He reflects on Syrian mythology which described how a pearl is formed when lightning strikes the mussel or oyster. So it becomes a creation from the impact of fire, the element of divinity, and water, the element of earth, and then is contained and nurtured within the creature of the earth. For Ephrem it is a vivid image which speaks of the human soul. A further example of the use of the pearl in literature is the Gnostic Hymn of the Pearl, found in a Syriac text. This tells the story of a boy, a son of the kings, who goes to Egypt to retrieve a pearl which has been entrapped by a serpent. He forgets his mission but is eventually reminded of it, retrieves the pearl and so carries out his quest. The pearl also is a theme of the *Kebrä Nägäst*, which describes how the pearl was hidden in the body of Adam, and wandered through history passing through generations of the righteous until it found fulfilment in Christ. Here the pearl is the essential truth of salvation, a kind of hidden identity of true human nature.

In all these examples, the pearl has a hard reality to it. It is not an abstract quality. It is specific to each individual, and is contained within him or her, a precious inner nature and reality, which gives it identity and meaning. If the soul is like a pearl then it is a precious and real part of human identity, not an abstract or intellectual quality.[25] This prehistory points to how Ethiopian theologians view the person of Christ. The words are poetic, synthetic and evocative, rather than philosophical or systematic. This is shown in the way words are used, with meanings which are not tightly defined.

When we turn to other words used to describe the identity of Christ, we find that these too point to his unique character. A word often used is *akal* or person. One writer defined *akal* as 'a visible tangible being combined and interwoven from head to toe with skin, flesh, nerves and bones' to which a soul has been united and is the subject of nature, of name and of operation.[26] The *akal* is united to the soul, and is the subject of nature, name and operation. *Akal* includes everything that a person is – both the common human nature shared with others, and also the actual individual existence, and both these aspects are included in the definition. *Akal* is referred to God as well as humans, so Christ is an *akal* or a person, as all humans are. The nature can also be described as *hellawé* or being. This further term relates to existence. It refers to something which has come into being and which exists.

All these words insist on the specific reality of the human person. The person's nature is always specific and resides in a person. It is not abstract or universal. Both *akal* or person and *bahrey* or other words meaning nature refer in different ways to a specific whole person.

FIGURE 7.1 The church of Däbrä Berhan Sellassé in Gondar has magnificent wall paintings, including this Holy Trinity, showing the Ethiopian way of depicting this subject.

There are no words available to describe the idea of a 'human nature' which is separate from real human beings. 'No nature occurs without person and vice versa', as put with unmistakable clarity by Ethiopian theologians.[27]

These comments about language and culture are tentative, and should not lead us to unjustified generalisation. But many authors and researchers have identified cultural characteristics which shape patterns of thinking and ways of expressing experience. The insistence on the completeness of the human person can be related to more general religious and social relationships. Religious insights are rooted in the understanding that people are complete persons, who belong within community, and are given identity and meaning through their relationships. It is expressed in the familiar saying of the Kenyan theologian John Mbiti: 'I am because we are, since we are, therefore I am.'[28] This idea is rooted in the strongly communal approach of Semitic thinking. People belong together. So when we speak of Christ in Ethiopia, we describe a complete person who is related to other complete persons. The philosophical debates about nature and person which were carried on enthusiastically in the philosophical academies of Athens do not work in Aksum.

The sense of completeness of the person can also be discerned in the forms of iconography. A popular subject for Ethiopian icon painters is the Trinity. The most familiar way of portraying this subject shows three white haired men sitting next to each other, all looking just the same. The presence of three persons in the icon illustrates the truth that there are three persons in the Trinity, and the identity of their features shows their identity as persons. It is an image derived from descriptions of the glory of God in the books of Ezekiel and Revelation. This form of icon is strictly forbidden in other churches, since God as he is cannot be comprehended or depicted. Instead icon painters often used the scene where three angels visit Abraham to point to the truth of the three persons and one divine nature of the Trinity. In contrast to all other parts of the Christian world, Ethiopian painters begin from the belief that there are three persons in the Trinity and, since this is our faith, then these should be the subject of the icon. In art, as well as in language and in theology, Ethiopia offers a fresh and distinct way of looking at the world and understanding our experience.

The Ethiopian Orthodox Church has included the word *tawehedo* in its recognised title. This indicates the central importance that the one incarnate person of Christ making both the divine and human present in one person has for the Christian church.

CHAPTER 8

Students and Teachers: The Oral Tradition of Scholarship

HISTORY: GONDAR AND THE ZÄMÄNÄ MÄSAFENT

Emperor Fasilädäs (1632–67) expelled the Catholic Jesuits and affirmed the Orthodox faith. He chose a site on a ridge to the north of Lake Tana to be the capital city of his kingdom. He began his building project at Gondar in 1636 by constructing a castle on the ridge, two churches and a stone wall to mark out the royal enclosure. This initiated a pattern of construction which gave shape to the city. A new emperor often built his own castle so that a spacious compound with several stone castles in a distinctive style of architecture with rounded battlements grew up. Further churches were built so that Gondar became known as the city of forty-four churches. This number referred at first to the number of churches over a wide area, up to 30 km distant from the city. Later the number forty-four gained a mythical significance as a symbol of royal power and piety.[1] Recently lists have been compiled to demonstrate where the churches were, and now the Muslim community is said to have set out to build forty-four mosques as a sign of its growing influence in this centre of Christian culture. The choice of Gondar as a permanent capital ended a period when the kings lived in traveling tent cities.

Fasilädäs intended his new capital to become the centre of a restored Orthodox Christian Solomonic kingdom, but the kings who succeeded him were unable to maintain their authority. There were destabilising influences which the kings were not able to

FIGURE 8.1 The castles of Gondar. A new king often built his own castle in the central compound in Gondar.

overcome. The church itself was divided by the controversies over the nature of Christ, and the Oromo were expanding to establish themselves throughout the kingdom. The nobility of the regions became too strong to be controlled by the kings, and gradually the power of the royal house diminished. Kings were confined to the royal compound, seldom venturing out, and were installed and soon removed by powerful warlords. Emperor Täklä Haymonot (1706–8) was assassinated by the armies; Yostos (1711–16) was poisoned; Dawit II (1716–21) was also assassinated; Iyoas (1755–69) was killed. This ended the line of Gondarine kings and ushered in a period called the *zämänä mäsafent.*

The name *zämänä mäsafent* or age of the princes or judges lasted from 1769 to 1855. The name is taken from the Old Testament period of the judges when, the Bible tells us, every man did what was right in his own eyes (Judges 21.25). Kings continued to reign in Gondar but without any real power. Instead local chiefs gained control of different areas, with centres of power in Gondar, Tigray, Gojjam and Shewa.

Insights into life in Gondar are given in the vivid descriptions of one of the great explorers of Ethiopia, James Bruce of Kinnaird, who lived in Gondar from February 1769 to 1771.

Bruce was 6 feet 4 inches with flaming red hair, and towered above the slight and slender Ethiopians. He had an extraordinary talent for languages, and spoke twelve at least, including Geez, Amharic, Arabic and Tigrinya. He travelled with a large company of assistants, servants and guides – with caskets filled with gifts and a formidable armoury of muskets and other weapons far more destructive than anything the Ethiopians had at their disposal. On his arrival at Gondar he proceeded to cure most of the royal court from small pox, including the favourite child of Esther, the prince's wife who became a close friend and lover; he got drunk and had a fight with the most powerful general in the royal entourage; he went riding with the noblemen and amazed them with his ability to shoot birds in flight while riding. 'Yagoube' became a favourite at court.

He settled in a house at Qusquam, near the palace of the Empress Mentewab on a hillside overlooking the ridge on which Gondar is built. She had grown up in a village near Gondar, and had been discovered by the courtiers of Emperor Bäkaffa the Inexorable (1721–30) who had sent them to find him a wife. She was described lyrically by the courtier who found her: she is 'a daughter of kings; her eyes are as stars; joyful as the clusters of the vine; her face is as bright as the olive oil; her hair as soft as the silk; her stature is like the palms; her lips drop modesty and honour; in truth she is lovely'. Bruce met her fifty years later, after she had retired from the court at Gondar to live in religious retirement on a hill a few miles outside the town, close enough to plot and use her power and influence to control successive kings – in the intervals between her prayers no doubt. The church of Qusquam is in a shady compound on the side of the hill. Beyond it the ruins of the palace of the wily empress and the house of the Scottish giant can still be visited. Trees overshadow them but the city of Gondar stretched along its long, low ridge can be clearly seen through the undergrowth.

Bruce describes the lawless society, the constant struggles for power, the cruelty of the noblemen and the debauchery of the feasting. A notorious often-quoted passage of the diaries records a feast at Gondar. It includes details of a live cow being brought in and pieces of meat cut off it while the unfortunate beast was still alive;

men being fed huge chunks of this raw meat by the women who sit on either side of him, since it is a sign of importance not to feed yourself and also to eat enormous mouthfuls; then of drinking cupfuls of the alcoholic honey drink, *tejj*; after which the couples take turns to move on to sexual pleasures accompanied by applause and encouragement from their neighbours.

After several years away from home Bruce finally returned to England and from there to his family home at Kinnaird in Scotland. He wrote a detailed account of his travels, which caused a stir. His fantastic tales of life in the Ethiopian court sold well. But people did not believe his stories. Dr Johnson, the writer of the famous dictionary, was inclined to the opinion that he had never even been to Ethiopia. He gained a reputation as a liar. One story tells of Bruce being asked if he had seen any musical instruments during his time in Gondar. He replied that he had on occasions seen a lyre. To which the reply came back, 'Well since you left at least there is one less liar in Ethiopia.' He was also ill-tempered, which was perhaps not surprising given the sceptical reception which his book received. Later of course other travellers confirmed his accounts, and the *Travels to Discover the Source of the Nile in the Years 1768, 1769, 1770, 1771, 1772 and 1773* have become a classic of African exploration.[2]

THE STORIES OF THE STUDENT AND THE TEACHER

Gondar was a place of violent political conflict with rough and crude activities, but was also a place of scholarship. The emperors did not manage to build a stable political order but they did ensure that the church and its culture was rooted and flourished in the churches which they built. Fasilädäs was succeeded by Yohannes the Pious (1667–82) who had been ordained a priest before he was emperor. He built two churches, and also a library which, we are told, he decorated with yellow plaster. As well as collecting manuscripts, he painted some of the illustrations himself. His successor, Iyäsu the Great (1682–1706), continued his scholarly interests. He built the church of Däbrä Birhan Selassie and arranged for 150 teachers to be attached to it. It is said that there were over 500 teachers in Gondar during his reign. At this period the theological studies of *zema*, *qené*, *aquaquam* and *mäshaf* were systematised and organised.[3] Even after the end of the line of Gondar kings, the cultural life of the city continued to develop. During the short reign of Täklä Haymonot II (1769–77), when the city was no longer under the control of the kings, seven more churches were built. One of them, Ba'ata Maryam, became the principal centre for the teaching of *aquaquam* and at the height of its influence was staffed by 276 teachers.

The tradition persisted amidst the political intrigue and anarchy of the eighteenth and nineteenth centuries. In this period we can gain a few glimpses of the cultural life of the city. Arnauld d'Abbadie, a French-Basque soldier and explorer, visited Gondar between 1850 and 1853. He describes young men attracted to the city, studying church art and the copying of manuscripts. Among the numerous teachers of Gondar was the famous poet and storyteller Aläqa Gäbrä Hanna, whose proverbs and wise sayings are still remembered and appear in literary anthologies. He was *aläqa*, or head, of the church of Ba'ata, and devised a new system of *aquaquam*, the art form of liturgical movement with prayer sticks and *sistrums*. His style had more gentle and rhythmical movements, which he claimed was inspired by the movement of the reeds on the shores of the nearby Lake Tana. Later he moved to Däbrä Tabor where he taught his new style and from there he travelled to the Shewan court of Menelek II.[4]

The education system is claimed to be among the oldest systems of learning in the world.[5] The tradition of scholarship was passed down in the earlier periods, but the syllabus was given shape at Gondar. This was the Ethiopian form of education, which produced the educated and administrative classes of society until the arrival of modern schools in the late nineteenth century. It is still widely taught at schools attached to churches and monasteries throughout Ethiopia. Gondar remains one of the main centres of learning in Ethiopia.

The description of the educational tradition given here comes from my own field research carried out during a three-month visit to the church schools of Gondar in 2008, and annual visits thereafter. During this period I visited many church schools, and interviewed teachers and students. The education system preserved by the teachers at Gondar is based on traditional teaching passed down over many generations, and, as will be seen, is radically different from theological education in any part of the Christian world. It is a distinctive branch of the Christian tradition which remains little known and often little valued.[6] It has developed a distinctive tradition in the churches of Ethiopia, but shows similarities to Islamic education in Ethiopia as well as other oral education systems.[7]

To grasp something of the character of Ethiopian Orthodox Church scholarship, here are two examples. The first is my diary note made after many nights spent at the church schools. The second is the record of a conversation with one of the teachers.

First, this is a note describing the life of a student at a church school teaching the traditional form of religious poetry, or qené:

> The day begins at sunset – the start of the Ethiopian day, 12 o'clock. I go with the students to the teacher's house. The teacher brings out a low stool and sets it in his doorway. We sit in rows on the ground in front of him. Some students have made cushions out of old grain sacks stuffed with bits of cloth. Others just sit on rocks. They ensure that my rock is conveniently placed and I am comfortable. Yeneta Gebre Mikael, the teacher, begins the qené lesson. First he prays. Then he teaches Ge'ez language. He repeats a series of words – working through the alphabet, first the Ge'ez word and then its Amharic equivalent. He is assisted by a senior student, called a *zerafi*, who stands in front of him. The *yeneta* or teacher says the word quietly then the student repeats it loudly, and then all the students shout it out. After he has worked through this vocabulary lesson which takes about twenty minutes, he describes the feast which the church celebrates that day or a piece of biblical narrative. He then moves on to the qené itself. He will recite several qené of different types, probably meditating on the events being celebrated in church. He says one line, to illustrate the structure of the verse and its meanings, and repeats it several times. Then the *zerafi* shouts it out. Then comes an extraordinary rolling and guttural wave of sound as all the eighty students together shout out the line of qené again and again. It is impossible to convey the impact of this blend of shriek, shout and chant which echoes around the dark compound. The teacher claps his hands and they stop. He repeats the next line. This goes on for two or three hours.
>
> Nobody takes notes, indeed it is too dark to see anyway. The students are clearly deeply attached to the teacher and speak of him with great fondness. Sometimes the teacher will address the class in a formal way, sometimes he speaks gently and affectionately, with jokes and humour. They are his students, he has accepted them to the school and he cares for them, assesses their progress and acts as a father to them throughout their time at the school.
>
> At the end of the teaching session, the students go back to their huts or to places around the compound, and sit in groups reminding each

other of what the teacher has said, and memorising the lessons. It is now about 10 pm. I am led to one of the stone buildings in the compound and given a bed. I lie there listening to the sounds of the students helping each other repeat the lesson for the night, their voices echoing in the still night. Around midnight they go to sleep for about four hours. Then early in the morning they get up and resume where they had left off the night before. They then meet for prayers, and the teacher may give another teaching session.

The morning is for more private study. There is an exercise called *näggara* – or speaking. The senior student – the *zerafi* – sits against a wall, his head wrapped in his blanket. The younger students line up and recite the qené which they have composed. They repeat the lines and the *zerafi* listens, correcting their language or the words they are using. When he is satisfied with the progress they have made he says firmly *lela*, next one, and the next student steps forward.

But they also have to live. Begging is an essential part of the day. The students go around the houses asking for food. If the people have it they will give them scraps of left over *enjära*, if not they will say to the student 'may God give you food'. If they are given food then they will eat. They dry the old bits of *enjära* in the sun, then grind it to a powder, mix it with the hot *berbere* powder which is an essential of all Ethiopian cooking. If they have it they might also add some chick pea powder, called shiro. The mixture is placed together in a pot with a little water and then cooked over a wood fire. It becomes a thick cake which they call *kochevo*. They don't allow me to accompany them on these begging trips but do invite me to taste the *kochevo*. Considering that it is made from old bits of unwanted *enjära* left over from the meals of other people, and a touch of hot pepper, I am surprised how tasty it is.

The school consists of a cluster of circular grass huts, about eight feet in diameter, in each of which about six students sleep. There are no desks or blackboards or teaching materials; there are no books; there is no food provided by the church and no money. Yet there is also no shortage of students waiting to join the college and no shortage too of the warmth, good humour and generosity which they show to all who come.

As well as spending time with the students, I also knew the teachers. One of the teachers described his experience of study:

'I was born', the teacher told me, 'in Selemte. It's a small village in the Simien region [these are spectacular high mountains in the north around Ras Dashen, at 21,000 feet the highest mountain in Ethiopia]. My father is a farmer and I have twelve brothers and sisters. But I was ill and now I find it hard to walk, so I could not work on the farm as I used to. So my parents decided I should study. When I was ten I started at the *nebab bet*, or school of reading, in the village. I stayed there for three years, going to the teacher in the mornings. We sat under a tree in the church, and the teacher taught me the letters of the *fidel*. It was a hard task for a boy as there are more than 200 letters to learn, but slowly I managed to learn them. Then I began to recognise words and sentences. Before long I knew the *hawariya* [the first Epistle of St John] by heart and many other passages of the Bible. I became proficient in reading, and was made a deacon at the church. I sang in the services, prepared the bread for the *qeddasé*, and assisted in many ways.

It was a good life, but I longed to study more. I left home, putting all I had in a bag, and went south. I had to beg as I went and soon I came to Kramare, not far from Debark [a bustling market town in the Simen region]. I found a teacher who accepted me in to his school to learn *deggwa*, or the hymns of the church. I stayed with him for four years, then I went on to Bet Simien, at the church of Dereshe Maryam at Wayna Giyorgis, where I learned *aquaquam* for a further four years; then to Wogera, near Gondar, to learn *zemmare* and *mäwase'et* with Mamher Pawlos for just a year. Then I moved to another church in Wogera called Dekkwa Maryam to learn qené for two years. Then the teacher told me I had made good progress and I could come to Gondar to finish. For this I had to satisfy the blind teacher Megabi Alef Henok so I came to Ba'ata. Ba'ata is a very famous place, it is the best for *aquaquam*. Here I stayed for another three years until Megabi Alef was satisfied. I received a certificate and am *mergieta*.

So I could now teach, but I wanted to study more. So I went to the church of Kidane Mehret here in Gondar. This is a famous place for Mäshaf, and here I could study the holy books. I taught here as well as learning. After six years I came here and here I have stayed.

The student's life is hard. There is little food and little sleep. You must be strong to finish. Often if we were not successful in our begging expeditions, I would eat meals in my mind.' He shows me the book lying next to him, large pages covered with Ge'ez characters. 'This is *Mehraf*, it is one of the collections of hymns we use most. You see, I have made my notes here. Now I know it by heart.'

These two examples come from contemporary Gondar, but have a timeless quality and could apply just as well to earlier times. They suggest the character of the education and culture of the church. It is an oral culture, with large amounts of material memorised.

The story of the teacher shows how he moves from teacher to teacher and follows a recognised course of study. After satisfying the

FIGURE 8.2 a + b A group of students in the traditional school. Several students share each hut.

FIGURE 8.3 A group of students, dressed for the festival, surround their teacher.

FIGURE 8.4 Cooking at the *qené bet*. A student cooks food for himself and his friends after begging.

FIGURE 8.5 A student proclaims his *qené* to an enthusiastic group of listeners.

teacher of his abilities, he received a witness paper, or certificate, to show he had reached a level to qualify him to teach. There are recognised centres for each of the separate theological disciplines, which will issue papers as proof of the abilities in the chosen area of specialisation.

The church schools lack buildings and financial resources, but there is a syllabus, a national course of study, a set of specialisations which lead to different career opportunities, and centres of excellence which issue recognised certificates. The system has evolved over centuries, and was set up in the Gondar period. First impressions of an informal and uncoordinated approach to study are misleading.

The educationalist Girma Amare argues that the education system can be fitted in to the framework of a modern education system. The separate parts of the tradition are taught at different levels. The four main stages are the primary level of reading; then the secondary level which is based on music and hymnody, and to this can be added movement or dancing; then the college level which is traditional poetry; and finally the university level of literature and commentary.[8]

It will become immediately clear that language does not convey the special character of Ethiopian culture. Western preconceptions of what hymns, poetry and dancing are need to be forgotten because the Ethiopian forms have little in common with these models. They are rooted in a culture radically different from anything encountered in other parts of the Christian world and are used here only because of the absence of any more accurate language.

NEBAB OR READING

First there is the *nebab bet* or house of reading. Everyone begins here, and receives a grounding in reading and writing. The *nebab bet* (plural *betocc*) are found in villages all over the country. In 1971 it was estimated that there were 14,500 of these schools, mostly in churches and monasteries. The tradition states that a boy can enrol on the fourth day of the fourth month of the fourth year of his life, but usually he starts at about the age of seven. Girls can attend the *nebab bet* but seldom do, since they require different and more domestic skills for the style of life in rural society. The children go to the teacher, meeting under a tree in the church compound or in a hut nearby or perhaps on a patch of ground in the middle of the village. The teaching day begins at 8.00 a.m. with prayers, and finishes at 5.00 p.m., again with prayers. Some children will come only for part of the day, since government schools operate a shift system, with pupils attending either in the morning or in the afternoon. This enables children to attend both the modern school and the church school, going to the *nebab bet* when they are not at modern school. This way it is possible to study in both types of school at the same time. Children are instructed in Amharic, the spoken language, and Ge'ez, the liturgical Ethiopic, learning to identify and read first letters, then words, then sentences. The text used to begin with is the *fidel hawariya*, which consists of most of the First Epistle of St John. Using this passage written out on a large sheet of paper the teacher shows the student how to distinguish first the letters, then the words and then the phrases. Some other texts are memorised, including many of the psalms. At the end of this first phase of study the student has learned large portions of the Scripture by heart, is able to read and write in both Amharic and Ge'ez, although as yet his knowledge of Ge'ez syntax and grammar is slight. His teacher is happy with his competence and a big party is held to mark his graduation. He may then decide to remain in the village where he has a certain standing because of his education, can help others to read and write when necessary and also help with the reading of church services.

ZEMA OR HYMNODY

The next step is the *zema bet* or house of music. This is the place where the church's liturgy is taught, and the student learns to take part in the singing and dancing of the church's liturgy. Zema is a general term for the music and hymns of the church. There is a huge body of musical material to be learned and it takes many years to master. At an early stage the student learns the three types of chant for the different season and occasions of the churches' year – *ezel, ge'ez* and *araray* – and over 200 types of singing and phraseology called *halleta*. By tradition students were expected to copy out their own hymn books, making the pages out of animal skin and the ink out of the soot scraped from the bottom of the cooking pot and mixed with leaves and water, then left to ferment in a ram's horn for three days. The production of a book using these traditional methods can take several years. Traditional crafts of book-making are sometimes practised but now books can be produced more simply. Since the cost of books puts them out of the reach of most students, they still copy material out by hand, and while the student may not be obliged to make his own paper and ink, it is still a laborious process. One teacher I visited showed me his liturgy book with a commentary inserted. It was a thick volume with board covers. It must have had several hundred pages, all written in his beautiful regular Ethiopic script. I realised on opening it that the paper was lined and obviously taken from a cheap exercise book. He had copied it, over years, to bring together the learning which his teachers had passed on to him, night after long night.

Within zema there are several parts, and these can be studied at different levels and with different aims in mind. The most basic is liturgy, which is studied at the *qeddasé bet* or house of liturgy. Here the student learns to celebrate the liturgy or *qeddasé*. *Qeddasé* means sanctification and is the name used for the Eucharist or Holy Communion. There are fourteen eucharistic anaphora to memorise as well as various absolutions and other prayers. These must be learned as well as several other services such as the *qidan*, or nine prayers of the Covenant, which is a service recited by the clergy in the early morning; the *sä'atat*, or hours, which is the Ethiopian form of the traditional seven services for the different times of the day, including Mattins and Evensong; and various other prayers. It takes more than a year to master liturgy, and many students decide at this point that they have studied enough. They have the qualification to be employed as priests or deacons at a local church and can receive a modest salary for carrying out a liturgical ministry. The level of education is still relatively low and so many teachers discourage students from learning *qeddasé* too early since they fear the student will be tempted to take the easy option of working as a priest at a church and will not progress to the more advanced disciplines. Completing the short course of study at the *qeddasé bet* is sufficient to be ordained as a priest, and as a result the clergy in Ethiopia have usually achieved only a basic level of education.

Those who want to advance must then become familiar with all branches of zema. There are many books to be studied. There is *deggwa*, a book of hymns; *Soma deggwa*, or the hymns used during the fasting seasons; *me'eraf*, sections of the psalms set to music, and various pieces of seasonal material; *zemmare*, which is a set of communion anthems; *mäwase'et*, hymns used at funerals; and *zik*, material used at specific festivals. These are all liturgical texts, used during the church's worship, and all must be memorised since books are not generally used in the performance of liturgy. Zema is a demanding course of study which takes several years to master.

The hymns are rich in poetry and theology, and contain within them the theological traditions of the church. They are said to have been composed by Yared who lived in the early sixth century.[9] As a boy Yared was sent to study but was lazy and kept running away, to avoid the hard work of study. During one of his periods of truancy he rested under a tree and watched a caterpillar laboriously climbing up the stem to find food. It fell many times but each time it started again until through perseverance it succeeded in its task. Duly chastened and instructed by the humble caterpillar, Yared returned and became a conscientious student. He worked hard, and God assisted him. Yared listened to the birds singing and from them learned a new style of chanting. His biographer recounts that this was a divine gift:

> God sent three birds to him from the Garden of Paradise in the likeness of the Trinity [...] One spoke to him in the likeness of a man thus: 'we were sent to you from the garden of paradise so that we might tell to you and declare to you how the praise of the twenty-four elders [of the Book of Revelation] is lifted up'.

After this lesson from the birds, he went to the cathedral at Aksum where he sang before the king and the court in the new style. The king was transfixed and inadvertently pushed his spear through the foot of Yared. Yared too was caught up in the melodies and was not aware of his wound until he finished singing. Previously the style of singing had been soft, a whisper in the throat, but after Yared it becomes a high tune and 'there is no-one who praises with a noise like the praise of Yared the priest who learned from the seraphim, because there is nobody to whom God revealed it except the people of Ethiopia'.[10]

The hymns attributed to Yared belong within the Middle Eastern Semitic tradition of poetry. The style is especially associated with Ephrem the Syrian, who lived in the fourth century and was known as the Harp of the Spirit. Following Semitic style the hymns build up a series of images and ideas, full of references to Scripture and pieces of teaching which combine to form an evocative style of Christian teaching.

Here is just one example. It is a hymn to Mary, used on the day of 21st Hidar in the Ethiopian calendar. It reflects on how Mary fulfils prophecy in the Old Testament, and refers to some of the passages often seen as prophecies of the Incarnation, which have also occurred in the *Kebrä Nägäst*. There is Noah's Ark, the Ark of the Covenant, the casket in which the Manna in the wilderness was stored, Zion the place of God, the lampstand which gives light to the temple in the prophecy of Zechariah and the door in the temple vision of Ezekiel which remains closed until the Messiah comes. The closed door prefigures the virginity of Mary.

> The golden lampstand of Zechariah
> Pure bridal chamber, the liberation of all who live,
> It is proper for all who live to sing of her greatness,
> She will deliver us to her territory [probably referring to Zion]
> And her prayers to the tranquil harbour.
> Of Zechariah the lampstand of gold,
> Of the prophet Ezekiel the closed east door,
> For your foundation he caused a pearl to shine.

Mary plead for us, truly let us be righteous.

Behold her beautiful and behold her fair,
whom the priests saw,
Moses saw her on the pure mountain
Zechariah saw the lampstand
Behold her beautiful and peaceful,
Zion the Holy Church.

This is Mary whom the holy prophets
Compared with the Ark of Noah,
Who had manna concealed inside her,
Wondrous white fleece of David,
Lampstand of Zechariah the priest,
Closed paradise, sealed pit,
Whom the prophets saw
wrapped with golden clothes made in a single piece.[11]

Yared's life took place in the period when the poetry of the church was being formulated across the Middle East. The Ethiopian hymns were developed and extended in the centuries which followed, and copied in manuscripts. The chroniclers recount that all the manuscripts of the *deggwa* were destroyed during the Islamic invasions of Grañ and it seemed as though Ethiopia had lost this great tradition of music and worship. But a single manuscript was discovered in the monastery of Bethlehem in South Gondar, which, as a result has remained a centre of the study of zema. It is one of the few places to which all who want to become recognised as masters of music can go to receive accreditation.

There is a further stage of study after zema. *Aquaquam* is a part of zema but takes the study on to a new level. While the singing of hymns is a part of the life of all eastern churches, *aquaquam* is found only in Ethiopia. The word *aquaquam* is derived from the verb meaning to stand and so could be translated as standing. *Mahalet*, as this part of the liturgy is called, takes place at every church, as part of all liturgy. At weekends and at major festivals in large churches, the *mahalet* continues all night, as I discovered in my various visits to churches. There are also lengthy performances of *mahalet* in public squares on festival days, which can involve over a hundred clergy. Sometimes *mahalet* is referred to as dancing, but this word does not convey the rich symbolic liturgical meaning of *aquaquam*. It is movement which expresses the meaning of the hymns, with a rhythmic structure provided by the shaking of *sistrum*, a kind of rattle, and by the beating of one or more *kerbero* or drums, and also with sweeping and coordinated symbolic movements of the *maqomiya* or prayer staff which the clergy carry.

It is a dramatic expression of the liturgy, carried out with dignity and at a slow pace. The singers stand either in a semi-circle in the church or in two lines facing each other. They hold a *sistrum* or rattle in one hand and a *maqomiya* or a staff with a cross-shaped end in the other. They may also be accompanied by two *kerbero* or drums. The movements are measured, stately and rhythmical, and gradually build up from a hymn sung by one singer, and then repeated several times with growing levels of rhythm and movement, until with a burst of clapping and ululation from participants and watchers it comes to a sudden end.

QENÉ OR POETRY

Next comes the study of qené, which forms the third stage.[12] Many students I met in Gondar chose to study qené after they had studied either *qeddasé* or the basic stages of zema, and so were around 17 years of age when they came to the *qené bet* or school of poetry. The study at the *qené bet* consists of thorough learning of the Ge'ez language, including grammar, syntax and sentence construction. Students listen to the teacher by night and then write their own dictionary and grammar after the lesson. This study requires between two and four years.

To learn the poetic method of qené, the student must master successively each of the nine basic types of qené and the variations on them. Each type has its own structure. There is a fixed number of lines, called *bet*, and phrases within the lines, called *hareg*. Each line usually ends with the same letter. There are nine basic forms of qené which begin with a simple two-line form and continue to a more complex eleven-line structure. There are further subdivisions so that altogether there are over 200 types of qené.[13]

The nine main types are these:

1. *Gubä'e qänä* – the assembly at Cana – two lines
2. *Za'amläkiya* – from my God – three lines
3. *Mibazhu* – how many – three lines with longer phrases

4. *Wäzémä* – the eve of a festival – five lines
5. *Sellassé* – the Trinity – six lines
6. *Zaye'ezé* – that which concerns the present – five lines
7. *Mawades* – praise – eight lines
8. *Kebre ye'eti* – this is glorious – four lines
9. *Etäna mogar* – the raising of incense – eleven lines

The mastery of qené requires a variety of skills – a meticulous and precise use of language, a careful selection of phrases, an attentive and prayerful meditation to reflect on the chosen theme. Unlike the other forms of traditional Ethiopian study which require an obedient memorisation, qené develops a different range of skills. It may seem as though qené is an exercise of creativity in contrast to the rest of the study, and it is, but it is a creativity which is the result of ascetic discipline rather than individual initiative.

Qené is a form of poetry much valued in both church and secular society in Christian Ethiopia. In secular society its allusive character and the humour contained in its hidden meanings has similarities with traditional forms of popular poetry, such as the verse of the *azmari* minstrels, who are often met in the bars and street corners of the Gondar region, improvising poems to suit all occasions, accompanying their songs on the single-stringed *masinqo.*

In churches qené has a set place in liturgy with local traditions defining what forms of qené should be recited at different liturgical moments. One scholar described how psalms and qené are recited together through the night prayers of *mahlet.* During Lent, these would include Psalm 3, with a *mibazhu,* then a *gubä'e qänä,* then Psalm 41 with another *mibazhu,* then Psalm 43 with a *mawades,* with this often composed by a visiting poet, and then further psalms and qené. Qené are also sung during and after the administration of communion at the *qedassé.* The style of qené in churches varies. Often the composer of the qené stands at the back of the group of *däbtära,* and quietly speaks his qené to another who proclaims it at full volume. After the *qedassé,* when the atmosphere is more relaxed, the recitation of qené has a festive, competitive style, with successful qené applauded and clapped. The recitation of qené illustrates the interpenetration of religious and secular culture.

First of all – it is spoken and not written. The *balaqené,* or qené master, prepares his qené for a specific occasion or reason – a church service perhaps, or a public recitation. He reflects and prays, and slowly his qené takes shape. He then proclaims it. It is not written down, and when the moment of performance passes, then the qené passes with it. It is intended as a way of study, teaching and celebration, and belongs to that specific moment. Some qené, especially those by the most famous of *balaqené*, are remembered and recorded, and there are some published collections of qené. But this is unusual, and only applies to some of the best-known and most celebrated qené masters.

The second feature of qené is the different levels of meaning. This is known as *sämena wärq* – or wax and gold. This image is derived from the art of the goldsmith. He prepares a wax mould and then pours the molten metal into it, so the gold is contained within the wax. So in qené there is an outer form of the words, like the mould, but also an inner meaning for those who have the insight to find it, like the gold hidden inside the wax mould. It is also called *westa wäyra* – or inside the olive. Just as the olive has a rough, uneven bark, within which is the richly coloured and grained wood, so qené contains a beautiful interior beneath the external words which those who can penetrate below the surface can discover. Some people say that in wax and gold, the double meaning is discovered in the individual words used, while in *westa wäyra* it is the whole qené which conveys something more.

Qené is part of Amhara culture and life. People love listening to qené and finding the hidden meanings. It is suggested that this comes out of the very formal and hierarchical character of Amhara society, with the traditional respect for authority and the memory of the complex and structured imperial court. This persists in everyday life in many ways. Even a simple action of meeting someone in the street leads to a series of greetings and asking after the health of different members of the family. Perhaps the formality governing relationships and behaviour hides deeper feelings which are only hinted at, and qené is a way of capturing both the formal outer and more deeply felt inner meanings in what is said.[14]

Here's an example of a well-known qené, known by many Amhara. The speaker is at the court of the nineteenth-century emperor Menelek II. He addresses the king, in Amharic.

Yigadlun indähon yihäw komkuläw
Yimatun indähon yihäw komkuläw
Yaläm tam Menelek kaya sadakakum

Translated this is:

> If you want to kill me I am standing here waiting
> If you want to kick me I am standing here waiting
> O Menelek you are a sweet scent which sweetens the world.

So the minstrel is humble, obsequious and respectful.

The twist comes in the third line. *Yaläm tam* means a sweet scent of the world. But if you pronounce it differently as one word then it becomes *yalamtam*, which means a festering gangrenous wound. The qené is now an insult and a protest against an authoritarian and brutal ruler.

> Menelek you are the gangrene and corruption which pollutes us all.

The wax of the courteous compliment becomes the gold of insult. The qené reminds us of the poetry of the fool in European history and literature, who had the liberty to insult or criticise the king in ways other people would not dare to.

Ambiguity and obscurity are built into qené. The qené master tries to see through the complexity of someone else's qené and compose one of his own, which is more obscure. So Girma Amare writes, 'The study of qené derives its significance from the fact that it is the most highly refined expression of Ethiopian culture, which, it is said, is characterised by ambiguity, vagueness and secretiveness. Qené may be defined as the art of detecting others' ambiguity while increasing the subtleties of one's own.'[15]

The qené of the church schools is religious in its subject and method. It follows different rules and looks back to a different origin. Church qené is a development of this traditional form of Amhara culture into a theological study, discipline and art form. The teachers in the qené school would object strongly to the suggestion that a qené is a poem and to the implication that it is vague or ambiguous or attempts to conceal its true meaning. The theologian composes qené to reveal a truth which is hidden, not to hide a truth which is plain. It tries to get round the great problem of faith, that we have to speak of God and yet God is so far beyond our experience that our words cannot reach him.

The roots of 'church' qené lie in the early Christian traditions of allegorical interpretation, and so are associated with theologians such as Origen of Alexandria in Egypt in the third century. Origen's allegorical approach had a huge influence on the church, and through the relation between Alexandria and Ethiopia it has passed to Ethiopia.

Origen realised that God is the reality which lies behind all human experience. He is beyond our grasp and comprehension, and so human thoughts and language cannot begin to grasp what God truly is or express this. But human language is all we have, and we can use it to hint at divine things and point towards them. The Bible is the example of this. It describes human events and words, yet concealed behind these historical, material and exterior words lies a deeper and interior meaning. Every verse has a spiritual meaning, to do with God and his dealings with the human race, and most also have a moral meaning, about how we should conduct our lives, as well. Qené is the Ethiopian form of that historical and theological tradition in the church which uses human language to speak of God and the things of God. So, in the church, qené is not intended to add obscurity to a plain meaning but to make plain what is hidden and profound, and to reveal the meaning which is already a mystery.

The word qené itself – the qené master at Selassie Theological College in Addis Ababa explained to me – points to this sense of double meaning, as both a divine truth and a human attempt to express it. It is derived from *qenäyä* which in itself has two meanings. It means 'sing' or 'make music' and so simply means a song. But there is an alternative meaning. It can mean 'make someone submit' or 'take prisoner', and so it calls to mind the need for the pupil to submit to the discipline. So here at the outset there is a double meaning. Qené is both a poem or a song, and the discipline required to become a qené master. This then points to a further meaning, which is that the call of Christ, which is celebrated in qené, calls us to the bondage of faith, and this in turn leads to the freedom and joy of song. The word itself conveys how qené works, with one meaning leading to another, and each stage a further discovery, which helps us to grasp and enter into the experience and practice of faith.

The sense of discipline is also indicated by the phrase used for 'compose qené': 'qené quänaquäna' which is best translated as 'measure' or 'count' qené. Clearly the care and accuracy required to follow the set patterns and to include the correct numbers of lines, phrases and syllables is the essential part of the discipline of qené, which in turn leads to thought of the care and rigour with which the spiritual life is followed. The composition or, we can now say, the measurement of qené, is as much spiritual discipline as it is poetic composition. So, as Mamher Haddis explains, 'qené is service to God and submission to the Holy Spirit, and Ge'ez language is also submission to the Spirit'.

As well as learning the language, the student practices an ascetic discipline so that his mind and heart can be conformed to God's leading, and his speech can be responsive to God's words. When the word qené is used in older examples of Ge'ez literature it has the meaning of hymn or poem, but also manual work or servitude. In response to my often-asked question, What is qené? one teacher in Addis Ababa offered me two phrases by way of definition. The first was 'to give your heart to the mystery of the Trinity' and the second was 'the woodworm', since studying qené slowly makes its way into your heart and lodges there. It would seem then that the harshness of the life of the qené student with its lack of food and sleep, its long hours of prayer and solitary composition of qené may not just be a result of living in a poor society, but also an essential part of becoming a qené master.

The relationship of master and student at the *qené bet* is at the heart of the experience of education. The teacher takes decisions about the student's progress, such as when he can move on to a new stage of qené composition and when he has gained full competence. When he nears the level required to become a teacher himself he should be able to interrupt and complete a qené started by another *balaqené* before the original composer has a chance to finish it himself. At this point the teacher will invite guests and summon the student to be examined. The guests ask the student questions about qené or about Ge'ez language, and if he answers these correctly, he is led to the teacher's chair and formally seated in it. He is then recognised as a teacher of qené.

Here are some examples of qené which show different ways in which meaning is both hidden and revealed, and in which the communication of theological truth is carried out. These examples are given first in Amharic, or Ge'ez, then in my English version. Then there is an explanation of the meaning.

The first is the *za'amläkiya* type, with three rhyming lines.

Läimä haläl wäld häwariya wängel bänaisu
Mäwibir imu tibäki bälbisu

Wäyi litä bihala inizä etiwäsaa näfisu

At such a young age the child-apostle did die
At his grave his mother clutched his robes and did cry
But his soul rises up and demands to know why.

This is about the promise of the Resurrection. The faithful servant of God has died young and his mother goes to the grave, clutching his clothes, which is all she has left of him. As she weeps at the graveside his soul rises up and asks her why she is crying. The hidden meaning here – the gold – lies not in language but in the reminder that the gold of resurrection is hidden in the wax of mourning. It is a statement of the truth of the Resurrection.

Now here is a very short qené but packed with allusions, of the *gubä'e qänä* type.

Itämäyit'ä kwasä mängäsä pädäk noha isikä
nätigä iminä miliatu mayä sayin ayisä

The horror of the eyes! The waters rise up until the rain clouds are dry
The crow! To the righteous man Noah it did not return nor come nigh

The wax is the story of the flood. The eyes are horrified because they see the waters which cover the surface of the earth, waters which have come from a double source, both rising from the depths and falling from the skies. The sorrow is compounded by the crow – or raven – sent out by Noah who flies away and leaves him, as is recounted in Genesis 8.6.

But the reference to eyes leads us to think of weeping, and so to a further idea. Jesus weeps for the sins of the world until he has no more tears, the water of grief, left. But ungrateful humanity, like the crow, turns away from him in hard-heartedness and ignores his grief. The qené tells of God's love which weeps over us who ignore him and run away from him, as the crowds did at Jerusalem on Good Friday.

There is still more hidden in these two lines. The idea of eyes weeping will bring to mind of the listener the great saint of Ethiopia Gäbrä Manfus Qiddus, an ascetic saint who lived on Mount Zuquala near Addis Ababa. His name means the Servant of the Holy Spirit, so he is the perfect example of a righteous man, like Noah. He is depicted in his icon weeping for the sins of the world and in his compassion allowing the birds of the air to drink his tears. Sometimes two birds – one black and one white – are drinking but while the white bird drinks in gratitude, the black bird pecks at the eye of the righteous man. So one accepts the compassion of the righteous man and the other rejects it.

Here just two short lines of the qené evoke a rich and complex set of memories and lead to a simple summary of God's love and human rejection of it.

Here is another beautiful qené of the *sellassé* type.

Sähäyä sämay yawegi hagar märek'é resuk
Enzä kirbto dädäkä eyamäwek
Zeni h'nedä mesalé sähäyä amoneyus lik
Kämä iyanekälekel bät'iyuk
Lä'ayenä hérodes krub enezä wäetu räkik
Läzärasak'u nägästä dibah tägehedä bäd dek

The sun in the sky does not heat high places nearby
But the deserts are far off become hot and dry
Here is an example from the Ammonius the wise
That something grasped is a building firm and high
The eyes of Herod were dimmed although he was nearby
But to the kings far in the east the truth drew nigh.

The idea here is that Christ is like the sun. The poet reflects that in Ethiopia the high mountain plateau is cold and frosty – even though it is high up and so it is physically nearer to the sun. The low-lying desert on the other hand is hot even though it is further distant. This leads to the thought that at Christ's birth, Herod lived in Jerusalem very near to Bethlehem, the place of Christ's birth, and so was near to the light of the world. But he did not recognise the coming of the Christ child. The three kings lived in a distant land, far off from the actual presence of Christ. Yet even though they were far distant, they were the ones who were enlightened by the truth. The third and fourth lines are an interpolation, referring to the biblical commentator Ammonius Saccas, and show how study can be compared to the construction of a house. So then, this suggests that the person who grasps the truth – like the three kings – can also be compared to the house which was unshaken.

And finally here is a qené which is quoted by Donald Levine in his book on Amharic culture, *Wax and Gold*:[16]

FIGURE 8.6 The holy man Gebre Manfus Qiddus, showing his hair that has grown so long that it covers his naked body, the wild animals who live in peace with him, and the bird drinking the tears from his eyes.

Yäbahetawi lijj sifälleg leullenna
Yäkristosu mist tälant wäshämäna
Qetäl betabäläw hono qärämänna

Levine's translation goes like this:

The son of a hermit, high rank to display
Made love with Christ's wife yesterday
When she fed him with leaves he faded away.

To grasp the significance of what appears to be a scurrilous and even blasphemous suggestion, we need to realise that the hermit's son is his hunger which inevitably comes as a result of his ascetic life. Christ's wife is the fasting itself since this was the discipline which Christ firmly adhered to in the wilderness. So the hermit's hunger and hence his virtue is enhanced by fasting but it diminishes when he eats the leaves, which is the traditional food of the hermit.

These are just a few examples of qené. They show the rich imagery and the allusive language which the *balaqené* uses. They suggest too how others will become enthralled by them, seeking to understand and then to compose their own. Part of the interest which they evoke is that you are never quite sure that you have understood them correctly or if there are other layers of meaning which are in the *balaqené*'s mind. There is the sense that the tradition of the church always is beyond us and has more to show us if we can just make that extra leap to grasp it.

MÄSHAF OR THE STUDY OF BOOKS

The fourth form of study is that of the interpretation of books, or the *mäshaf bet*. Here we are at Girma's university level. As in the case of advanced study in the other disciplines, students come to the *mäshaf bet* when they are mature. The number of students is smaller than at the previous schools, and the students include both young men continuing their studies and elderly monks studying the literature of the church. In the two *mäshaf bet* at Gondar students receive a modest salary, live at the church and preach in the surrounding villages. Teaching is done in the mornings, at 9.00 a.m., although private study continues through the day. There are five sections of the commentary tradition – Old Testament, New Testament, dogmatics or the study of the Church Fathers, the Books of the Monks and law. Traditionally a school teaches only one of the branches of mäshaf, and several years are required in order to become competent in each discipline.

In the churches of the West, this tradition is contained in books. A Western theologian studies texts which are written, published, read and discussed – and so are dispersed, disseminated and communicated widely. This is convenient, and makes faith accessible to a very wide audience. But it is a private activity since a book is read alone and in seclusion.

Before the age of mass publication, the production of a book was an activity engaging a wide cross-section of the community. The production of a manuscript of a theological or hagiographical text involved the collection of stories, documents and texts; a team of copyists who worked together on writing down the material; correctors who found alternative manuscripts and checked theirs against others; and more. Printing has changed the nature of a book. Instead of being a product of the life of a community, it has become the mass production of a set form of words. The Ethiopian-style of study of books – mäshaf – reminds us of the older approach to books and to study and to tradition and to faith.

The tradition of faith is preserved and held in churches. These are the places where it is spoken, explained, memorised and taught. Since there are not large numbers of printed books there is not the physical possibility of wide dissemination. Instead the tradition of faith remains within churches; something real, almost tangible, and located in monasteries on hilltops and in villages within this vast land of mountains and gorges.

Christian tradition begins with the Bible. Although the Bible is written and copied, or later printed, and so becoming a book, the Christian faith believes that it is more than a book. It contains the word of God. If this is the case, then it follows that the word of God cannot be limited to a set of words on pages of a book. It is living and active, listened to and reflected on, built up and refined over generations. From this point of view we can say that the Word of God is not just the Bible, but the Bible as is has been reflected on, prayed over and passed on by generations of believers. It can be spoken and listened to in various ways. There is a book or rather a set of books which we call the Bible, but these books must be read and interpreted in the church, and the church therefore interprets how this word is found.

The Western churches have agreed on a fixed text of the Bible. It includes thirty-nine books in the Old Testament and twenty-seven books in the New Testament – a total of sixty-six, and if we add the books of the Apocrypha then this figure increases to seventy-three. The Ethiopians have more books in the Bible than other churches, and a more flexible approach to deciding which books are to be included. Ethiopian scholars consider that the Bible includes eighty-one books, or sometimes eighty-two, and differ as to which books are to be included. The figure of eighty-one has entered popular speech. 'All the clergy and laity commonly use the term "eighty and one" whenever they speak of the Bible in their religious encounters.'[17] Lists of books are found in medieval texts, the *Fetha Nägäst*, or law of the kings, and the *Sinodos gessaw*, written sometime after the thirteenth century, and the later *Gadla Märqoréwos* or the Acts of Merkorios, from the seventeenth century. The various lists include some little-known works, such as the book of Jubilees, the Apocalypse of Ezra, pseudo-Josephus, the books of Sinodos, the books of the Covenant, Clement, the Ethiopian Didascalia, and the Miracles of Jesus. Among them is the Book of Enoch, recognised as an important early text, and transmitted only in its Ethiopic form. Within this mass of material which is the Bible, not all is read in church. As in other churches, selections are made for reading at the *qeddasé* and other parts of worship. But all is holy and part of the word of God as it is received and studied by the church.

These books and others, such as the book of monks, are listened to and learned at the *mäshaf bet*. The now-familiar procedure is followed. The teacher sits in the teacher's chair and one of the students squats in front of him on a low stool and reads from the book which is placed on a reading desk. The students sit around the sides of the room. After the student has read a short passage then the teacher gives the traditional commentary. The students listen and memorise. Afterwards they remind each other what the teacher has said. This method ensures that the content of the commentary is passed on from previous ages, and retains an unchanging character. Of course the teacher might make small variations but he must avoid novelty. If he changes the content of the commentary the people will say 'the tobacco plant never lacks verdure nor a heretic his interpretations' or 'who can compete in a tree with the brood of a monkey or in speaking with the brood of the heretic'.

Bible commentary is called *andamta*. The word *andamta* is derived from the word *andam* meaning 'and (there is) one (who says)' which is the form which introduces many of the comments. The Ethiopian tradition claims that the *andamta* came to Ethiopia with the group of priests who accompanied Menelek I in the tenth century BC, but the present form can be attributed to the Gondar period. There are three strands of material contained in the *andamta*. First, there are translations of the commentary of patristic writers such as John Chrysostom and Basil of Caesarea. Then, second, translations of later Syriac, Coptic and Arabic texts. Then, third, original Ge'ez material.[18]

Andamta, as it has reached the church today, is claimed to have been known by Yared during the Aksum period, and developed through the following centuries until it reached definitive form at Gondar in the seventeenth and eighteenth centuries. It has now been published and some sections have been translated into English by Roger Cowley and others. But the place where it truly belongs is in the *mäshaf bet*, where generations listen, learn and then pass on to others.

Andamta should not be understood as a text of Scripture with commentary as is customary in a literary culture such as there is in the West. Instead it is a presentation of the way that the church has understood the word of God. This understanding has taken shape by being added to. The text of Scripture can be understood as having three forms, and these were illustrated to me by the late Sayfa Selassie, a scholar in Addis Ababa, by a verse of Luke's Gospel – Luke 13.32. This is a saying of Jesus referring to King Herod who has opposed his preaching. 'He (Jesus) said to them "Go and say thus to that fox for me."' The first form is the literal translation – which I have just written – 'say thus to that fox'. The second form is the interpretative translation, which gives further insight into meaning, so this verse would then read 'say thus to Herod', explaining that the fox is a way of speaking of the king. There is also a third form in which the tradition is set out, and that is *andamta*, in which various interpretations of a passage are given.

Roger Cowley suggests that this approach might have originated with marginal notes inserted into the manuscripts. 'Marginal annotations [...] are closely associated with the development of the written *andem* commentary tradition, and are probably the actual literary nucleus around which the oral tradition crystallised and was reduced to writing.'[19] In this way comment on Scripture developed as the text was copied and passed on, and was an integral part of it.

The later comments preserved in the *andamta* should not be seen as later compositions nor human interpretations, but as part of the tradition, handed down from the beginning and explaining the God-given meaning of the holy texts. The *andamta* commentary is a form of translation rather than commentary. The Amharic word *targum*, means both translate and interpret. It is also used in Judaism to refer to the comments of teachers on the text of Scripture. Translation is not seen as a literal and wooden rendering of a word into a different language but is rather an act of communication which is explanation and interpretation.

In *andamta*[20] a piece of Scripture is followed by a list of interpretations, sometimes as many as fifteen. In this list, there are several possible ways of interpreting the text. There is a simple translation, or a paraphrase, or a comparison of the text with a parallel statement, or a sentence explaining an apparent discrepancy in the text, or an illustration from experience – and each form has its Ge'ez title. The *andamta* should therefore be seen not as a free commentary such as a Western scholar might produce but more as a version of the Bible as it is read and reflected on by the church. The *andamta* version is a form of the Bible.

Here is an example from a text in one of Roger Cowley's translations, showing the original verse, a more creative rendering of it and then a series of interpretations. It is the passage of the book of Numbers where a plague of serpents bite the people, and Moses makes an image of a bronze serpent and places it on a pole and whoever looks on the serpent is cured (Numbers 21.9).

> (Ge'ez original) And Moses made a serpent out of bronze and raised it up to be shown as a sign and whenever a serpent bit a man he would look to that bronze serpent and he would be saved.
>
> (Amharic version) Moses made a serpent of bronze and he raised it up in a place where it could be seen, whenever a snake bit a man he would look at that serpent and would be saved; this is a symbol: the snake is of the devil, the bronze serpent is of the Lord: when a living animal the snake which bit them, the bronze serpent would save them; the devil is living by nature and harmed them, the Lord suffered and died in his body for salvation, this is a symbol.

Andam: the snake which has poison bit them, the bronze serpent saved them – the devil who has the poison of sin bit them, the Lord who is pure in nature saved them, this is a symbol.

Andam: the snake is a symbol of Adam, the bronze serpent of the Lord, this is a symbol of those who were bitten by the poison of the snake, the bronze serpent saved them, Adam was bitten by sin, the Lord by his goodness saved him.

Andam: bronze is pure and the nature of the Lord is pure.

Andam: bronze is red, for the Lord having broken his flesh and poured out his blood, saved the world.

Andam: the sound of bronze is heard from afar off, for the suffering and death of the Lord from one border to another is heard.

Andam: bronze is found in hot lowlands and in temperate highlands, the Lord will beget children from the nation of the Jews and the nation of the Gentiles, and the Apostles are those who were saved, having heard his voice and seen his face; those saved having just heard his voice are the believers who are raised up until the day of his coming.[21]

This is a complex list of meanings. Not all sequences are so long. Here is a commentary on a familiar verse from the first chapter of the book of Genesis. It shows how, although the student may not necessarily reproduce the words exactly as spoken, he does have to absorb the traditional interpretation as an essential part of his reading and understanding of the text.

God created man in his likeness
Andam (there is someone who says): that the man is like God in his person
Andam: man is immortal in his soul like God.
Andam: man is placed under God to rule the world
Andam: man is the representative of God in this world
Bo (there is also someone who says): man is like God in his person
Bo: man is like God by his immortality
Bo: man is like God by his authority under God.

Ethiopian scholars are men of deep learning, of a kind which is difficult for a Western mind to grasp. They commit huge amounts of Scripture, hymns, commentary to memory, in the course of years of dedicated and absorbing study. The tradition of the church has become part of them, and they in turn have become a part of the tradition, witnessing to it and handing it on to the next generations of students and scholars. So the tradition is broad and extensive. It is liturgy, it is Scripture, it is the way Scripture has been read and understood, it is singing and movement, it is fasting and feasting – in fact the whole of the life of the church.

When we grasp this inclusive approach to the idea of tradition we understand further why books are not essential. A book can never capture the richness and depth of this oral tradition. Books can be useful but could never replace the process of learning and living. In Ethiopia books are used as notebooks to aid memory. This is why the student needs to write out his own text by hand, and keep it for reference to help him to practice and live out what he has learned. A book is useful – but its use is limited. An Ethiopian might point out – with sadness and sympathy – to a Western Christian, that if we rely on books we are reducing the living word of God, loved and nurtured through the ages, to a dry and lifeless set of words captured and frozen on bits of paper. An oral tradition sets us free to live within the church – while a written tradition traps us and restricts us. We need to hear God's words, not read God's books.

THE DÄBTÄRA

Those who have studied at the higher schools of zema, *aquaquam* and qené become *däbtära*. *Däbtära* are found only in Ethiopia, and have an essential ministry in the church. Western commentators translate the word *däbtära* in various ways, none of them satisfactory. They have been called 'lay ecclesiastics', 'lay canons', 'choristers', among others. A better word is 'scholar' since a *däbtära* is someone who has studied at a church school to high level, usually having completed zema, *aquaquam* and *qené bet*, a course of study which lasts at least ten years. In addition to formal church education the *däbtära* may study divination, fortune telling and other esoteric branches of knowledge. As a result he has a varied set of skills. His role in the local community has many parts. He is a chorister, poet, dancer, scribe, painter, herbalist and wizard.[22]

There is no ordination to enter the class of *däbtära* and participation in the ministry of the *däbtära* is flexible. Some are employed by the church, while others have a less formal attachment. The *däbtära* has a liturgical role in performing the *mahalet*, or liturgical singing and movement, which takes place in the *qené mahlet* of the church. On a major festival large numbers of *däbtära*, often over a hundred, meet to carry out this ministry, which lasts through the night until the *qeddasé* begins at dawn. They also sing after the *qeddasé* and at public festivals.

The most probable derivation of the title *däbtära* is from the Ge'ez for 'tent' since in the Old Testament the Ark of the Covenant was kept in the tent, and the Levites danced before it. *Däbtära* are said to descend from the families which came from Jerusalem with Menelek. There are reports of *däbtära* in the medieval period. Alvares says that large churches had a 'great' or 'infinite' number of *däbtära*. He counted 200 *däbtära* at Yemrehanna Krestos, 400 at Makana Sellassie and 4000 at Lalibäla where they were shared out amongst eight churches.[23] It is unclear from Alvares's account whether, at this time, the *däbtära* were ordained as priests, but since he distinguishes the *däbtära* from the priest it seems likely that they did not then, as now, become *däbtära* through an act of liturgical ordination.

Däbtära have a reputation for scholarship, and are consulted for advice in times of need. Alongside their church studies they may learn traditional forms of medicine, and some will have learned magical formulae and techniques – surreptitiously since this is pagan and frowned on by the church authorities. They can write amulets to protect against the power of evil spirits, assist in problems of life such as passing exams or finding a partner. Their powers make them respected but sometimes feared.

The order of *däbtära* needs to be understood in the context of the tradition of the church. The *däbtära* is the person who has absorbed and knows the church's tradition. He holds the tradition, performs it during liturgical celebration, and passes it on to those who come to learn. Since the tradition has the power to overcome evil, then it follows that the *däbtära* is the person who can use this power to overcome devils and carry out acts of power. This is a broader role than that of priest and deacon whose function is limited to sacramental and religious actions. The *däbtära* does not enter the *mäqdäs*, but, like the Levites of the Old Testament, stays outside the tent. His role is of great importance and significance. The tradition of power, handed down from the times of the New Testament, is entrusted to him, to preserve, to perform, to use and to pass on.

FIGURE 8.7 A group of *däbtära* with *sistrum* and prayer stick singing after the service.

CONCLUSION: THE SPOKEN WORD

We have become more aware of the importance of speaking and listening in the proclamation of growth of faith. Not only did Christ, the Word of God, communicate through preaching, conversing and uttering words of power, but the first apostles are described in the Acts of the Apostles as thinking through and articulating their message as they preached sermons. They lived in a culture which valued the spoken rather than the written word. Plato compares writing to speaking in the *Phaedrus*. One of the protagonists is sceptical about the use of the written word.

> You who are the father of letters, Thamus says to the god Theuth who invented writing, have been led by your affection to ascribe to them a power the opposite of that which they really possess. For this invention will produce forgetfulness in the minds of those who learn to use it because they will not practise their memory [...] written words are useful as a reminder of what we already know.

Socrates pithily comments that 'writing is the illegitimate brother of speech'.[24] Patristic writers commented that before the Fall, Adam and Eve had direct access to God's wisdom and did not need the clumsy practice of speech to know this.

Speech has a double significance. It is the result of the Fall by which the human race lost its direct apprehension of God's wisdom, but it is also the gift of God, and his word, by which we can regain access to God. As Christianity spread it took root in Greek-speaking cities where education was in the seven liberal arts, three of which built up skill in speaking – grammar, rhetoric and dialectic.[25]

This is the root from which Ethiopian theology has grown. The tradition of biblical exegesis is a huge mass of memorised theological interpretation, spoken, listened to, memorised and communicated. Alongside the passing on of this tradition, language is learned, the rules of qené poetry mastered, and the skill of speaking acquired. When we listen to the qené master proclaiming his poem, we are in the same cultural world as the teachers of the early church, creating a living and powerful spoken tradition, and passing it on faithfully.

[illegible]

CHAPTER 9

Evangelicals and Pentecostals: New Ways of Believing

HISTORY: THE FORMATION OF MODERN ETHIOPIA

The process of the formation of a modern state of Ethiopia began on 11 February 1855. On this day the warlord Kassa Hailu was crowned *negusä nägäst,* king of kings, or emperor, and chose to be known as Téwodros II. He began the process of building a centralised state, with a taxation system, a standing army, a justice system and the regulation of the church. It all ended tragically with the king descending into an erratic brutality, and a defeat by the British army under General Napier in 1868 sent to rescue a group of missionaries who were being held hostage on the mountain fortress of Maqdala. In the attack the king killed himself.

He was succeeded after a short interval by another Kassa, this time from Tigray in the north, who overcame his rivals and was crowned as Yohannes IV in 1872. He was deeply pious and enforced an end to division within the church at the council of Borru Meda, after which he set about a forcible conversion of the people of Welo to his new unified Christian Church. The well-being of the church and the state became joined, so that secular nationalism and religious mission were integrated to form the basis of modern Ethiopia. He died in 1888, shot in battle at the town of Metemma fighting against invaders from Sudan.

The next king was Menelek II, who ruled over Shewa to the south of both Téwodros's Begemder and Yohannes's Tigray. Menelek had been imprisoned by Téwodros on the fortress of Maqdala, from where he had escaped, returned to his native Shewa and there built up a power base, from where he was able to succeed Yohannes. He established the boundaries of modern Ethiopia through a series of military campaigns. At Adwa in Tigray his army of 100,000 soldiers confronted a smaller but better-equipped Italian army of 14,500. In a three-hour period between 6.00 a.m. and 9.00 a.m. on 1 March 1896 the superior numbers of Ethiopians overcame the superior armaments of the Italians. Thus Ethiopia became the only country in Africa to defeat an invading European army and so resist colonisation – and the first African general to defeat a European power since the conquest of Italy by the Carthaginian Hannibal in the Second Punic War of 218–212 BC. Menelek's military campaigns in the south were more prolonged and just as significant. These had been taking place in the years before Adwa and continued after it, and through them he had gradually extended the boundaries of Ethiopia southward. His reign effectively ended in 1908 when he suffered a debilitating stroke, although he did not die until 1911.

FIGURE 9.1 Menelek's palace at Entoto on the ridge above Addis Ababa from where he moved down the hill to found the modern capital.

Haile Selassie dominated the twentieth century. He became regent in 1916 and was the most influential figure in the government during the final years of Menelek II, the period when the Empress Taytu and then *lijj* Iyäsu ruled. He was crowned Emperor in 1930, and ruled until his death in 1974. His reign was interrupted by the Italian occupation between 1935 and 1941 when he went into exile. During this long period he was seen as first a moderniser, but towards the end of his reign became a reactionary figure.

Ethiopia had once again expanded to reach the borders of the great medieval kingdom. The campaigns of Menelek trebled the size of Ethiopia, and increased its population. Not only had the European imperialists been resisted but Ethiopia itself had become an imperial power, ruling over a multi-ethnic empire with eighty ethnic groups. There had been other attempts at an African imperialism, by the Mahdiya in Sudan, the Fulani in Nigeria and the Zulus in South Africa, but only Ethiopia succeeded in its imperialist ambitions.

The new Ethiopia consisted of a strong centre based on Addis Ababa with a dominant language and faith. This was a new Ethiopia with a large part of it consisting of new territories, with many ethnic groups and languages, and with most people following various traditional forms of faith. When the Ethiopian kingdom had expanded 500 years previously the monks had a monopoly on mission. But now there were other alternatives. Western missionaries had arrived, bringing their form of Christianity to Africa, and infiltrated Ethiopia. There were now several brands of Christianity on offer. These had different understandings of mission and different strategies for evangelism.

The end of the process was a growth of Evangelical Christianity mainly in the south and west. These churches grew alongside the traditional pattern of faith of the Orthodox Church and proved attractive to many people. The spread of Evangelical Christianity was uneven and varied across the regions. Within the process there were different forms of Western Christianity, but also common patterns which enabled Evangelical Protestantism to become established and – eventually – grow and thrive.

ORTHODOX MISSION METHODS

Orthodox priests and monks arrived in the newly conquered areas at the same time as the invading armies. The campaigns in the south had been taking place since 1880, and had begun for financial reasons. Menelek needed money to pay a large twice-yearly tribute to Yohannes IV. An indication of the scale of the financial demands made on him by Yohannes is shown by the tribute he paid in December 1880. This was the equivalent of £50,000 worth of cotton goods and £30,000 in money, which he delivered on 600 mules, with a similar amount payable six months later. His own lands in Shewa could not produce enough to pay this and so he developed the practice of sending out raiding expeditions at six-month intervals, to coincide with the end of the rainy seasons, called *zamacha*. Both Amhara and Oromo were among those attracted by the prospect of wealth and land and set out on these adventures into the south. With a large army equipped with modern rifles, Menelek encountered little effective opposition. On the return of the parties the treasures were shared with half going to the king and half to the warriors who had carried out the raid. Sometimes the original ruler was left in charge of the lands conquered and sometimes power was given to Menelek's supporters.[1]

Menelek's armies set up new garrison towns. These were called *kätäma*, a word which means height, and had earlier been applied to the mobile tent capitals of the medieval Solomonic kings, and was used here because the new town was often set up on the top of a hill. Sites chosen were near local markets, and controlled trade routes. There would be fences and fortifications, tents for the soldiers and occupiers, a house for the governor and lodgings for soldiers who also were landholders, called *neftenna* or rifle-bearers, since they had the legal right to carry guns. As well as these occupiers there were also priests, bringing the tabot, which had accompanied the raiding party and was surrounded by the threefold division of the church. The clergy formed an integral part of the new *kätäma*.

At the centre of the kingdom was the new capital city of Addis Ababa, or new flower. This was founded in the 1880s. It was connected with the *kätäma* network to reach across the new empire. The *kätäma* provided a foothold and a bridgehead for the occupying forces, from where Menelek's rule, the Amharic language and the Orthodox Church could extend further into the countryside. The church with its clergy, set up at the centre of the *kätäma*, became not only a place of worship but also a centre of mission. As in the Middle Ages when monasteries were established in areas conquered by the armies, so now the church had its place within the new settlements.

However, while the medieval monastic settlements had been in rural areas, the churches of the nineteenth-century expansion were in the towns. The Orthodox faith was introduced, but did not penetrate the countryside as effectively as the medieval monasteries had done.

Throughout its history the church had grown and extended its influence through two methods. These continued to be practised in the south as well as the north.

The first and usual method was transmission within the kinship group – as a part of the life of the community, governing the rhythm of the seasons, the way of understanding the world, and managing the tragedies which afflicted and challenges which exercised. Those who were born into the community of faith in the mountains of Ethiopia were Orthodox because they were part of the Orthodox community. This missionary method applied especially to traditionally Orthodox areas, although once established in new areas and with communities established, new members and their families became integrated into a Christian society.

The second method was the extension of that community through conquest or other means. As the community expanded into new areas by military conquest, commercial exploitation or migration, so the conquerors brought their faith with them. Among the pressures which led to movement of population in this period was disease, which devastated the highlands in the 1890s killing millions, which led many Amhara to move south to escape the epidemic, and so to the further establishment of churches.[2] The Christian faith was brought to new areas as part of an imperialist expansion which included political domination and economic exploitation. This accounts for both the strength and the weakness of growth of the Orthodox Church in the nineteenth century.

It was strong because there were many attractions in becoming Orthodox. Local people were attracted to this new faith brought by new rulers for many reasons. Among these was the greater security which it gave, since it was not permitted for Christians to be sold into slavery, and so converts to Christianity were, at least in theory, immune from risk of being carried off as part of the thriving trade in human commodities. Adoption of the Orthodox faith brought privilege, but also required new members to learn a new language and follow a new culture. Faith could become associated with the rule of the oppressors.

But this mission method also had weaknesses. The Orthodox brought the Christian faith, but they did not attempt to integrate it into the culture and language of the new ethnic groups of the Ethiopian Empire. This left a vacuum which awaited the new missionaries from Europe, and of which they were to take full advantage. The Orthodox churches had introduced the Christian faith to the region, and Evangelicals were to build on this by providing a form of faith using local languages and customs, and, as we shall see, providing other benefits as well. The Orthodox had prepared the way, and the missionaries benefitted. As an Orthodox theologian, Habtämaryam Worqenéh, commented, looking back at the success of Evangelical missionaries in attracting former Orthodox, 'Where there is roast fish, why struggle with the ocean?'

FORMS OF EVANGELICALISM

The arrival of missionaries from foreign lands was a familiar theme of Ethiopian history. Egyptians had brought episcopal government in the fourth century; Syrians and others introduced a popular form of monastic life in the sixth century; and the Portuguese had tried – less successfully – to bring the church under Roman Catholic authority in the sixteenth century.

After the Portuguese Jesuits were expelled in 1632, there was a period of isolation. Few foreign visitors reached the Ethiopian court. An exception was Peter Heyling, a German Lutheran from Lubeck who arrived in Gondar in late 1634 or early 1635. He was known as *muallim Petros*, or Doctor Peter, and translated the Gospel of John into Amharic. He left around 1652. It is reported that followers of his Protestant biblical approach can still be found in parts of rural Ethiopia.[3]

Protestant missionaries of the nineteenth century were more numerous and came from more countries. They introduced a style of church life which had more radical differences from Ethiopian forms. The varied strands of missionary styles and objectives led inexorably to the complexity of modern Ethiopian Christianity. The successive waves of missionary arrival can be divided into several types.

The first main influx of missionary enthusiasm took place in the reign of Téwodros II. These missionaries were sent by the British Church Missionary Society, although many of them were recruited from the training institute of St Chrischona in Switzerland, where training in practical skills was combined with Christian witness. They wanted to work within the Ethiopian Orthodox Church, bringing the same kind of reforming movement which had brought into being the Protestant churches of Europe. Missionaries were at first welcomed by Emperor Téwodros but later he came to distrust them and this led to their imprisonment and the dramatic relief operation led by General Napier.

Some of this group set up a mission to the Falasha Jews. They preached an Evangelical faith but encouraged converts to be baptised into the Orthodox Church. The Society for the Promotion of Christianity among the Jews continued to work in the region around Gondar until 1920.

The next to arrive were from the Swedish Evangelical Lutheran Mission. They came by sea and maintained a presence along the Red Sea coast in Eritrea, but had a longer-term plan to evangelise in the south of the country, among the Oromo, which they hoped would provide access deeper into the interior of Africa. The prospective Oromo converts were followers of traditional African religions and so the aim here was straightforward conversion, although some still thought that converts should be baptised into the Orthodox Church. Access proved difficult, and most of the first Swedish missionaries remained in Eritrea, although a small base was established in Addis Ababa. Mission stations were eventually set up in western Ethiopia, at towns including Nekemte and Dembi Dolo. Other societies joined them – the United Presbyterian Mission of the USA, the Swedish Bibeltrogna Vänner (or Bible-true friends) who had split from the Evangelical Lutheran Mission, and the Hermannsburg Mission. These made little impact until the persecutions carried out by the Italians after 1935, but then grew. They, along with other Lutheran groups, eventually formed the Ethiopian Evangelical Church Mekane Yesus, or place of Jesus, in 1959.

A further group of missionaries arrived in the early twentieth century, from Baptist groups within the USA. Many were sent by the Sudan Interior Mission, who interpreted the location of Sudan in a sweeping fashion to include Africa south of Egypt. They set up hospitals and schools, and had some success in building small Evangelical communities. They were expelled during the Italian occupation, but the movement grew under local leadership. The churches supported by the SIM missionaries grew, as had Lutheran churches, and eventually formed the Kale Hiwot, or Word of Life, Church, which is now the largest Evangelical church in Ethiopia.

Throughout the period there was a Roman Catholic presence, which had begun with the arrival of Justin de Jacobis as Apostolic Prefect of Ethiopia in 1839. This took two forms. Members of de Jacobis's Lazarist religious order worked in Eritrea and other parts of the north, and followed the traditional Ge'ez traditions of liturgy and practice, asking only acceptance of the authority of the pope and relying on local clergy. Meanwhile Guglielmo Massaja, supported by French Franciscan Capuchins, went south, and required conformity to Latin forms of worship. The two congregations of Ge'ez in the north and Latin in the south persist into the present.

Anglicans came later, in the twentieth century. There was a chaplaincy in Addis Ababa, serving the Anglican community, and a mission sent by the Bible Churchmens Missionary Society, later renamed Crosslinks.

More Evangelical communities could be added to this list, but these separate strands of mission activity show the variety of Evangelical practice and these groups formed some of the traditions of Protestant Christianity which have grown in Ethiopia. These missionaries found that they had come to a country which was proud of its independence from the colonising European powers, had suddenly expanded to include a much greater diversity of ethnic groups, and was slowly and unevenly entering the modern age. They settled and oversaw the beginnings of new Protestant churches. This period came to a sudden end with the invasion and occupation of Ethiopia by Italian troops in 1935. The missionaries, with a few exceptions, were forced to leave.

Their work was shaped by the society in which they had settled. They reacted to the wider political movement of imperial expansion, the desperate poverty of many of the people and the desire for education and medical care. The stories of the missionaries here mentioned show how they reacted to the conditions they found in Ethiopia and how they tried to establish missionary communities.

THE SOCIAL CONTEXT

The missionaries came to Africa as part of the great movement of European peoples known as imperialism. Although they were responding to an evangelistic calling, they could not avoid entanglement in the politics, economics and diplomacy of the imperialism of the nineteenth century. They belonged to one side of an unequal relationship between Europe and Africa. In his study of missions and politics, Donald Crummey has commented, 'The missions [were] one factor in a three sided process of religious impulse, African society, and European government, each component of which maintained its autonomy of interest, but whose driving force lay in the European economy.'[4] Ethiopia is proud to be one of the only two African countries not to have been colonised – the other is the much newer state of Liberia formed as a place for returning slaves. While its victory over the Italians at Adwa in 1896 saved it from conquest, it could not isolate it from the pervasive influences of Western imperialism in Africa. The progress of imperialism in Ethiopia followed a different pattern from in the rest of Africa, since Ethiopia fell under direct rule from Europe for only a brief period between 1936 and 1941. Political independence did not free Ethiopia from entanglement in the history of European expansion, and missionaries found themselves agents of this expansion. An outcome of the victory at Adwa was that no one colonial power controlled Ethiopia, and there was instead an easier access for a wide range of national missionary groups. The diversity of Ethiopian Evangelicalism was a result of, in part, its successful resistance to imperialist aggression.

There are many examples of the intertwining of political and religious motives. In the early nineteenth century, George Annesley, Viscount Valentia, visited the Red Sea region as part of a plan to counter French expansion in North Africa under Napoleon, and sent Henry Salt into Ethiopia on two visits in 1804–5 and 1809–10. Valentia later became president of the Abyssinian subcommittee of the British and Foreign Bible Society, and so combined evangelistic and political interests in Ethiopia. This dual concern is expressed in Henry Salt's analysis of the situation at Gondar. 'At the present moment [. . .] the nation, with its religion, is fast verging to ruin; the Galla [Oromo] and Mussulman tribes around are daily becoming more powerful; and there is reason to fear that, in a short time, the very name of Christ may be lost among them.'[5]

The interaction of religious and political interests also lay behind the dramatic series of events in the reign of Téwodros. Samuel Gobat,

Bishop of Jerusalem, had enlisted the help of the Pilgrim Mission in an evangelistic enterprise. The mission was based at Basel and trained its personnel at the St Chrischona-Pilgermission Institute in practical skills like weaving, building and woodwork, so that they could carry on quiet and pious lives doing useful work and building a Christian community around them by example and presence. A party of four arrived at the camp of Emperor Téwodros in May 1856. At first they were enthused by the king's support of a Christian mission. 'He is the only man in Abyssinia who possesses the fear of God', one of them commented. The 'King's attitude to us lets us expect auspicious things for the future'.[6] However, as the king's position became insecure his demands changed and the missionary-artisans found themselves required to use their skills not in road-building and teaching but in casting cannons which the king hoped would provide him with a weapon which would give him an overwhelming advantage over his enemies. As his reign advanced, his violence increased and, if overcome, his enemies were treated with extreme cruelty. Téwodros wanted to build his state through alliances with the European powers and so made overtures to both England and France, writing formal letters in October 1862. The British government made no response, and in reaction to this perceived insult, Téwodros kept the missionaries as hostages. This then led to outrage in England, and so to the massive military campaign by General Napier who had led voyages to India, Ceylon, the Red Sea, Abyssinia and Egypt in the years 1803, 1804, 1805 and 1806. A large military force was sent across the mountainous region of the north of Ethiopia, attacked Téwodros's fortress at Maqdala, at which point the emperor killed himself and missionaries were released and escorted – reluctantly – out of the country. Here, as at other times, evangelistic, military, economic and political currents flowed together in a complex interaction.[7]

Catholics too sought to extend the influence and interests of their homelands. The Capuchin Justin de Jacobis kept in close contact with the French government, and sent regular reports to Paris between 1840 and 1860, expressing the hope that the French government would assist in the total conversion of Ethiopia, writing – somewhat naively – 'Abyssinia in its entirety is preparing to become Catholic in the very near future.'[8] His contemporary, Massaja, favoured Italy. He replied warmly to an invitation from the Piedmont Foreign Office sent in January 1857 to provide political intelligence, assist in commercial opportunities and even represent Piedmont in negotiating treaties. Massaja's promotion of the Latin rather than the Ge'ez rite intended to bring Ethiopia and Italy closer together. He wrote of the

> supreme advantages which implanting the Latin rite in these savage countries would produce [. . .] coming to us with the European rite and literature to attach themselves essentially to us, and to the mother church with the vehicle of the language which can communicate to them infinite treasures of the science and the spirit.[9]

The colonisers of Africa brought with them the culture and also the scientific knowledge and technological achievements of Europe. The kings of Ethiopia welcomed the support that this could give them in their building of a modern society. Téwodros had been optimistic that that the missionaries who arrived at his court would help him build his modern state and would provide him with the military hardware to enable him to overcome his enemies. His successors also looked to Western arrivals to provide the knowledge, technology and skills which would give economic and social support to their political order. They hoped that the foreigners would become allies in the struggle for power with feudal landowners, and help to provide education and medical services. They also encouraged missionaries to set up schools and hospitals.

The role of missionaries in development of the state, and also the potential of this role both to advance and to undermine the missionary endeavour, is shown by the rise and fall of Thomas Lambie (1885–1954). Lambie was an American missionary who served with, first, the United Presbyterian Church of North America and then, from 1927, the Sudan Interior Mission. He was a doctor who went first to work in the Sudan and then, in 1919, received an urgent appeal to come to Wallaga, in the west of Ethiopia, to provide medical care during an influenza epidemic. The success of his medical work led to his fame spreading and three years later, in 1922, he was asked by Emperor Haile Selassie to set up the first modern hospital in Ethiopia, in Addis Ababa. He became field director of the Sudan Interior Mission in 1928, and was given permission to set up mission activities in other parts of the south of the country. He built more hospitals and clinics, and was awarded Ethiopian citizenship by the emperor in recognition of his medical work. Lambie came as a missionary, established a reputation, and then was given the opportunity to carry out evangelistic work as a consequence of the success of his innovative medical work. He provided modern medical facilities and spread Evangelical Baptist Christianity. He was, unfortunately, unable to manoeuvre his way through the complexity of the politics of the Italian invasion from 1935–41. He wanted to support his churches through the difficult times of Italian occupation and so he tried to gain Italian sympathy by publicly retracting his earlier condemnation of the use of poison gas by the Italians. This action was considered to be treachery by Haile Selassie who withdrew Lambie's citizenship when he returned to Ethiopia in 1941. Lambie left the country and did not return.[10]

The expulsion of Lambie did not affect Haile Selassie's reliance on missionaries to help develop education and medicine. The need to modernise led the emperor Haile Selassie to issue decree 3.11 on 27 August 1947. This decree divided Ethiopia into 'Ethiopian Church areas' and 'open areas'. In the latter, mostly in the south and west, 'missionaries were permitted to teach and preach the Christian Faith of their own denominations without restriction'. Alongside this went encouragement to open schools and hospitals. Even in closed Orthodox areas missionaries were allowed to establish hospitals and carry out non-denominational work. The missionaries responded to this invitation. Lutheran Evangelicals were among those who developed a holistic approach to mission, and made it their aim to serve both the material needs of the body and the spiritual longings of the soul.

The society in which the missionaries found themselves was poor and so provided opportunities to establish relationships and gain adherents through offering practical help. Ethiopia was a feudal society, with many living in extreme poverty. Peasants, in most areas, were *gebbar* or serfs, cultivating land owned by others. The land they farmed could be given or sold to a landlord who could take their crops or evict them, leaving them homeless. Those who farmed the land were required to comply with numerous and arbitrary exactions. A tithe of produce was paid to the church, taxes of varying amounts to maintain the court and the army, and arbitrary payments to local officials. The Swedish missionary Carl Cederquist lamented, 'how can you expect these people to have time and mental peace to attend schools and listen to the gospel?'[11]

There was a thriving slave trade, with traders benefitting from a business deeply rooted in society and forming a traditional and profitable part of the local economy. Slavery was common throughout Ethiopia. From the tenth century there had been an active trade in slaves from Ethiopia, with many exported to Arabia. A ruler of Yemen, Said ibn Negah, is said to have bought 20,000 *habasha*, or Ethiopian, slaves. When the missionaries arrived it was estimated that 25,000 slaves a year were captured and traded.[12] Emperors tried periodically to legislate against slavery – Yohannes IV in 1884, Menelek II in 1889, the empress Zawditu in 1918 – but without ending the trade. The trade in slaves was a source of concern to the international community, and was a reason for refusing Ethiopia admission to the League of Nations when it was founded in 1919. Haile Selassie was determined to bring this practice to a close, and to enable Ethiopia to become part of this international network. On 15 September 1923 he passed another law which prohibited slave-trading on pain of death, and allowed all slaves to be given freedom and the right to return to their home country. On 28 September, Ethiopia was admitted to the League of Nations by a unanimous vote of members. While this had some effect, it is said that slavery persisted in some parts of the south-west as late as 1990. Their concern for the situation of the slaves led to attempts by missionaries to care for individuals caught up in the trade.

There are many eyewitness reports in which the devastating effects of slavery are described. The missionary Onesimus Nesib reported meeting a slave caravan in 1886. There were 700 slaves, and apart from a few castrated boys and some young mothers, all were girls between eight and sixteen years old. The missionaries were deeply distressed but could do nothing about this sad procession.[13] It led not only to human suffering but economic devastation. A British Frontier Agent, H.A.C. Darley, reported on a visit to an area of the south-west in 1923:

> A strip of territory three hundred square miles has been depopulated and devastated by slave traders, and in this area over a million people have been killed and removed into bondage [. . .] the route lies through country which was formerly a garden but now nothing can be seen but skeletons and devastated houses.[14]

Slavery was an opportunity for the missionaries to combine humanitarian action with evangelism. Slaves were purchased, set free and then provided with an education at missionary schools.

An early mission school run by the Swedish Evangelical mission in Massawa relied on finding freed slaves to be the recruits for enrolment in the school. A piece of legislation to restrict the slave trade was enacted in the late eighteenth century. As a result of this, only government agencies were allowed to purchase and free slaves, so that merchants would be unable to continue the trade under pretence of purchasing slaves in order to free them. A result of this enlightened legislation was to dry up one of the sources of pupils of the Swedish school. In 1875 the principal of the school was concerned that it was impossible to obtain slaves as pupils because the authorities sent very few. In the following year there were only five students left due to the difficulty of finding slaves to buy and liberate, now that the slave merchants were being put out of business.[15]

Liberated slaves, educated in mission schools, sometimes became leaders of the Evangelical churches. Some of these boys became able students, and progressed to pioneering roles in the missionary enterprise. An early convert was Onesimus Nesib (*c.*1856–1931). He was born in the west of Ethiopia to an Oromo family and given the name Tika, which means interpreter or opener, a name which proved prescient in view of his later career. He was captured by slave traders at the age of four, after the death of his father, and had been sold and resold four times before being bought by Werner Munzinger, a missionary, at the age of fourteen. He was the first pupil at the Swedish Evangelical school at Massawa, and was an enthusiastic pupil. He was renamed Onesimus by his new protectors, using the name of the slave who was the subject of one of the epistles of St Paul in the New Testament. He was invited to Sweden for five years to study at a theological training centre from 1876 to 1881. But he longed to bring the gospel to his own people, and it is told that he would pray long into the night with the words, 'How long, how long Lord, will it be before you send a preacher of the gospel there?'

He was handicapped in his own ability to do this because he had been taken from his home at the age of four and could not speak the local Oromo language. So it was a happy chance that, in 1886, living on the Eritrean coast and looking for an opportunity to travel as an evangelist to Oromo regions, he met an Oromo woman called Aster Ganno Salbana, who shared his enthusiasm. They set up a fruitful partnership and together produced Oromo Christian literature, including a translation of the complete Bible. He used the Amharic version of the Bible and translated while she helped him to find an idiomatic and fluent style of the language. He supervised the printing of the Oromo Bible at St Chrischona in Switzerland and returned with this task completed in 1899. In 1904 he was finally able to settle in Oromo Wollaga, at Nekemte, where he remained until his death.

He died on Sunday 21 June 1931. He had arranged to preach at the Evangelical Church and set out with his grandson. His grandson recalled that it was Onesimus's practice to walk slowly, greeting and talking to people whom he met on the way. This time he ran so fast that his grandson could not keep up with him, and said he was in a hurry because he was going to die that day. When he arrived at the church he collapsed with a stroke and died that evening – with, among others, his fellow translator Aster with him.[16]

A more cynical use of slaves as converts was the offer from slave holders to provide hundreds of congregation members upon payment for this service. The minister concerned, Carl Cederquist, declined the offer.[17] Ethiopian Orthodox had also benefitted from the desire of peasants to escape the threat of slavery. Following the conquests of southern areas by Menelek II, many peasants took advantage of the law which forbade the enslavement of Christians, and implored the emperor to allow them to be baptised into the Orthodox Church.[18]

It was not only freed slaves who developed into leaders. Conversion to evangelical religion became an escape route from poverty. Gidada Solon was born in 1901 at Dembi Dolo. At the age of 5 he became blind as a result of small pox, in an outbreak in which his mother and three of his siblings died. One day the boy could feel the heat of the fire on his face but could not see it, so he swore using God's name. His father slapped him, telling him not to use the name of God in vain. As a teenager he used to sit by the roadside begging. He was told about the missionaries and he went to see who they were. He was invited in to listen to Thomas Lambie as he preached. As he listened he realised that they were talking about the same God whom he had sworn about and then his father had slapped him. He thought to himself that if you are the God who gives to the blind beggar a chair in the house of a missionary then I'll serve you. He went to school and had an amazing memory and did well. He became a pastor, being ordained in 1940. One of his sons, Negaso, became the first President of the Federal Republic of Ethiopia, after the fall of the Derg, from 1991 to 2001.[19]

The vivid stories of Onesimus and Gidada show the impact of missionaries in poor communities, and the promise offered to those with little prospect of a better life. They, along with others, provided a hagiography of inspired leaders which provided some of the momentum for the growth of Evangelical churches.

The churches recognised the importance of humanitarian activity. As early as 1871, the board of the Swedish Evangelical Mission stated its aim of providing material support for the poor. 'It appears evident that our mission should not only be a mission of preaching but also a mission of service which in the beginning lays more stress on caring for those in need.' 'You have made life easier for us and our children', said a local believer in 1916.[20] Western churches have continued to provide material benefits as well as spiritual teaching. Evangelical church leaders claim to be concerned for the whole person, and offer a holistic ministry and not just a spiritual message. This has been attractive to many Ethiopians but has aroused suspicion and hostility from Orthodox who have not had the resources to provide similar opportunities and material support.

There are many examples of the mixing of the spiritual and the material. A missionary in the west of the country reported that he was concerned that street children at his school could not attend lessons because they needed to beg to survive. He decided to make a daily payment to these children to make up what they had lost from begging. In 2013 the minister of a congregation in Addis Ababa arranged funding from a Western source for a project to provide poor children from the neighbourhood with breakfast before going to school. He reported to the church meeting his concern that he was not offering more than just food to these children, and started Bible classes to provide spiritual food to supplement the material nourishment. Material support went hand in hand with evangelistic preaching.

EVANGELICALS AND ORTHODOX

Evangelical missionaries came to bring the gospel of Christ to places where this saving message was not known. This mission purpose was the subject of a resolution at the first meeting of the Church Missionary

Society, founded in 1799, that 'it is a duty highly incumbent upon every Christian to endeavour to propagate the knowledge of the gospel among the heathen'.[21] In Ethiopia, as in other parts of the Middle East, the missionaries came to a country which had been Christian for far longer than their own homelands. This set them new challenges, and they had to decide on a strategy in this setting. It evoked various reactions. Protestants often compared Ethiopia to pre-Reformation Europe, and saw their vocation as assisting the Christians of Ethiopia to achieve the benefits of a reformed and so renewed faith. It is a view expressed by the Anglican missionary David Stokes:

> Today the Church of Ethiopia, that honourable church which has stood and withstood for so long, lies in darkness and in the thraldom of superstition. The old foundations have been forgotten, the old paths abandoned, the Scriptures neglected, tradition become supreme [...] [T]he situation greatly resembles that pertaining in England in the early days of the fifteenth century.[22]

So in the case of the mission to an ancient church, such as the Ethiopian Orthodox Church, the task of evangelism became the task of Reformation.

Lying behind the varying experiences was the attitude of missionaries to those they found themselves among. We have already noted the different approaches of Pero Paez and Alfonso Mendes. This contrast was to be repeated whenever Western Christians encountered Orthodox, and are illustrated by the changing reactions of missionaries of the Anglican Church.

Among the earliest missionary arrivals were Samuel Gobat (1799–1879) and Christian Kugler (1801–30). Both were Swiss Lutherans, trained at the institute of St Chrischona and sent out by the Anglican Church Missionary Society. They arrived in Ethiopia in 1829. Kugler considered his role to be translation work, made little attempt to adapt to life in Ethiopia, argued with his hosts and became a cause of irritation, and died in the following year. Gobat, on the other hand, had a longer and warmer association, which he described in vivid detail in his journals.[23] He established relationships with some of the contenders for political power, and travelled to Gondar where he arrived in February 1830. He wore Ethiopian dress, shared food and lodging, and liked to meet and talk to people wherever he went. Once settled in Gondar there was a stream of visitors to his house eager to talk to him and discuss doctrinal matters. He based his conversation on Scripture, referring to the relevant texts, and if he could not find a suitable passage declined to respond, saying that 'God has not revealed that to us in his Word.'[24] He thought that if the episcopate could be expanded so that there was more effective governance, the Bible translated and education improved, then necessary reform would follow. This would result in greater trust in grace, and additions such as the veneration of Mary or the saints, fasting and some other parts of traditional devotion would naturally diminish.

He had copies of the Bible to distribute, although this was not always a welcome gift. On receiving this gift of God's word, King Gigar (1821–30) summoned Gobat a few days later and returned it, pointing out that he already owned several books and would prefer 'a piece of cloth, silk or linen'. Among his friends was the *echägé* Filpos. The two men engaged in regular dialogue. After one conversation, in the presence of another monk, Filpos wondered if Gobat might fill the currently vacant position of Abuna. 'We are agreed on all principal points. I have found the abuna that we want', he said. Not surprisingly, this proposal came to nothing. Gobat was dubious, commenting in his diary that he thought that 'a man who fears God and keeps his Word cannot be abuna unless people would submit to a general reform of their religion'. Filpos fell out of favour with the king and was replaced as *echägé* later that year. Gobat consoled his friend suggesting that God had permitted his dethronement to save him from the temptations of high office, a comment which Filpos repeated to everyone who came to see him, saying how Gobat was a man of faith and sincerity. Commenting on this episode, the Ethiopian historian Taddesse Tamrat notes the naivety of the missionary who took seriously the flattery of this impossible mock offer.[25]

The experiences of Kugler and Gobat illustrate attitudes which have marked the relationships of missionaries and local Ethiopians throughout their meetings. While Kugler was insensitive and made little effort to meet and engage with local people, Gobat was warm and direct. His devout, serious and respectful character enabled him to establish a positive missionary base. But while he had good personal relationships he remained dismissive and unsympathetic to many aspects of the faith of Ethiopians. When travelling to Gondar during the fasting season, he pointed out passages from the Bible showing that fasting was of no spiritual value. His hosts responded generously and ensured that goat or a sheep, as he desired, would be slaughtered for him personally every evening. At Kugler's death he did not allow the clergy to pronounce the prayers of absolution on his colleague because these prayers were nothing but 'superstitious ceremonies'. He confided his true opinions to the privacy of his correspondence:

> Christianity in Ethiopia is entirely degenerated into superstition [...] there is still left sufficient of it to attach us to the Christians of that country and to engage us to consider them as brothers who have alienated themselves from our common Father and have reaped as fruits of their errors, misery and degradation.[26]

Many of his successors made the same discovery that genuine and generous personal relationships can be developed alongside firm evangelical theological convictions to produce constructive missionary endeavour.

The first Anglican chaplain to be sent to Addis Ababa was the unusual and eccentric Ethelstan Cheese. He was appointed in 1926 and stayed for a year. He proved to be an unreliable chaplain but a remarkable evangelist. There was at that time no Anglican church building in Addis Ababa and little to keep him rooted in the city. He could not settle, he was unreliable, he could not organise anything. His bishop sighed as he wrote in a letter, 'it would take a special kind of stickfast flypaper to hold Cheese, for he is forever wanting to slip away from the job he is specially selected for'; then a month later in a further letter, 'our worst fears are realised and Cheese, the peripatetic friar has gone into the blue as I expected he would'. After a year as chaplain, he left to carry out a peripatetic ministry in the Somali region of Ethiopia. He walked from place to place, mostly in the Somali desert but sometimes extending his travels into the Arabian peninsula and the Middle East. He worked at producing Somali versions of texts, including not only the Bible but also John Bunyan's *Pilgrim's Progress*.

There are many stories of this period of his life. He would sometimes be discovered on his wanderings by police or army vehicles sitting under a thorn tree with his briefcase and an empty water bottle in a remote area miles from the nearest waterhole. He would be unconcerned. On one occasion his rescuer asked him, 'What would you have done if I hadn't come along to give you a lift?' 'Ah, but you did come along, my dear boy, didn't you? Don't you see?' An army officer wrote about a meeting with him in 1941:

> He arrived at our camp. He approached us. His face was pale coloured, and he was tall and spare and thin. He had a straggle of beard and dusty clothes. 'How do you do?' he said in a high-pitched Edwardian voice. He coughed. 'Do you happen to know what day of the week it is?' We asked him to stay with us but he wouldn't take any of the camp-beds we offered him. 'I have got out of the way of using them, you know, I am really just as happy on the ground.' 'You must at least have a blanket' we said 'to wrap around you.' 'That would be very nice' he conceded. 'I did have one but I gave it to someone a few days ago.' Next morning he left us while the colour of dawn was still in the sky. We watched him walk up the road and disappear. In the town that afternoon we asked about him. 'Oh yes', the people said 'we know him. We all know him. He is a Holy Man.'

He continued this life until 1953, when he was persuaded to return to England.[27] Ethelstan Cheese showed throughout his life a sacrificial dedication to people he loved, which did not fit easily into the ministry of a church organisation.

Later Anglicans of the Bible Churchmens Missionary Society, later renamed Crosslinks, followed a consistent strategy of supporting the Orthodox Church. In 1940 they sent David Stokes to work in Ethiopia. He, along with others, including Austin Mathew, who was Anglican chaplain in Addis Ababa from 1928 to 1968, Eric Payne and the distinguished Ge'ez scholar Roger Cowley, were determined to build positive and supportive relationships with the Orthodox Church. They were invited to teach at Ethiopian Orthodox schools in Addis Ababa and Mekelle, but, unlike other missionaries, rejected opportunities to open their own schools, in case Orthodox suspected them of trying to lure Ethiopian boys into Anglicanism. Instead they patiently built relationships of trust and confidence, and always made it clear that they had no intention of proselytising. Austin Mathew wrote to his superiors in London,

> It is very easy to see the weak points of any institution and the weaknesses of the church here are patent to the most casual observer. It required knowledge and sympathetic enquiry to find out what good underlay its obvious faults [...] I am not prepared on the partial evidence before me to agree with the other missionaries that the church is dead and the only thing to do is to replace it with other purer forms of Christianity.[28]

A sign of the commitment to work with and support the Ethiopian Orthodox Church was the reluctance of chaplains to receive Ethiopians into the Anglican congregation. Ethiopians who asked for membership of the one Anglican congregation in Addis Ababa were directed to the local Orthodox Church. The Constitution of the Anglican Chaplaincy of St Matthew, drafted in 1976, stated that the Anglicans 'respect the Ethiopian Orthodox Church as the established church of the country and therefore refrain from all spiritual work among Ethiopian nationals'.

A new stage of the life of the Anglican community began with the setting up of a church in the western town of Gambella and then in camps hosting refugees from the war in neighbouring southern Sudan. Some of those who fled the fighting were Anglican, and others were attracted to the Anglican forms of church order and liturgy. A church was founded in Gambella in 1996, and further churches followed in local communities and in refugee camps along the border. The number of churches has grown, a theological college to train clergy has been set up and the Anglican church is now the second largest in the Gambella region. A bishop was appointed in 2007, and his successor, Grant le Marquand, presides over the church from the centre in Gambella. The desire of the church to serve its members, especially students who travel to other parts of the country, and also others attracted to the distinct Anglican mix of liturgical order and an evangelical biblical message has led to a revision of its previous reticence to receive Ethiopians into the church. It retains a commitment to build good relations with other communities but is open to the possibility of setting up new congregations. The Anglican Church has become a small but growing Evangelical church with a clear mission alongside others. Its changing practice illustrates different possible kinds of relationship with the indigenous Orthodox Christians.

USES OF THE BIBLE

The backdrop for the Protestant mission was the imperialism of the Europeans, and an opportunity to gain acceptance in society came through various forms of social and economic improvement. But the missionaries had not come to this area of the Horn of Africa to provide assistance to the government. While they were concerned to

FIGURE 9.2 Anglican clergy at the area synod at Gambella.

bring education and health, the heart of their message was religious. They came with the good news of salvation, and this message was the Bible. This book contained the simple message that Jesus Christ has died for our sins and that faith in him is all that is needed for forgiveness and eternal life.

So we can date the true beginning of the evangelical mission to Ethiopia not to missionary preaching but to the work of an Ethiopian Orthodox monk from Gojjam, called Abraham. Abraham had led a peripatetic life visiting Egypt, Syria, Persia and India, adding knowledge of a variety of languages and cultures to his traditional grounding in Ethiopian church traditions. At the age of 50 he became seriously ill while on a visit to Cairo and was tended – or, as he put it 'snatched from the arms of death' – by the diplomat and scholar Asselin de Cherville who was the French vice-consul in Egypt. The two men became friends and decided to undertake the task of translating the Bible into Amharic. They worked on Tuesdays and Saturdays for ten years, with Asselin referring to Hebrew, Syriac and Greek versions, and Abraham seeking the best Amharic rendering. The work done, Abraham set off again on his travels and died shortly afterwards, in 1818, of the plague in Jerusalem. Abraham's great work was a volume of 9539 handwritten pages 'in the handwriting of the translator, Abu Rumi, which is a bold and fine specimen of the Abyssinian character'.[29] Asselin then sold it for £1250 to the British and Foreign Bible Society, which had been founded a few years earlier in 1804, who published the full Bible in 1840. It came to be known as Aba Rumi's Bible, and can be considered as the foundation moment of evangelicalism in Ethiopia.

The spread of a biblical faith was continued by other Ethiopians. Taye Gäbrä Maryam (1860–1924) started life with a traditional education in the Ethiopian Church. At the age of 18 he went to Massawa looking for a lost uncle, and there met members of the Swedish Evangelical Mission, including Bengt Lundahl. He wanted to enter the Swedish school but Lundahl thought he was too old since he was eighteen years old. His persistence was rewarded and he was eventually admitted. Three years later he decided to join the Bethel Evangelical Congregation at nearby Imkullu. Throughout his life he remained committed to his Ethiopian Orthodox roots and also to the study and preaching of the Bible, as a member of an evangelical style of Christianity. He was received at court by Emperor Menelek and was granted permission to preach – which he did on numerous occasions. As well as enjoying the friendship of the emperor, he provoked the hostility of traditional monks and others, led by abuna Matéwos and traditional members of the church. Conflict quickly developed. One conversation is recorded in which the abuna in frustration asked Taye, 'Where did you come at your religion, you ass?' To which Taye responded, 'Alas we really have made stupid asses of ourselves by putting aliens like you in office.'[30]

On being asked to provide a scholar of Ethiopian studies by Germans to teach at Berlin, Menelek sent Taye, and so he studied at the Oriental Institute of Berlin University, from 1905 to 1907. As Menelek declined in health, so the opposition to Taye grew in strength and he was later imprisoned for a year from 1910 to 1911 for his theological views. He left an extensive literary contribution in Amharic and Ge'ez including a History of the People of Ethiopia, a book entitled *Mäzgabe Qalat* or Treasury of Concepts, and many hymns in Geez and Amharic. His importance is in his commitment to an approach to Christianity both fully Ethiopian and also Evangelical. His career shows the possibility of an Evangelical Bible-based Orthodoxy. He died after a short illness in August 1924. Controversy followed him to the end, as his wife's request that he should be buried at a church in the centre of town was refused, and the suggestion of traditionalist priests that his grave should be in bushes outside the church compound alongside Muslims was unacceptable to her, and he was finally laid to rest in a cemetery provided for foreigners on the edge of town.

Alongside the discovery by Ethiopians of the attraction of the simple Bible message went the colportage labours of the missionaries. Protestants hoped for a Reformation of the Orthodox Church, as had happened in Europe in the preceding centuries. They printed and distributed Bibles and encouraged people to read them for themselves, meeting in small groups to discuss and discover biblical truth. A few groups started to read this new Bible. One place where this happened was the Tigrayan town of Tseazaga. Some time around 1860 a book was discovered hidden in a crack in the wall at the church of Giyorgis at Tseazaga. Unlike the other books in the church it was printed and in Amharic. It turned out to be a copy of Aba Rumi's Bible and had probably been brought to the village in the first wave of CMS activity twenty years previously, left in the church and forgotten. The clergy studied the Bible together and grew in understanding. Ten years later, they received a visit from two Swedish missionaries, Lager and Hedenstrom, who encouraged them in their new-found conviction of salvation in Christ alone, and arranged for further visits from nearby missionaries. Some of the deacons who had studied the Bible were taken to Adwa to be ordained priests by abuna Atenatéwos, who was bishop from 1869–76, who exhorted them to 'teach the gospel in their own land and if possible even beyond'. This contact led to suspicion that they had adopted the faith of Westerners, and from May 1873 their views were attacked in a series of public disputations with the traditionalist monks of Däbrä Bizen, as a result of which the 'Bible-readers' left Tseazaga, and only returned when political change led to freedom of religious faith in 1889.

The 'Bible-readers' were not just promoting a new translation but a different Bible and an alternative kind of faith. For Orthodox the Bible was a holy book, written in the sacred language of Ge'ez, read in church by the priest or the deacon, then wrapped in a rich brocade cloth and held out to be kissed by the faithful after reading, who would bow and cross themselves before approaching this holy book which contained a power against evil and a cure for illness.

The arrival of missionaries was bound to provide a challenge. The potential for conflict is shown by a story told to me by Rachel Weller. She told me how, in the early days of the arrival of American Presbyterian missionaries, they agreed to work together with Orthodox colleagues in teaching the non-Christian people about the importance of the Bible. The Orthodox offered their holy book to be treated with reverence and awe, but the Americans – bringing printed versions of the sixty-six books translated into Oromo – distributed it as widely as possible, encouraged open and free discussion and used it as the basis of preaching about faith in Jesus. The conflicting views of holiness inevitably led to tensions, and when followers of the Americans died, once again, as in the case of Taye Gäbrä Maryam, the place of burial exacerbated the conflict. The Orthodox clergy would not allow them to be buried in consecrated ground. Soon after this the first congregations of the Evangelical Church Bethel were formed.

THE FORMATION OF NEW CHURCHES

Western missionaries started out by teaching the Bible, and tried to find sympathetic Orthodox clergy who would baptise and support Evangelical Christians. Their purpose was to bring reformation to the Orthodox Church. At first they intended that new converts would be baptised into this traditional form of Ethiopian church. It was not long before differences in emphasis, teaching and practice led to the formation of separate churches.

Bengt Lundahl (1848–85) set up his school at Massawa in 1870, and began to receive a small number of students. Two years later, on Advent Sunday 1872, he celebrated a communion service for four of his pupils. He was aware of the significance of what he was doing and this simple act of worship was later recognised as the beginning of the Evangelical Church of Eritrea. His colleague, Lager, opposed this action and remained committed to the plan to reform the Orthodox rather than set up an Evangelical church. At almost exactly the same time a church was formed at nearby Imkullu, with steps in the direction of a formalised church taken at five-year intervals. The first Eucharist took place in December 1872; then a ministry was inaugurated in 1877, a council of elders in 1882 and then a standing committee to administer funds in 1887. By 1889 there were eighty-four communicants. In 1893 the Evangelical mission made a formal decision to set up an Evangelical Church alongside its mission to bring Reformation to the Orthodox.

The mission in Addis Ababa, under Carl Cederquist, avoided becoming a church for longer. Cederquist arrived in Addis in 1904, and carried out his first communion service after fifteen years in the capital. He formed a council of elders and so set up an Evangelical church in 1921. A year later the first Ethiopian pastor was appointed.[31] Swedish Lutherans were pragmatic. Their main concern was to bring reformation to Ethiopia. If their approach to Bible study could be contained within the Ethiopian Church and sympathetic clergy found to baptise and administer communion to Evangelical Christians, then they referred their converts to these. When this proved impossible they formed Evangelical communities.

The American missionaries of the Sudan Interior Mission had no interest in founding churches. They were a non-denominational society, and understood their mission as bringing the gospel – not setting up a church. The missionaries preached a firmly Christo-centric message, showing that all Scripture pointed to Christ, even if allegorical interpretation was required to show this. Bondage to the spirits was replaced by freedom in Christ, and believers were summoned out of the darkness of traditional religion into the light of Christ. They were known as 'Jesus people' and formed informal communities based around a prayer hall rather than a church. Later, in the twentieth century, these groups formed themselves into the Kale Hiwot or Word of Life Church. The SIM mission decided to retain a distinct identity. They did not become members of the new church but worked alongside it.[32]

At the end of almost a century of missionary endeavour there were small communities of Evangelical Christians, with schools and hospitals, present mainly in the south of the country. This patient work was brought to a halt by the expulsions under the Italians. At this point there were ten mission agencies working in Ethiopia, with a total of 181 foreign missionaries and an estimated 150 believers attached to each of the ten societies.[33] This small but significant foothold of evangelical gospel teaching was brought to a halt after the occupation of the country by the Italians in 1935.

Missionaries were expelled, not so much because the Italians were determined to spread Roman Catholicism but because the missionaries were suspected of sympathising with the enemies of Italy in the Second World War. In fact French Capuchin friars were expelled along with Swedish and American Protestant missionaries – all suspect because of their ethnic origin. Only the German Hermannsburg missionaries remained, being the majority of the eighteen foreign missionaries who remained – out of 180 in 1935. They left anxious that the work to which they had given so much effort would be weakened and come to an end.

When Haile Selassie returned in triumph to Addis Ababa in 1941, so did the missionaries. They had to wait before being given permission to return to their mission areas. There was long debate by the government over the place missionaries could have in the restored Ethiopia, which eventually resulted in the mission decree of 1944, with its distinction between 'closed' areas, where Orthodox were in the majority and missionary activities were strictly limited to medical and educational work with teaching of general recognised religious principles, and 'open' areas, which were the regions of the south and west where few people were Orthodox. As these discussions slowly continued, the missionaries had to wait impatiently in Addis Ababa, uncertain what they would find left of the small and scattered communities whom they had left behind three years earlier.

At last they received permission to go south. In 1943 Giles Playfair, the Director General of SIM, set out to see if anything was left of their mission work. He was unprepared for the experience which awaited him. He wrote reporting 'the mightiest movement of the spirit of God of which we have heard in our day is now taking place'. One group of believers in Wallamo had grown from seventeen baptised believers in 1935 up to forty-eight when the missionaries left in by 1937; but now, in 1943, the number had exploded to 10,000.[34] He reported that this pattern had repeated itself throughout their mission area. Instead of bringing decay and collapse, the departure of Western leaders had opened up the opportunity for a dramatic growth.

Out of these two mission initiatives the two largest Evangelical denominations were formed. The churches which grew out of the Swedish Lutheran missions were eventually constituted as a national church on 21 January 1959 with the title Ethiopian Evangelical

Church Mekane Yesus. Later, in 1971, the various Baptist churches which had arisen out of the SIM missions became Kale Hiwot Church.

It turned out that the expulsion of the missionaries by the Italians had the opposite effect from what they feared. Instead of weakening the Evangelical churches it gave new life as local leaders took over the guidance of their own communities. Independent communities had been formed. Now they had become national church movements.

A further wave of revival took place with the rise of Pentecostal churches. The roots of Pentecostal prayer groups lay not in the rural communities of the south, influenced by the preaching of Evangelicals, but among students and factory workers in the cities, who were young and often from Orthodox backgrounds. Movements of Pentecostals were begun and then spread in several cities, including Harar, Nazareth and Addis Ababa. Conferences were held in Hawasa in 1956 and in Addis Ababa in 1966. Out of these a local leadership took shape, and the Mulu Wengel or Full Gospel Believers Association was formed in 1968. Their slogan was 'The Gospel for Ethiopia by Ethiopians'. Foreign involvement was not welcomed nor was foreign money accepted.[35] Later further Pentecostal churches were founded, among them the Ghennet, or Paradise, Church and Hiwot Berhan, or Life and Light, Church in 1977 and 1978.

I talked to several people who described those early days to me. Almaz's story captured something of the searching, personal encounter and mutual support behind Pentecostal prayer groups. She was a student in Addis Ababa in the 1980s:

> I studied medicine at Addis Ababa University. It was the time of the Derg and I was reflecting on my ideals, and was searching for some kind of meaning. One day I was in a queue for the canteen, and another student who had always impressed me by her character was standing in front of me. I spontaneously spoke to her: 'What have you got that is special', I asked. The reply came back – 'Jesus.' That led me to join my new friend in a student Christian fellowship. It was not denominational, and we studied the Bible together secretly. It was Derg time and the churches had been closed. So I found faith.

Here a missionary, Rachel Weller, remembers the early days of Pentecostal revival in the Evangelical church:

> Kurt Holgren was teaching students, and they were reading Acts. The students asked if the things they were reading about at Pentecost still

> happened. Kurt suggested that we pray and find out. So they went home after the gathering and prayed and had similar experiences to the apostles at Pentecost. I'm not sure that they saw tongues of fire but they certainly spoke in tongues. This revival started in the 1970s, and caused controversy in the missionary community. It created an underground church which defied the authorities, many went to prison, and witnessed to the guards with boldness. They simply lived the Book of Acts. When the Derg was no more they suddenly emerged from the underground. Many of us found this hard to come to terms with – after all we Presbyterians were known as God's frozen chosen back home. But we could sense the energy.
>
> There was a Bethel Church in Addis. People said it was too big and called it a white elephant. But in the Derg time it was full. There were three services on a Sunday. People came in at the back and after the service they were asked to leave by the door at the front to make room for the next congregation, otherwise they would just stay to worship again.

Pentecostal Christians were persecuted both under Haile Selassie and the Derg regime. In spite – or because – of this they attracted an increasing number of young people, who were educated and intelligent, uncompromising in their hostility to the Communist government, and so were seen as offering a threat to the government. Throughout the closure of churches and imprisonment of believers, Mulu Wengel continued to grow. The church reports a total of 50,000 members in 1974 and then 500,000 in 2000. When the first church reopened in Addis Ababa after the fall of the Derg in 1991, 15,000 people flocked to the church on the first Sunday.[36] The largest church in Addis Ababa today is the Mulu Wengel building at Ketena Hulett, near the ring road. It can seat 5000 worshippers, and there are plans to replace the present building with a new larger church to accommodate the growing congregation.

TWO CHRISTIANITIES

The result of Evangelical evangelism is a second style of Christianity in Ethiopia. Alongside the Orthodox Church which has been identified with Ethiopia throughout its history as a state, is now a growing number of independent Evangelical churches. These vary from small churches drawing members from an ethnic group, locality or place, to the large Pentecostal churches with large numbers

FIGURE 9.3 The choir at the Mulu Wengel church at Ketena Hulett in Addis Ababa. The church seats 5000 worshippers and is being rebuilt to make it larger.

of members, to the main denominations with connections to worldwide Christian churches.

We have already described the mission style of Orthodox as 'integrative'. Its aim is to bring new members into the Christian church by integrating them into a new political and religious society. People become Christian by becoming part of Ethiopian society through acceptance of the language, the customs and the pattern of festivals and fasts, which forms the life of the Orthodox Church.

The Evangelical churches have a different method of mission. This can be described as the 'extractive' approach, and was the method of Western missionaries. The extractive style is based on an understanding that all people are part of one human family, with a shared common humanity, and so all are members together. This common humanity is prior to the kinship group or the culture of the particular society. Mission is 'extractive' since the convert is taken out of his social group and incorporated into a new form of universal Christian society.

While familiar in Western forms of mission, this was a departure from Orthodox approaches. The new Evangelical community formed by this extractive style of mission is ready to use whatever language was familiar to the convert – instead of incorporating them into society through learning a common shared language. It includes people of various ethnic groups without requiring them to adopt unfamiliar cultural forms. And it uses a form of worship and prayer which fits into local culture. The new 'extractive' approach uses ideas such as vocation, conversion and repentance, all of which suggest the need for a change of life, a leaving behind of what is familiar and emphasising that the church is new, discontinuous and different from existing society. These terms are not generally used in an integrative approach.[37]

The growth of Evangelical churches demonstrates the attraction of the communities formed through the extractive method. A student at the Trinity Theological College carried out a survey of a sample of young Orthodox who became Evangelical. His conclusions refer to the beginning of the twenty-first, rather than the nineteenth, century.[38] They suggest some of the factors which attract Ethiopians now, and which provide insights into the place of new churches in society and the social pressures on young people.

The researcher, Melkamu Mengesha, began by noting the integrative character of the Orthodox Church. The church is rooted in the life of the community and so has an integrating and unifying effect, while Evangelical churches, because of their individualistic approach to faith, have a divisive and disintegrating effect. Conversion from Orthodoxy to Evangelicalism is 'a complete and radical change [...] a sudden transition from a traditional indigenous community oriented solidarity based form of religion to one which is individually oriented closely linked to globalisation and which separates spirituality from everyday life'.

His survey indicates the reasons why people convert. He lists the reasons in order of significance, measured by the number of people giving them. He found that many converts from Orthodoxy to Evangelicalism were young, economically deprived, detached from their home communities and living in the cities. He lists the reasons they give for the attraction of Evangelical churches:

- The churches are well funded and offer good wages and financial support.
- The evangelisation techniques are intimate, and person to person.
- Faith and practice is flexible and accommodating, with little emphasis on dogmatic controversy. Faith is enough.
- People feel liberated from strict regulations over matters like fasting, and so it is more convenient for people who don't like strictness.
- The Evangelical churches use local languages.
- Minority ethnic groups associate the Orthodox Church with Amhara dominance.

The growth of Evangelical churches has added a new dimension to the religious composition of Ethiopia, which happened alongside the formation of the modern state and the incorporation of a wider mixture of ethnic groups. The two traditions of Christian faith are both well established in Ethiopia. They coexist with a blend of cooperation and suspicion.

CHAPTER 10

Survival and Growth: The Ethiopian Orthodox Tawehedo Church in the Modern World

HISTORY: THE LAST FIFTY YEARS

Emperor Haile Selassie returned to Ethiopia in 1941 after six years of exile. He was escorted by British troops who already had colonial interests in East Africa and hoped to extend their influence into Ethiopia. The emperor quickly asserted his independence and Ethiopia was declared a sovereign state in 1942. He strengthened his authority and personal control of government, with the power of the monarch affirmed in a new constitution promulgated in 1955. His intention was to use this power to develop Ethiopia into a modern state, but in spite of some progress, the country lagged behind its neighbours. Since schools and hospitals were concentrated in Addis Ababa and in centres of population, large parts of the country were overlooked. Haile Selassie was seen as increasingly reactionary and thought to be holding back progress, and so discontent grew. There was an attempted coup in December 1960, when Haile Selassie was out of the country, led by two brothers, Germame and Mengistu Neway, but this was overcome by loyal troops. The stifling of this revolt did not end the resistance. As discontent grew, a group of army officers went to the Emperor's Palace in Addis Ababa at 6.00 a.m. on 11 September 1974 and instructed Emperor Haile Selassie I to appear before them. As he stood in full army uniform they read a proclamation of deposition, bundled him into the back of a yellow Volkswagen Beetle car and drove him to army headquarters. Later he died, said to have been strangled by the new leader, Mengistu Haile Mariam. And so a line of Christian kings tracing its origins back to King Solomon came to an end.

A group of army officers ruled Ethiopia for the next seventeen years. The first four years were dominated by a vicious power struggle between two groups, MEISON or the all-Ethiopia Socialist Movement and the EPRP or Ethiopian People's Revolutionary Party. There was a shoot-out at the palace in 1977 followed by a period of brutal terror tactics in which Colonel Mengistu Haile Mariam eliminated his rivals. Government was run by a committee, called in Amharic the Derg, which was dominated by Mengistu. The government sought financial support and ideological legitimacy from the Soviet Union, and set up the Workers' Party of Ethiopia to carry out Communist policies. Development was centrally directed, and there was disruption caused by enforced movement of peoples in the villageisation process. A succession of bad harvests and disruption caused by repression led to the famines of 1984–5. The news reports about these had a powerful impact around the world and led to an outpouring of international aid and concern – and also established an image of Ethiopia as a country of starvation and destitution.

There was persistent war with several opponents, with Somalia and Eritrea from 1974 to 1978, and then again with a northern coalition of groups from Eritrea and Tigray from 1983, which spread to other groups to the west, east and south. The protracted fighting came to a sudden end when Russian military support for the Derg dried up following the collapse of European communism in 1990. In May 1991 Mengistu boarded a plane and went to Zimbabwe, where he still lives, and the guerrilla army from the north finally made their way into the capital city of Addis Ababa which they had fought for through campaigns lasting many years.

The new government of the EPRDF – the People's Revolutionary Democratic Front – has retained power since then. Its leader, Meles Zenawi, was 36 years old and a seasoned military commander when Addis Ababa fell in 1991. He was described by the then British Secretary of State for International Development, Clare Short, as 'the most intelligent politician I have met anywhere in the world'. His thesis at the Erasmus University at Amsterdam was entitled 'African Development: Dead Ends and New Beginnings'.[1] He has argued against Western democratic ideals, stating that effective development needs stable and continuing government, which is not subject to policy changes at the will of a fickle electorate. Generally the government has won elections with overwhelming majorities. An exception was the close and hotly contested election of 2005. After this there was a change of direction away from the policy of ethnic federalism which had devolved power to the regions and towards centrally driven developmental policies. Meles died in 2012, and leadership passed without major disruption to a Pentecostal Christian from the south, Hailemariam Dessalegn – the first leader of the state to come from a non-Semitic-speaking ethnic group. There has been consistent economic growth since 1995, speeding up from 2008 into double digits, although this has not reached into all sectors of the population and many economists have questioned the effectiveness of this recorded growth.

CHANGES IN RELIGIOUS LIFE

The Ethiopia of Haile Sellassie and his predecessors was defined as an empire with a Christian king, an Orthodox Church and the Amharic language. These three characteristics came to an abrupt end with the series of dramatic events which in a few months ended a political and religious arrangement which had persisted, although with modifications, since the conversion of King Ezana in the mid-fifth century. The destruction of the imperial state extended into the Orthodox Church.

The church lost its lands and income soon after the Derg took power. An early act of the new military government was to proclaim a Declaration of Socialism, on 20 December 1974, which set out the goal of public ownership of national resources. On 4 March 1975 Proclamation 31 nationalised all rural land, establishing peasants' associations to manage the process. Then on 26 July Proclamation 27 nationalised urban land, with new kebele associations as a counterpart to peasants' associations. Thus the landed wealth of the church, which traditionally owned a third of Ethiopia, was taken away.

The next major loss of power for the church came with the arrival of the new government in 1991. During the time of the Derg the Orthodox Church had held on to its position as the church of the nation, and the anti-religious policies of the regime were directed against Evangelical and Pentecostal churches – with the exception of the Mekane Yesus Church, whose development activities were useful to the regime. This changed in May 1991 when the new government issued the provisional constitution, with an article concerning the separation of state and religion. This declared that 'The Ethiopian state is a secular state; there shall be no state religion, and the state shall not interfere in religious affairs neither shall religion interfere in the affairs of the state.' With this the traditional pre-eminence of the Ethiopian Orthodox Church suffered a further blow, and it changed from being an integral part of the nation into one of several religious organisations.

A more gradual change throughout this period has been the establishment of a modern education system, with schools and colleges set up by successive governments. This led to a further diminishing in the influence for the Orthodox Church, which lost its role as the principal provider of education.

While the Orthodox Church was losing its traditional power and influence, the Evangelical and Pentecostal churches were enjoying a new freedom. State repression was relaxed, and the new churches benefitted from the new opportunities to recruit new members and spread to new places. There was a dramatic rise in the size of the Evangelical churches, from 5 per cent of the total population in 1984, to almost 20 per cent in 2007. Ethiopia was becoming a major force in world Evangelicalism. Up until 2000 it did not appear in the list of countries with large numbers of Evangelical adherents, but this was changing. In 2000 Ethiopia was seventh in the list of Evangelical countries with 13 million members of Protestant Churches. This figure is projected to increase to 49 million by 2050, making Ethiopia the country with the second largest number of Evangelical Christians, after the USA.[2] An inevitable consequence is a decline in the proportion of the population who declare their membership of the Orthodox Church.

It has been concluded from this growth in Evangelical faith that the Orthodox Church is in dramatic, even terminal, decline and that it belongs to a vanished age and is in need of reformation. It seems that people are leaving the Orthodox Church and joining new Evangelical and Pentecostal churches.

This is too simple a view. The last fifty years has been a time of radical and complex social change. A more careful examination of census figures shows a changing situation with a strong and vibrant faith showing itself in growth in membership across all faith groups, including Orthodox (Table 10.1). Several conclusions can be drawn from these figures.

The category of Evangelical churches includes a wide variety of churches and of forms of Christianity. Since 1991 there has been a huge growth in the number of church denominations. Under both Haile Sellassie and the Derg, the formation of new churches was restricted, and with the removal of this prohibition, it was inevitable that existing Evangelical churches would emerge from their underground existence, and that new churches would spring up. The new churches include traditional Bible-based Evangelical churches attached to worldwide Evangelical denominations, new independent Pentecostal churches and smaller churches drawing membership from specific ethnic groups. Since 1991 growth has continued. New churches have been introduced from Kenya, South Africa and the USA. Some pastors have left existing churches and formed their own communities. The more traditional national grouping of the Evangelical Churches Fellowship of Ethiopia has been supplemented by the Ethiopian Pastors Conference, bringing together Pentecostal churches. As well as these two main groupings, new churches, unattached to either, are appearing. In 2007, 628 different Pentecostal denominations were registered with the Ministry of Justice, of which the majority, 85 per cent, were not affiliated to either of the two main networks. These churches are generally known

TABLE 10.1 Membership of Ethiopian faith groups

	1984	1994	2007
Total population	*39 m*	*53.5 m*	*73.8 m*
Orthodox	54.02%	50.6%	43.5%
	(21 m)	(27 m)	(32 m)
Evangelical	5.48%	10.2%	18.6%
	(2.13 m)	(5.45 m)	(13.7 m)
Catholic	0.98%	0.9%	0.7%
Muslim	32.9%	32.8%	33.4%
	(12.8 m)	(17.5 m)	(24.6 m)
Traditional	5.79%	4.6%	2.6%
Non-religious	0.83%	0.9%	1.2%

in Ethiopia simply as Pente, a name which includes a wide variety of theologies, worship styles and ethnic allegiance. It is changing constantly. The growth in Evangelical churches is a sign of the arrival of modernism, the fluidity of society growth and access to many religious movements. Change is continuing. The growth of Evangelical churches is part of a movement which has taken place across Africa, rather than an internal shift away from traditional Orthodox faith.

The Ethiopian Orthodox Church is also growing. When considered as a proportion of population, the Orthodox community may seem to be in decline, but the total number of Orthodox Christians is increasing and increasing fast. The total membership of the Orthodox Church grew from 21 million in 1984, to 32 million in 2007 – a growth of over 50 per cent in twenty-three years. Few churches can claim a growth of this magnitude. One survey of worldwide Christian membership trends lists Orthodox countries in order of size of membership of their churches. In 1900 Ethiopia was seventh on the list with 2.7 million members; then by 1950 it had moved up to fourth place with 8.7 million. In 2000 it was second with 28 million, only exceeded by Russia which had 69 million. By 2050 it is projected that the Ethiopian Orthodox Church will have 56 million members, and will have outstripped Russia, which will have diminished to 32 million. In this case it will be the largest national Eastern Orthodox Church.[3]

The modern era is not a story of decline of the Orthodox Church but of adaptation to changing historical circumstances, a search for an understanding of its true identity and mission, and a continuing engagement with contemporary society. The Ethiopian Orthodox Church may have lost its head, its land and income, as well as its position in the nation and its role as national educator. Yet instead of declining and disappearing as might have been predicted, it has redefined itself and discovered a new strength and identity. It is vibrant and growing. Estimates provided by the Patriarchate in Addis Ababa suggest that there are 35,000 churches in Ethiopia, a figure which can be increased to nearer 50,000 if churches in the diaspora are added; 500,000 clergy, including priests, deacons and *däbtära*, and 10,000 church schools. This is a growing, not a declining, church.

The political changes in the Ethiopian state since 1974 have been dramatic yet need to be seen as part of a longer-term process of modernisation, which has been continuing since the mid-nineteenth century. In the life of the church there have been corresponding changes. While these are complex, interlocking and uneven, nevertheless they have – broadly speaking – been successive, with one following another, and bringing about change in a church for the modern age. These stages were, first, the struggle for an autonomous episcopate, independent of control from the Coptic Patriarchate in Cairo, which occupied the church from about 1850 to 1950. Then, second, was the setting up of a sustainable and democratic form of local church life, which happened especially in the time of the Derg. Then, third, came an emphasis on education and teaching, which has accelerated after the fall of the Derg. These three movements have helped the church to sustain its life and to grow in the changed social and political situation of modern Ethiopia.

AN INDEPENDENT EPISCOPACY

As Ethiopia grew in size and self-confidence, as a political entity, from the mid-nineteenth century, the requirement that there should be a single Egyptian archbishop was more and more restrictive and anomalous. In the following century people began to express their dissatisfaction and their desire to be free to order the life of their own church. Both lay intellectuals and clergy were indignant at the many scandals arising from the oddity of a large and thriving church being dependent on a leadership supplied from a foreign capital. An early expression of this resentment came in the press in April 1926. It was reported in the newspaper *Berhanena Selam* (Light and Peace) that forty boys had been drowned in the Blue Nile River as they were travelling to Addis Ababa to seek ordination as deacons. Further incidents were then uncovered amounting to at least seventy-seven deaths by drowning in that month alone. Other articles followed, pointing to further abuses. One correspondent described how he had counted 1777 boys aged between age seven and eight on the road south of Däbrä Marqos on their way to Addis Ababa to be made deacon. Another reported that he had seen many boys begging in the market place to raise the money needed to pay the charge levied by the abuna for ordination. As the century progressed, so protest grew. A church synod in 1945 received letters from clergy pointing to the anomalous situation whereby the Egyptian church with only

1 million members and subject to the pressure and control of an Islamic government should have power over a church in the Christian country of Ethiopia with a membership estimated at somewhere between 7 million and 20 million members, a number varying according to the estimates made by the correspondents.[4] These expressions of nationalist aspiration and frustration with dependence on a foreign church had been growing throughout the modern period, and had been a driving force behind the slow emancipation of the Ethiopian Church.

The end point towards which nationalists worked was an independent episcopate free of influence from Cairo, and an autocephalous church with a patriarch who was empowered to consecrate other archbishops. It took a long period of time and the painful negotiation of a succession of political obstacles to arrive at this outcome.

The first step had come in 1881 when Yohannes IV persuaded Patriarch Kyrillos V of Alexandria to send four bishops, instead of one, who were assigned to different regions of Ethiopia. But these were still Egyptian, and not all welcomed this development. When Abuna Luqas, the archbishop in Shewa died, a replacement was sent from Cairo, but the emperor Menelek did not receive him and sent him back to Egypt.[5] He preferred to rely on the archbishop of Shewa, Matéwos, who crowned Menelek as emperor, king of kings, at Entoto in 1889, and retained close contact with the emperor.

The next stage of the struggle took place after the death of Abuna Matéwos in 1926. Once again the Ethiopians tried to secure the appointment of an Ethiopian. Three years of negotiation followed which ended when a new Coptic patriarch, Yohannes XIX (1928–42), chose a new abuna, Qérelos. While the abuna was Egyptian, three Ethiopians were also consecrated as archbishops. One of these, Sawiros, was the *echägé*, and since he combined both positions, the two forms of leadership, episcopal and administrative, were united.

The final break with Cairo was precipitated by the Italian occupation. On the arrival of the Italians, abuna Qérelos retreated to his homeland of Egypt, and the Italians declared the Ethiopian Church to be independent. As with much that happened in this period, this declaration had a political context, since Egypt was under the influence of England, which was on the opposite side to Germany who was the ally of Italy in the Second World War. When Haile Selassie returned he restored the link with Egypt and abuna Qérelos was able to return. But now Qérelos was regarded as someone who had deserted the country in its time of need, and this weakened his position. Actual power over the church was in the hands of the *echägé* Täklä Giyorgis, who had been with Haile Selassie for some of his exile and accompanied him on his return to Ethiopia. Abuna Qérelos found his position untenable and once again retired to Egypt in 1942. On his death in 1947, a series of negotiations led to the consecration of Täklä Giyorgis as archbishop Baselyos in 1951, which was a major step towards an independent episcopacy, but he still had to be consecrated in Cairo, and other bishops still had to be approved by the Coptic patriarch. At last, in 1959, after further negotiation and a change of Patriarch in Cairo, Baselyos became the first Ethiopian Patriarch of Ethiopia. Since 342 the patriarch of the Ethiopian Church had been a foreigner – and now after 1600 years the head of the church had been born in the country over which he presided.

The church was now defined as autocephalous, and so fully independent with no need to seek approval from Cairo for episcopal appointments.[6] Baselyos retained the title and position of *echägé*, and combined the sacramental and the administrative leadership of the church. Alongside this process of slow emancipation, the number of other bishops gradually increased, and new dioceses were set up in Ethiopia and overseas. In 2002 there were forty-six bishops.

While the church might have become independent of Egypt it had not escaped state control. In 1951 a Church Assembly met to choose the Archbishop, following the death of the Egyptian Qérelos four years earlier. Of the 105 electors only thirty-nine were appointed by the church, and the other sixty-six were lay members of the government. Through this composition of the assembly the emperor kept his influence in the choice of the first Ethiopian abuna. State intervention continued under the Derg. Opponents of the regime were purged, and the wave of accusations reached the Patriarchate. Téwofilos was accused of corruption and supporting counter-revolutionary movements. He was deposed in February 1976 and executed three years later. New elections were held in which over 1000 people took part. A late candidate was a peasant monk, abba Melaku Wolde Mika'el, from the south who happened to be in Addis Ababa on business and was detained by the authorities. Although an unlikely choice, he was an anti-establishment candidate and so preferred by the government to a candidate from among the bishops. He found himself elevated to become abuna Täklä Haymonot.

After his death in 1988, a new patriarch, Märqoréwos, who was a supporter of the Communist Derg government, was chosen. He survived for three years until the new government ousted the Derg. He, in turn, was forced to abdicate and placed under house arrest. A new patriarch was elected in 1992. Abba Gäbrä Medhin, who became Patriarch Pawlos, was a Tigrayan, born in Adwa, who studied in America, was imprisoned by the Derg and then fled to America again, from where he was summoned to take up the position of patriarch. The new government presented this appointment as a restoration of the rightful succession of patriarchs following the usurpations of Täklä Haymonot and Märqoréwos. Meanwhile Märqoréwos had been helped by supporters to escape from Ethiopia to Kenya in 1993 and then travelled to the USA in 1997. Here he set up a rival hierarchy of bishops to form a 'Legal Holy Synod in Exile'. It claims over sixty churches in North America and other diaspora communities. In response the Patriarchate in Addis Ababa works hard to form links with churches outside Ethiopia. This schism continues.[7]

In a surprising turn of events the two leaders of church and state, both from the small town of Adwa, Pawlos and Meles, died in the same week at the end of August 2012. While the next prime minister, Hailemariam Dessalegn, was a Protestant from the south, thus setting a new trend, the new patriarch, Mathias, was a figure of continuity. He was born in Tigray like his predecessor and had lived in Jerusalem and America since 1978, where he had been associated with opposition to the Derg.

A further consequence of the connection between church and state is provided by the separation of the church in Eritrea. After Eritrea became independent of Ethiopia, the church was granted autocephaly in 1994, and abuna Philipos was consecrated. A third patriarch, abuna Antonios, was enthroned in 2004. He was known for his energetic reform of church institutions and his readiness to resist government interference. As a result he was deposed in 2006, and detained either in a remote monastery, according to some sources, or in a darkened room in Asmara, according to others. Patriarch Dioskoros replaced him in May 2007. This church claims the membership of approximately half of the population of Eritrea, yet is divided between the supporters of two patriarchs, and there are reports of imprisonments and of priests required to serve for long periods in the army, leading to the closure of churches.

While the communist government of the Derg and the present government of the EPRDF affirm secular principles, the connection between state and church is maintained. The state has continued to show its concern to ensure a loyal and supportive head of the church. Patriarchs are chosen who are acceptable to the government of the day, and this influences other appointments.

The involvement of government in church life and influence in ecclesiastical appointments are consequences of the close historic connection of church and state. The church is deeply rooted in the structures of society and cannot be easily extracted from political involvement and hence state influence.

The phrase 'the Great Tradition' has been used to capture this religious character of Ethiopian national identity. The idea of this great tradition describes a church which is a mixture of social customs and ideals, which have grown up in society, rather than a community with personal faith commitments. While the growth of ethnic federalism has made the 'great tradition' anachronistic, the social character of Christian faith remains. Commentators have tried to capture the elusive spirit of this religious nationalism. For example: 'it was neither a single powerful church dignitary nor the priests as a class who had power over the state [...] but rather the spirit of tradition – the church as the embodiment of Ethiopian culture – that transcended church and politics'; or 'Any Ethiopian institution tends to crumble away on close approach and the church is no exception, it may be best defined in terms of the prevalence of certain attitudes and the influence of certain individuals which are closely bound up with Orthodox Christianity.'[8] The practice and culture of the church have formed Ethiopian society and are inextricably a part of it. The church remains rooted in society.

A CHURCH OF THE PEOPLE

More bishops meant that the church could be organised differently. When there was a single archbishop, his role had been sacramental, and his main function had been to ordain clergy and consecrate tabots. As the number of bishops increased, the possibility of a more active involvement in the running of the church opened. Dioceses were formed.

Yohannes IV had sent his four bishops to the main regions of Ethiopia: Tigre, Shewa, Gojjam and Begemder. As the number of bishops grew so their geographical distribution became more widespread, with bishops and their residences scattered more evenly around the country. It was a new experience for churches to discover that they were part of a diocese and had a bishop to care for them, and there was, at first, little motivation for them to be obedient to the bishop. Local churches had grown up in a haphazard way. Often they had been given lands by the king or by members of the local nobility, named *balabet*, and so had their own property and income. Personal loyalties had built up around churches so that a community of worshippers formed, with many coming from a wide area on the monthly feast day of the church. In the case of churches which were royal foundations, the king appointed the clergy. Many monasteries, most notably Däbrä Libanos, also had a network of churches which were dependent on them. As a result, churches looked to a mixture of different places for their support and their guidance. They did not have a sense of loyalty to the bishop or to the diocese, but to those who had provided land and resources, or to the communities who supported them. The bishop was a remote figure who had little impact on daily life.

The second Patriarch of Ethiopia, Téwofilos, tried to bring order to the new dioceses. He issued a decree in 1972 setting up parish councils which would be under the authority of the bishop, would be composed of elected members and would prepare a budget to be approved by the bishop. For the first time there was a legal definition of a parish. But there was little reason for churches to accept the decree, and its ineffectiveness is shown by the need to reissue it in 1978 and 1981.[9]

This changed with the arrival of the Derg. The churches lost their lands and their income, and so a new form of government and a new source of income became urgently needed. As compensation for the loss of historic landed income the Derg allotted an annual sum of 5 million birr to the church, to be administered by the bishops. While the sum was small in comparison to what had been lost, it strengthened the influence of the bishops who controlled the allocation of these funds. A General Assembly of Parish Councils was arranged by the Patriarchate in June 1983, and this led to an effective and widespread implementation of parish councils.[10]

The formation of parish councils was part of a democratisation process which affected all parts of society. Alongside the military grasp of power, there had been popular uprisings of poor against rich, and this contributed to the removal of the previous holders of power. The centres of protest were the university and the colleges, the army and factories. The day before Haile Selassie was removed, state television showed a version of an earlier BBC film showing the extent of the famine in the north of the country, and another showing the luxurious lifestyle of the emperor. This careful piece of programming aggravated the hostility against the wealth of the emperor and nobility, and fuelled the passions of the first stages of the revolution. In the early days of the military government, in April 1974, 100,000 Muslims, with support from some Christians came out on the streets to demonstrate in favour of equality. There were protests from clergy in many areas against the opulent lifestyle of bishops, and these led to demands for higher salaries for clergy. Other workers demanded better pay and conditions, which caused difficulties for some churches. Evangelical churches had set up hospitals and schools and found themselves unable to respond to workers' demands. In 1977, Evangelical missionaries from SIM closed one of their largest hospitals, in Sheshamane, not because of direct political pressure but because they could not afford to meet the demands from workers, which were supported by the courts.[11]

As power shifted away from the previous holders to new parts of society, so the nature of church influence changed. Traditionally the church was thought to own a third of the land, and this was lost when land in both rural areas and the city was nationalised in March and July 1975. The use of land was entrusted to the administration of peasants' associations to allocate according to clear guidelines.[12] While this led to a loss of income, the peasants' associations were often more sympathetic to demands for new churches than the landlords of the Haile Sellassie era had been. Often clergy were chairmen and secretaries of the peasants' associations, and their identification with the farmers led to a more popular power base for the church.

In the year after the nationalisation of land, in February 1976, Patriarch Téwofilos was removed, after being accused of numerous crimes including collaboration with the Italians and the misappropriation of funds. He was imprisoned and later executed in 1979. The new patriarch Täklä Haymonot, as we noted earlier, was an unlikely candidate. He did not come from a traditional Orthodox area but from the south, and was an ordinary monk, with no formal education, no experience of church administration or government, and who followed a simple lifestyle. His election opened the way to a dismantling of the power of bishops. Under the new patriarch, many of the bishops who had been appointed with the approval of the emperor were retired or transferred to a diocese where they would have less influence.[13]

Some commentators have criticised Täklä Haymonot for his ignorance and naivety. But he was also much loved and turned out to be a leader for the times. He followed a simple and ascetic lifestyle. He seldom wore shoes and donated his salary to various development or church projects, and while he was not able to oppose government directives over the removal of former bishops, he was able to encourage and inspire a growth in popular support of the church. Parish councils became more effective and many new churches were built. He appealed to the new peasants' associations who already sympathised with the church, and so supported the programme of church-building. It is difficult to obtain accurate statistics but records of Patriarch Täklä Haymonot show that during his time as patriarch there were 764 churches built, five new monasteries set up, and 216 churches renovated. By 1986 over 13,000 parish councils were in existence.[14] The separation of the church from the state and the removal of its money and political power was a time of loss and difficulty but also turned out to be a time of freedom and liberation. Support for the church was taken on by local communities and congregations.

ASSOCIATIONS

There is a strong tradition of community association and mutual support within Ethiopian society. People come together in community associations for various reasons, and many associations are connected with churches. They have become a source of lay involvement and new initiative in the development of church life.

Church associations are called *mahabers*, which means unity or togetherness, and take various forms. A *mahaber* could be a monastic community but now is more likely to be a group that is connected to a local church. The *mahaber* might be dedicated to the commemoration of Mary or of a saint or a martyr. Members meet together for a shared meal on the monthly celebration of the saint, and often invite others to join them. These regular shared meals form a focus for the life of a church community as well as providing a means of mutual support for members and care for the poor.[15]

The *mahaber* tradition provided the opportunity for a popular and influential lay movement within the life of the church. The loose forms of church government over many centuries have allowed the formation of associations. These can be described as spaces within the church, outside the control of the hierarchy, which then encouraged growth of lay initiatives and movements which have helped to shape

FIGURE 10.1 This *mahaber* is attached to a church in Addis Ababa. It meets each month. These groups are an important focus of parish life.

a modern church. The importance of *mahabers* grew after the beginning of the Derg government, since when they have grown in number, size and range of activities.

An early lay movement was the Haymonote Abaw Students Association, formed in November 1957. Its founding membership was drawn from the students of three colleges in Addis Ababa. Haile Selassie was the patron, and Abuna Téwofilos was the chairman. It was set up in reaction to the new radical student groups which opposed the emperor, attacked the church as outdated and obscurantist, and gave itself the aim of developing a mixture of traditional faith and modern culture. It became involved in development issues such as housing and health, and attracted several thousand members. Membership had declined by the time that the Derg took power and its activities had reduced. Attempts to reconstitute it after the fall of the Derg failed, as new groups developed to take its place.[16]

Its place in the active ministry of the student community was taken by Mahabere Kiddusan, the Community of the Saints, which was formed in 1991 at the end of the period of the Derg. Students who were sent by the government to Belate military training camp decided to meet together as an association to serve the church. After the government fell, they returned to their colleges where they continued their commitment to the church. Other associations joined, and in 1992 Mahabere Kiddusan was recognised by the Patriarchate and was incorporated into the new Sunday School Department. It has grown dramatically since then, and now has many thousands of members. It draws its membership from university students, who remain members through their lives. These pay 2 per cent of their income to the association, make annual visits to a monastery for spiritual direction, and provide professional services to the association free of charge. The central office is Addis Ababa in an eight-storey building opposite the entrance to the Patriarchate.

Mahabere Kiddusan has become an effective agency of renewal in the church, supporting monasteries and traditional church schools, publishing three journals and a large selection of books in various languages, and broadcasting on radio and television. There is also a research section which has published accounts of plans by Evangelicals, Muslims and groups within the Orthodox Church to infiltrate, subvert and attack the Orthodox Church and the Ethiopian

FIGURE 10.2 The main offices of Mahabere Kiddusan in Addis Ababa.

state. Their findings have contributed to an atmosphere of suspicion and distrust between religious groups. Another department checks all publication of the association to avoid any elements of error.

Mahabere Kiddusan describes itself as combining a traditional approach to faith with a modern form of presentation. It is doctrinally and spiritually conservative. This influences not only the policy and strategy of the church as it seeks to adjust to a changing society, but also the nature and character of the emerging style of church life. While it is supported by some bishops, others are concerned at the extent of its power and influence.

A member of Mahabere Kiddusan summarised the work of the association as having three elements:

> First – the survival of church traditions in the monasteries and church schools. Projects include new buildings at several churches and traditional schools, with one building at a leading school in Gondar, Ba'ata, being constructed with a budget of 5 million birr. Then there's a fund of 1.5 million birr for selected traditional teachers. And in some schools grants of 70 birr a month to a number of pupils and 500 birr pcm for teachers.

Secondly – monasteries. These preserve the rich culture. Many places are remote and beyond the reach of the bishops. Mahabere Kiddusan is providing food, and setting up projects to build working communities with agricultural projects. All this aims to build more modern styles of management.

Third – there's work in evangelistic work in society at large. Mahabere Kiddusan wants to encourage financial probity, anti corruption, and the spread of literacy.[17]

Something of the fervour and freshness of the movement is conveyed in this recollection by a founding member of the society.[18]

Mahabere Kiddusan was founded in 1991 at a military camp. In fact I was there at its founding. I was a freshman at Addis Ababa University and had completed my first semester. Then I was sent to the military camp. There were 10,000 students sent by the Derg to this camp, called Belate, in Sidamo in the south of the country, to be trained to fight the EPRDF. We used to keep the festivals together. On Ginbot 1 we gathered in a big hall and founded Mahabere Kiddusan.[19] Only a few days later Addis Ababa fell to the EPRDF – on Ginbot 20. We students were told to leave the camp on Ginbot 19. We set out on foot. Some went to Kenya. I stayed at Hawasa for ten days, and then was brought to Addis Ababa by the Red Cross on Ginbot 27. I went to stay with my family. Some of my friends went back to their home village. Later the university reopened.

Our central building in Addis Ababa is a mechanism by which we can unite people, and so change the world. The idea for the building started nine years ago. Our association applied for land for the building. Then Abuna Pawlos gave us permission to build inside the Patriarchate compound. But there were some tensions and hidden conflicts between MK and some people in the church. So we bought a rented house on our present site. The members of MK committed one month's salary a year for three years to provide funds to build our new offices. All the costs of the building were met by members of MK. For example the third floor was paid for by members from USA and the fourth floor by members from Europe. The professionals all gave their time free of charge. One construction company gave us use of a bulldozer free of charge – worth thousands of birr.

An example of what we do is a formal school owned by MK. It's been a struggle. In the first year we lost 40,000 birr, but then things improved. We have one main mission, which is ethical. We want to introduce children to high ethical standards. Our children behave differently from children in other schools. The school is at present in

> a rented house. We want to buy the school outright which will cost 24 million birr. We'll do it by selling shares in the school to our members.
>
> We are planning big. We have to.

CHURCH EDUCATION

The church education system has been the source of learning and literacy for the people of Ethiopia throughout its history. The demanding syllabus which we described earlier fostered a disciplined and intelligent class of scholars. These provided teachers for local communities, and administrative officials for the government. It enabled social mobility since education was open to all, and it provided an opportunity for social advancement for even the poorest in society.

Now the future of church schools is threatened by the spread of modern schools. As modern education extends and schools are set up in all areas, children are obliged to attend at least primary schools. These reduce the attractiveness of church schools since they open another path to educational achievement. Poverty in rural societies provides a further challenge for the schools, and makes it harder to fund the teachers. Teachers at church schools receive small salaries – typically £50 a month. And, as living conditions become harder, so Christian households are less able to provide food and students often go hungry.[20]

Church schools are responding to this in various ways. Boys often attend church schools first, and when they have completed parts of this education go on to attend modern schools. Some church schools provide teaching at times to fit in with modern schools – which usually teach on a shift system with pupils attending either in the morning or afternoon, thus leaving time in the day for attending church schools. Sometimes boys spend the summer holidays at a centre of church education. Some schools provide facilities for girls. Projects are being set up to fund new buildings or income generation for the schools.

There are also Sunday Schools in many churches. The Sunday School movement can be traced back to 1951 when two Egyptian teachers working at Selassie Theological College trained students to become Sunday School teachers, going to churches to teach young people after the *qeddasé* had finished.[21] This approach grew – with the church of Mizkaye Hizunan Mehdane Alem in north Addis Ababa becoming a centre for education and training from 1957 onwards. Both girls and boys attend teaching sessions at weekends and sometimes on weekday evenings. These follow a three-year syllabus covering a variety of biblical, liturgical and other subjects. Most teaching is done by students with those who have completed their study there and then become teachers of the next generation. The Sunday School Department, which was founded in 1971, states that there are 10 million young people connected with the Sunday School movement with 4 million actively involved.[22]

The vigour of the Sunday Schools became clear to me as a result of a visit to one school at the outskirts of Addis Ababa. There is an ambitious education programme at the church of St Peter and St Paul in western Addis Ababa. The school is called the Fre Haymonot, or Fruit of Faith, Spiritual School. One of the teachers invited me to visit the school. We met on a Friday afternoon and set off in a taxi. When we arrived we went to an upstairs hall. There were about 450 students who all came from one high school where he used to teach. This group meets from 3.00 to 5.00 p.m. several days a week. There is also a morning shift of similar numbers, and there are groups from other high schools on other days. They teach a three-year syllabus and the teaching is done by young graduates of the school. When I went, there was a lecture by a young man of about eighteen years of age, with the subject of the background to the Gospels and the differences between the evangelists' accounts. The school students also arrange programmes for the public. There's a monthly programme at the church for taxi drivers. Sunday School members who are taxi drivers invite other taxi drivers. They explain church tradition. Faith is 'stolen' (they mean caught or absorbed) by others. It's this approach rather than an active evangelisation which is effective in Orthodox churches.

Alongside Sunday Schools there is a growing practice of preaching at the 'fifth hour services' or *Meriha Gibur*. Many larger churches arrange daily services of preaching in the early evening, often led by theological students. In attending many of these, I have been struck by the confidence of the preachers, often young men in their early twenties, the clarity of the preaching and the large numbers attending, often several hundred.

The church is also concerned to support the traditional schools of theological study, using oral methods to teach the traditional disciplines of *zema, qené* and *aquaquam*. There are signs of revival here too. Donald Levine reports that when visiting Gondar, a centre of church education, he found less than a hundred students at the church schools. The number has increased consistently, with the numbers now exceeding 3000 students in around fifty schools.[23] As well as the increase in numbers, the schools are approaching the challenge of maintaining these traditional schools in various ways. The important centre of education in Gondar at Ba'ata is building a large new building to house 200 students in modern conditions, a project funded by Mahabere Kiddusan; other schools are setting up agricultural projects to improve nutrition; a new school at Qusquam is located near the medical training school and encourages students to attend evening classes in theology after their studies at the medical school are over for the day. Another major centre at Däbrä Libanos receives students from government schools during the holiday periods, with visitors reporting that over 2000 young people attend for these short courses. Some schools are arranging facilities for girls as well as boys.

Some educationalists are looking to church schools to develop a role in providing effective education. Attendance at government schools is increasing, and the millennium development goal of providing all children with the opportunity to attend primary school is well on the way to being achieved. However, conditions in many schools, while improving, remain poor and educational standards low. While the government provides buildings and teachers, they provide only minimal funds for teaching materials, which pupils have to pay for. Many would argue that a good education system needs strong church schools, with their tried-and-tested methods and strong educational outcomes, to flourish alongside government schools.

Providing clear and thorough teaching is essential to Orthodox mission and ministry. The church does not have a strong tradition of evangelisation, but does try to educate its members. So the renewal of traditional education and provision of new forms is a key part of the present mission of the church.

TADISO: AN ALTERNATIVE FORM OF RENEWAL

Mahabere Kiddusan and other groups like it root their mission work in the historical traditions of the Orthodox Church, supporting monasteries and traditional schools as part of the tradition of faith which has grown and flourished in Ethiopia. Other groups have followed a different approach, and have set out to reform the church on biblical principles, as understood by Evangelical teaching. There is a variety of approaches referred to by the general title of *tadiso* or renewal, or, more succinctly, Ortho-Pente. These groups claim that 250,000 people supported this movement in 1998.

Supporters of the Tadiso or renewal movement look to the various reform movements in the history of the church, and claim that there is a long tradition of protest and radical opposition to the authorities of the church. They point to the moral teaching of Bäsalotä Mikael and the monks, the Stephanite monks of the fifteenth century, which, supporters of Tadiso point out, predate the European Reformation, and argue that there have always been attempts to renew and reform the church, and they stand in this tradition of reform. The more immediate starting point for the Tadiso movement was the arrival of Western Evangelical missionaries and their preaching of a reformed Evangelical style of Christianity. Tadiso followers discovered that the teaching of the Evangelicals could be held within the Orthodox Church and they discovered a coherence between the two forms of faith. They set out to bring a new reformation to the church as they read the Bible and discussed its teaching. This process gained momentum as students learnt and discussed within the Sunday School movement. Some reformers trace the origin of the present-day Tadiso to the teaching and evangelism of Haymonote Abaw student fellowship.

The reform groups developed at the same time as and alongside more traditional movements such as Mahabere Kiddusan. These were set up in the later years of the Derg and have grown since then. Commentators discern three different approaches adopted by Tadiso groups. Some consider themselves loyal members of the Orthodox Church, and seek a reformation by studying the Bible, teaching in Sunday Schools or preaching at churches. They consider that the approach of Evangelical teaching is consistent with the writings of Orthodox Church fathers. A leader of this tendency was Aläqa Meseret Sibhat Leab. He was born in 1921 in Aksum and studied in traditional Orthodox church schools. He travelled to Addis Ababa where he was influenced by Evangelical and reform groups, and was invited to teach at the Mekane Yesus seminary of the Evangelical

Church. He remained at the seminary for thirty years, teaching and writing. He founded the Mahabere Bkur, community of the firstborn, and set up the journal *Chora* in order to express its views.

Other reformers adopted a more radical position, avoiding membership of any church denomination, and considering the church comes into being whenever the Bible is preached and responded to. An influential figure in this Bible-truth Ministry was a founding member of Mahabere Kiddusan called Seyoum Yami, who after his time as a student in Ethiopia went on to further study in Germany. He became converted to an Evangelical faith and returned to Ethiopia with a mission to reform all churches according to an exclusively biblical message.[24]

A third group of Tadiso reformers felt increasingly alienated from the Orthodox Church and left to found new church groups – of which various Ammanuel churches are examples.[25]

Tadiso is controversial within the Orthodox Church. Its members and supporters consider that it is carrying on the tradition of reform and renewal which has been a part of the history and the tradition of the church. They are aware of the need to be faithful to the gospel message, and to oppose corrupt or superstitious intrusions into the gospel message of the church. They are not surprised that they, like other earlier reformers in history, are persecuted, and even excommunicated. This, they say, is the fate of the true prophet.

For others, who follow traditional Orthodox teaching, Tadiso subverts and undermines the church. It rests on study of the Bible rather than church tradition. This leads to the view that Tadiso claims to be Orthodox but teaches Protestantism. It is a new kind of proselytism aimed at converting the church rather than individuals. Several Tadiso organisations have been condemned by the synod of bishops. These include Mahabere Bkur, or Association of the Firstborn, and its journal *Chora*. Critics claim that *Chora* places icons and Ge'ez texts on the front cover but inside attacks Orthodoxy. The growth of Tadiso groups raises the question of identity. Tadiso can be seen as a legitimate form of Orthodox church life, seeking to renew the church; or as a different form of Christian faith which should be recognised as a different church and its adherents encouraged to find a place outside Orthodoxy. The synod of bishops has excommunicated Tadiso groups, showing the view of the church that traditional forms of worship and practice should be affirmed and Evangelical influence rejected.

A DISPUTED LANDSCAPE

The new openness to churches and faiths has changed the religious climate of Ethiopia. Competition has developed between faiths. This has been described by the anthropologist Tom Boylston as a 'religious market place', by which he means that different communities are seeking to occupy public space, often literally.[26]

The struggle shows itself in many ways – in icons and pictures placed in shops, taxis and other spaces, in the use of loudspeakers to project both the Islamic call to prayer, and Orthodox preaching and liturgies over a wide space, in the growing numbers attending mass rallies and celebrations.

Above all it shows itself in the building of mosques and churches. Boylston cites the experience of his project area of the Zege

FIGURE 10.3 The small Muslim community in the strongly Christian area of Zege has ensured that its new mosque is the tallest building in the area.

FIGURE 10.4 The local community has built this new church of Mika'el in a prominent position in the hills to the north of Addis Ababa. The committee chair stands in front of it.

peninsula. This is a traditionally Christian area, with seven monasteries and churches stretched along the shore of lake Tana. There are 10,000 inhabitants of which a small proportion are Muslim, yet this community has constructed a large mosque in the centre of Afaf, the market town of Zege, the tallest building in the town and dominating the landscape. The response of the local Christian population has been tolerant, accepting the freedom of the Muslim community to build a mosque and worship, even in this historic Christian area. However, they have also set in place a building programme and have constructed two new churches in strategic locations on the peninsula.

In my own visits to Addis Ababa I often attend the church in an area to the north of the city called Jesus *and arba*, or Jesus 41, since that's the number on the bus route which goes to it. Here there is a large church dedicated to Gännäta Jesus or the paradise of Jesus. Next to it in the same compound is a second new church dedicated to Maryam since it is a part of faith that Jesus and Mary his mother belong together. A few minutes' walk away, on top of the hill overlooking the town, there is a small church of St Michael, and here a large new basilica-style church is nearing completion. The motivation for this is clearly not the pastoral needs of the community, already well served by the two churches of Gännäta Jesus and Maryam. But since the hill dominates the north of the city, it is important that this space is consecrated by a church which asserts the spiritual power and presence of the Orthodox Church, asserting the sacredness and identity of the landscape, and showing to all that this is a Christian place.

The years since 1991 have been a time of development and growth for the faith communities of Ethiopia. They have also been years of political, social and economic change. We can be sure that change will continue, in unexpected and radical form. The vitality and tenacity of the Church in Ethiopia in adapting to the changes and challenges of the past gives hope for the future.

CONCLUSION

A Traditional African Church

During the last century Christianity has become the dominant faith in sub-Saharan Africa. Table C.1 shows the pattern of growth, especially in the period following independence.[1]

This has taken many by surprise. A little over a century ago, in 1910, the World Missionary Conference met in Edinburgh in 1910. It brought together Christians from around the world with a strong representation from East Asia, especially China and Japan. Honorary doctorates were distributed to the leaders of these churches, to recognise their potential leadership in world Christianity. No one from Africa was invited.

Yet as the century continued the growth of African Christianity gathered pace. The phenomenon we have already noted with the growth of Evangelical Christianity in Ethiopia after the withdrawal of Western missionaries was reproduced across the continent. It was part of a realignment of the church with a shift of emphasis away from a Christendom with its centre in Europe, to a world Christianity, which spread in Africa, Latin America and East Asia.

In an Africa where new states were being formed in place of a disintegrating European imperialism, Ethiopia's tenaciously held independence, through victory at the battle of Adwa in 1896, and then restoration of the monarchy after the short-lived Italian occupation during the Second World War, made it into a model and example for new nations achieving independence.

New churches, as well as new states, looked to Ethiopia. They remembered the ringing phrases of the Old Testament prophecies,

TABLE C.1 Global patterns of Christian growth, in millions

	1900	1970	1980	2000
World population	1619	3610	4373	6250
Christian population	558	1216	1432	2019
Christians in Africa	8.7	115.9	164.5	323.9
Christians in Europe	273	397	403	555

especially that promise contained in Psalm 68.31 concerning the faithfulness of Ethiopia, 'which will lift up – or stretch out – its hands to God'. This claimed a direct descent from the faith of the Old Testament, which entered Africa from Israel and was not mediated through the churches of Europe. When African Christians in South Africa set up new churches independent of Western colonial forms of Christianity, they called themselves Ethiopian. The first founder of an Ethiopian Church was Mangena Mukone in 1892. Other African church leaders chose names which recalled the roots of African Christianity in Ethiopia. Among the churches of South Africa were the Ethiopian Star Church of God, the Ethiopia Church of Abyssinia and the Coptic Ethiopian Church Orthodox of Abyssinia. Figures appeared in South Africa such as 'His Royal Highness Ras Michael Sultan D [...] of the Ethiopian Imperial Delegation Office, organising unity between South Africa and Abyssinian Chiefs'. However, there was no Abyssinian delegation in South Africa.[2]

Ethiopia also caught the attention of African Americans. The Jamaican printer who founded the Universal Negro Improvement Association in 1914, Marcus Garvey, used Ethiopia as a rallying call to evoke an image of Africa and to express a longing for return. He wanted Africans to see themselves as made in God's image, and God as a model for them. He wanted them to see 'God through the spectacles of Ethiopia'. Later, one of his disciples, Arnold Josiah Ford, settled in Ethiopia and composed the 'Universal Ethiopian Anthem' in 1930. This was the year in which Ras Tafari Makonnen was crowned as Haile Sellassie emperor of Ethiopia, 'conquering lion of the tribe of Judah, elect of God and the light of the world'.[3]

The new Ethiopian Churches of South Africa and the religious movements of the Caribbean did not grow as a result of direct contact with the churches of Ethiopia. Missionary evangelisation by the Ethiopian Church came later. It was not until 1940 that an Ethiopian Orthodox Church was set up in the Sudan. Then there was a mission led by Abuna Yesehaq to South Africa in 1990 in the course of which he ordained four priests and baptised several thousand people, and new parishes in Kenya, Ghana, Nigeria and Uganda were established in the 1990s. But these are recent and comparatively modest movements of evangelisation.[4]

The evocative looking towards Ethiopia arose not from communication in the present but from a sense of the importance of the past. New churches were aware of the place of Ethiopia in the Bible with its selection of references placing it in the purposes of God. They also recognised the long presence of the Christian church in Ethiopia and Egypt, the 'unbroken historical continuity of the churches of Egypt and Ethiopia of today and the ancient world [...] [churches which had witnessed] a Christianity that was established in Africa not only before the white people came, but before Islam came'.[5]

The historian Adrian Hastings described the growth of African Christianity in the period of nationalism. He ended his study with the suggestion that the roots of African churches should be looked for in Ethiopia, rather than in Europe. He calls this 'village' Christianity, and wonders if this, rather than the Christianity of Rome, Geneva or Canterbury, is the model which lies behind the Christianity of Africa. Ethiopia, he wrote, nurtured

> a form of Christianity which seems almost archetypal in a number of important ways for the rest of the continent [...] 'village' Christianity in contrast to 'mission' Christianity; inclusivist rather than exclusivist; mass rather than elite; community generating structure rather than structure generating community; yet never without structure; never without its lines of demarcation, even on occasion exclusivist. It is this model of historic Ethiopia which increasingly prevails: village Christianity with very little superstructure had been present all along together with much symbolic ritual now making its way right across the continent.[6]

He ends his story at that point and does not provide further description of this Ethiopian village Christianity. The Christian faith of over 300 million people living within a vast continent is too diverse to be traced back to a single origin. The large Pentecostal churches of the big cities are more likely to find their inspiration in communities in the USA or Canada than in the villages of Ethiopia. It was from Zion Illinois that African Zionist churches take their title rather than the Zion in Jerusalem. African Christianity has taken many shapes as it has spread across the country.

Hastings's remarks remind us of the statement that the Ethiopian Church is the only pre-colonial Christian Church of sub-Saharan Africa. It developed a form of faith which arrived in the early centuries of the Christian era and grew on African soil. It provides a historic link between the churches of contemporary Africa with the earliest period of Christian history. This history diverged at an early date from that of the rest of the Christian world so that it has taken its own distinctive shape.

The observations made in this study show what shape the faith of Christ took as it was introduced and took root on the continent of Africa. It began at the place where the religious ideas of the Old Testament and wider Semitic world encountered the worldview of Africa. It was a community which was conscious of its relationship with the God of the Old Testament as well as the New, of the continuity between Old and New Testaments, and the place of social regulations, including over diet, in giving structure to that society. It was one community, bound together under a king who had a sacred task entrusted by God. It was served by a large class of sacred ministers, whose position was authenticated through connection with the worldwide church and enabled a relationship of the people with their God. Its worship was carried out in sacred places, which were those points in the natural world where the divine and spiritual were already recognised as present. Here power was offered and experienced, and was guarded by communities whose ascetic lifestyle ensured their place in the offering of the divine power to heal and save. The wisdom and knowledge which preserved this salvation were carefully preserved, memorised and handed on. It was aware of its common roots with the other faiths of the region, Judaism and Islam, and was ready to share in pilgrimages and festivals with people of these different faiths. When it finally came into contact with Christians from other regions, it affirmed the unique quality of the faith it preserved, and resolutely avoided assimilation into other forms of Christian practice.

This account of the Ethiopian Orthodox Tawehedo Church is the record of a witness to the faith of generations of Christians living in the mountainous region of east Africa. It is one of the traditions which has entered the new churches of Africa. It belongs in the history of the peoples of Africa, as well as being an integral part of the story of the worldwide Christian faith.

Notes

INTRODUCTION A TRADITION OF FAITH

1. Edward Ullendorff, *The Ethiopians: An Introduction to Country and People* (Oxford 1960), p. 32.
2. Zewde Gebre Sellassie, *Yohannes IV of Ethiopia* (Oxford 1975), p. 10.
3. Gérard Prunier and Éloi Ficquet (eds), *Understanding Contemporary Ethiopia* (London 2015), pp. 1–2.
4. Tawehedo means 'united' and refers to the church's belief in the single nature of Christ. This will be discussed in Chapter 7.
5. The *Encyclopedia Aethiopica* was published by Harassowositz in Wiesbaden in 2003–15.
6. Stuart Munro Hay's books and articles are listed in the bibliography.
7. Donald Lockhart (tr.), *Itinerario of Jeronimo Lobo* (London 1984), p. 160.

CHAPTER 1 PLACE AND IDEA: IDENTIFYING ETHIOPIA

1. The Central Statistics Agency of Ethiopia gave the figure of 90.1 million in 2015.
2. For these figures, see John Reader, *Africa, A Biography of the Continent* (London 1997), p. 205.
3. Ibid., pp. 206–7.
4. Reader, *Africa*, pp. 64–5; Stuart Munro Hay, *Ethiopia, the Unknown Land: A Cultural and Historical Guide* (London 2002), pp. 17–18.
5. David W. Phillipson, *Ancient Ethiopia* (London 1990), p. 33.
6. See Emmanuelle Vagnon, 'Comment localiser l'Ethiopie? La confrontation des sources antiques et des témoignages modernes au XVe siecles', *AÉ* 27 (2012), pp. 21–48, at p. 23.
7. Adrian Hastings, *The Church in Africa, 1450–1950* (Oxford 1994), p. 326.
8. Harold Marcus, *A History of Ethiopia* (Berkeley and London 2002), pp. 97–9; Philip Marsden, *The Chains of Heaven* (London 2006), pp. 275–91.

9. For these and other references from Greek authors, see Donald Levine, *Greater Ethiopia* (Chicago 1974), pp. 3–4.
10. This claim was made to me by many people in the course of conversations during field visits.
11. For reference to this debate see ibid., pp. 27–8.
12. For a convenient summary of these passages see Edward Ullendorff, *Ethiopia and the Bible* (London 1968), pp. 5–12.
13. The homeland of this Ethiopian is demonstrated in F.F. Bruce, 'Philip and the Ethiopian, the Expansion of Hellenistic Christianity', *Journal of Semitic Studies* 34/2 (1989), pp. 377–80.

CHAPTER 2 SEMITIC AND CUSHITIC: A MEETING OF CULTURES

1. For linguistic origins see Harold Marcus, *A History of Ethiopia* (Berkeley and London 2002), p. 3, and Donald Levine, *Greater Ethiopia* (Chicago 1974), pp. 26–30. Levine argues from this the modern expansion of the kingdom under Menelek II was a reunion of a set of peoples who had come from the same origins, rather than the subjugation by Amhara of alien peoples.
2. The temple is described by David W. Phillipson, *Ancient Churches of Ethiopia* (New Haven and London 2009), pp. 35–7. Pre-Aksumite culture at ibid., pp. 4–11, and Marcus, *History*, pp. 3–4.
3. Edward Ullendorff, *The Ethiopians* (Oxford 1960), p. 137.
4. The *Kebrä Nägäst* is translated by E.A.W. Budge, *The Queen of Sheba and Her Only Son Menyelek* (London 1922). For the identification with the Queen of the South see ibid., ch. 21, p. 16.
5. *Kebrä Nägäst* chs, 29–32; Budge, *Queen of Sheba*, pp. 33–8. There are several versions of the name in the manuscripts. Bayna Lekhem, Budge's name, is probably derived from Arabic, ibn al-Hakim, son of the wise man. Menelek, which is in eighteenth-century tradition interpreted as the Amharic *min yelek*, 'what brings you here?' being the question of Solomon when his son returns to Jerusalem. See G. Piccadori in *EA* vol. 1, pp. 920–1.
6. *Kebrä Nägäst*, ch. 68; Budge, *Queen of Sheba*, pp. 113–14.
7. For this dating see Stuart Munro Hay, *The Quest for the Ark of the Covenant* (London 2005), p. 80.
8. For these events see Chapter 4.
9. The text of the colophon is in Budge, *Queen of Sheba*, p. 228, and there is a more modern translation using a better text in Ralph Lee, *Symbolic Interpretation in Ethiopic and Ephremic Literature* (London 2011), pp. 43–4.
10. For this argument see Stuart Munro Hay, 'A Sixth-Century Kebra Negast?' *AÉ* 27 (2001), pp. 43–58.
11. This is the analysis of David Hubbard, *Literary Sources of the Kebra Negast*, PhD thesis (St Andrews University 1956).
12. The name Copt is a form of the Arabic word *gibt*, used in Arabic. For fuller discussion of this council see Chapter 7.
13. Arguments for an early date are in Irfan Shahid, 'The Kebra Negast in the Light of Recent Research', *Le Museon* 89 (1976), pp. 133–78, and David

Johnson, 'Dating the Kebra Negast: Another Look', ed. T. Miller and J. Nesbitt, *Peace and War in Byzantium* (Washington D.C. 1995), pp. 197–208; and are rebutted by Stuart Munro Hay, 'A Sixth-Century Kebra Negast?' For other texts from that period which show that people of that time looked to the Ethiopian kingdom for support, see Marie-Laure Derat, 'Roi Prêtre et Prêtre Jean; analyse de la Vie d'un souverain éthiopien du XIIe siècle Yemrehanna Krestos', *AE* 27 (2012), pp. 127–48, at pp. 133–4.

14. J. Lobo, *A Voyage to Abyssinia* (London 1735), p. 310.
15. For *däbtära* see Chapter 7.
16. These points of resemblance are discussed in Edward Ullendorff, *Ethiopia and the Bible* (Oxford 1968), pp. 73–115.
17. See the comments of Levine, *Greater Ethiopia*, p. 43.
18. The Judaism of Khazaria is summarised in Diarmaid MacCulloch, *A History of Christianity* (London 2009), pp. 459–61.
19. Taddesse Tamrat, *Church and State in Ethiopia* (Oxford 1973), p. 211.
20. Cited in ibid., p. 201.
21. The story of Qozimos is in the life of Yefqeranna Egzi, summarised in Carlo Conti Rossini, 'Ethiopian Hagiography and the Acts of Saint Yafqeränna Egzi (14th Century)', in Alessandro Bausi (ed.), *Languages and Cultures of Eastern Christianity: Vol. 4, Ethiopia* (Farnham, Surrey 2012), pp. 329–54, at p. 343. For Sabra see Steven Kaplan, *The Beta Israel (Falasha) in Ethiopia* (New York 1992), p. 56.
22. Maxime Rodinson, 'On the Question of "Jewish Influences" in Ethiopia', *Journal of Semitic Studies* 9 (1964), pp. 11–19, at pp. 17–19.
23. For this see H. Polotsky, citing A. Dillmann, in 'Aramaic, Syria and Ge'ez', *Journal of Semitic Studies* 9 (1964), pp. 1–10 at p. 5. Lists of loan words have been collected by Witold Witakowski, 'Syrian Influences in Ethiopian Culture', *Orientalia Suecana* 37–9 (1989–90), pp. 191–202, at p. 192.
24. Manuel de Almeida, cited in J. Spencer Trimingham, *Islam in Ethiopia* (Oxford 1952), p. 17.
25. This citation is used by Levine, *Greater Ethiopia*, p. 47, as part of his identification of common cultural traits within Ethiopia making it into a 'cultural area'.
26. The myth of the origins of the zar is found in J. Tubiana, 'Zar and buda in Northern Ethiopia', ed. I.M. Lewis et al., *Women's Medicine: The Zar-Bori Cult in Africa and Beyond* (Edinburgh 1991), pp. 19–33.
27. While the importance of spirit possession has declined in western forms of Christianity, the victory over spiritual powers is referred to in several familiar passages of the New Testament.
28. For the Chinese iron bracket, see David W. Phillipson, *Ancient Ethiopia* (London 1990), pp. 67–8, and for the coins of Däbrä Damo, see Philip Marsden, *The Chains of Heaven: An Ethiopian Romance* (London 2006), p. 251.
29. Enrico Cerulli, 'Perspectives on the History of Ethiopia', in Bausi, *Languages and Cultures*, p. 18.
30. I am grateful to Dr Mangala Frost for pointing this out to me.
31. For a brief account of this novel see MacCulloch, *History*, pp. 231–2.
32. Cited by Donald Crummey, *Priests and Politicians: Protestant and Catholic Missions in Orthodox Ethiopia, 1830–1868* (Oxford 1972), p. 9.

33. This phrase is used by Enrico Cerulli, and the quotation is in *Storia della litteratura etiopica* (Milan 1956), pp. 12–13; see also Levine, *Greater Ethiopia*, pp. 64–8. Levine traces this tendency in the absorption of Sudanic agriculture in the third millennium BC, also art and musical motifs in later periods.

CHAPTER 3 KING AND ABUNA: THE FORMATION OF A CHURCH

1. Mani lived from *c.*216 to *c.*274. This remark is often cited, for example in Stuart Munro Hay, *Ethiopia, the Unknown Land* (London 2002), p. 236.
2. Rufinus, *Historia Ecclesiastica* in PL 21, 478–80. He says it came from Aedesius, 'ipso Aedesio referente'.
3. Alternatively Sälama may be simply a proper name.
4. Constantius warned that Athanasius was guilty of 'ten thousand crimes'. See Athanasius, *Apology to the Emperor Constantine*, PL 25, 626F. This evidence is discussed in Steven Kaplan, 'Ezana's Conversion Reconsidered', *Journal of Religion in Africa* 13 (1982), pp. 102–9, at pp. 102–3.
5. Towards the end of the period of Egyptian domination, in 1939, it was estimated that there were 7 million Ethiopian Christians, and 1 million Egyptian Christians.
6. By Sawirus ibn al-Mukaffa, in *History of the Patriarchs of the Egyptian Church*, discussed in Ayele Tekle Haymonot, 'The Egyptian Metropolitan of the Ethiopian Church', *Orientalia Christiana Periodica* 54 (1988), pp. 175–225, at p. 183.
7. Ayele, 'Egyptian Metropolitan', p. 184.
8. For the decline of the church of Nubia see W.Y. Adams, *Nubia, Corridor to Africa* (Princeton 1977), pp. 525–46.
9. The *Fetha Nägäst* dates from the fifteenth century, and was widely observed from the seventeenth century. It remained the religious law code of Ethiopia until the fall of Haile Selassie in 1974. For the text of the pseudo-canon see Mansi II, bd 964 and 994. It was introduced into Ethiopia at the time of the emperor Zär'a Ya'eqob and caused concern. One text donated by the emperor to the Ethiopian monastery in Jerusalem alters this passage to say that the Ethiopians should appoint the metropolitan, but this is clearly a forgery; see Wudu Taffete Kassu, *The Ethiopian Orthodox Church, the Ethiopian State and the Alexandrian See: Indigenizing the Episcopacy and Forging National Identity 1926–1991*, PhD thesis (University of Urbana Champaign Illinois 2006), p. 37.
10. This statement by M. de Maillet is cited by Stuart Munro Hay, *Ethiopia and Alexandria, the Metropolitan Episcopacy of Ethiopia, from the Fourteenth Century to the Zemana Mesafint* (Warsaw 2005), p. 115.
11. Ayele, 'Egyptian Metropolitan', p. 192.
12. The 'house of Éwostatéwos' was a Judaising movement which had its main strength in the north. See Chapters 2 and 4.
13. See Stuart Munro Hay, *Ethiopia and Alexandria, the Metropolitan Episcopacy of Ethiopia*, vol. 1 (Warsaw 1997), p. 192; *Ethiopia and Alexandria*, vol. 2, p. 72.
14. Charles F. Beckingham and G.W.B. Huntingford, *The Prester John of the Indies* (Cambridge 1961), vol. 1, p. 120, vol. 2, pp. 349–52, 356–7.

15. Richard Pankhurst, *A Social History of Ethiopia* (Addis Ababa 1990), pp. 31–2; citing Beckingham and Huntingford, *The Prester John of the Indies*, pp. 118–19, 126, 236.
16. An estimate provided by a colleague working in the Patriarchate. It includes priests, deacons and *däbtära*. An approximation indicates the large numbers of ordained clergy. For comparison note the Church of England has 16 million members and 27,000 licensed ministers.
17. Gadla Aron cited in Munro Hay, *Ethiopia and Alexandria*, vol. 2, p. 13. For the monastic expansion see Chapter 4.
18. Monophysitism is discussed in Chapter 7.
19. Pankhurst, *Social History*, p. 183.
20. Payment was in pieces of salt, or *amolas*. Abuna Qérelos charged four *amolas* to ordain a priest, two for a deacon and one to confirm a child. Since there had been a gap of fifteen years since the previous abuna died, there was a large backlog of ordinations. A contemporary visitor comments that Qérelos had made ordinations into a 'farce'. Pankhurst, *Social History*, p. 181, citing E. Combes and M. Tamisier, *Voyages en Abyssinie* (Paris 1838).
21. R.P. Dimotheos, *Deux ans de sejour en Abyssinie* (Jerusalem 1871). I am grateful to Dr Kindeneh Endeg for this reference.
22. For the christological schools see Chapter 7.
23. He chose this name since a prophetic work, the *Fekkäré Iyäsus*, had looked forward to a messianic king with this name. There is a lively and evocative biography of Téwodros by Philip Marsden, *The Barefoot Emperor* (London 2007).
24. Donald Crummey, *Priests and Politicians, Protestant and Catholic Missions in Orthodox Ethiopia 1830–1868* (Oxford 1972), p. 141; for the career of Salama see S. Rubenson, 'The Interaction between the Missionaries and the Orthodox: The Case of Abune Salama', in Getatchew Haile et al. (eds), *The Missionary Factor in Ethiopia* (Frankfurt 1998), pp. 71–84; and the comment on Salama's position, p. 84.
25. Ayele, 'Egyptian Metropolitan', p. 210.
26. See Chapter 10.
27. These texts are in Ernest Barker, *Social and Political Thought in Byzantium* (Oxford 1957), p. 174; Nicholas Cabasilas, *Life in Christ* 3.1 tr. de Catanzaro (New York 1974).
28. A figure given by the fifteenth-century traveller Francisco Alvares.
29. In Pankhurst, *Social History*, p. 28.
30. Beckingham and Huntingford, *Prester John of the Indies*, vol. 1, pp. 267–71, vol. 2, pp. 323–8.
31. Charles Beckingham, *Travels to Discover the Source of the Nile by James Bruce* (Edinburgh 1964), vol. 2, p. 607. See Pankhurst, *Social History*, pp. 23–8, 89–92.
32. Eike Haberland, *Untersuchungen zum Athiopischen Königtum* (Wiesbaden 1965), especially p. 104, discusses kingship in the area. The impact on Rastafarians is discussed in my Conclusion.
33. Beckingham and Huntingford, *Prester John of the Indies*, vol. 1, pp. 240–1.
34. Téwodros was a successful general from Quara in the west of the country, Yohannes from Tigray, Menelek II from Shoa and Haile Selassie from the east.

35. However, Marie-Laure Derat questions whether Yemrahännä Krestos was in fact a priest. See 'Roi Prêtre et Prêtre Jean', pp. 128–9.
36. Donald Crummey, *Land and Society in the Christian Kingdom of Ethiopia from the Thirteenth to the Twentieth Centuries* (Urbana, Illinois 2000), p. 84.
37. Zewde Gebre Selassie, *Yohannes IV of Ethiopia* (Oxford 1975), p. 25.
38. Stéphane Ancel and Éloi Ficquet, 'The Ethiopian Orthodox Tawehedo Church and the Challenges of Modernity', ed. Prunier and Ficquet, *Understanding Contemporary Ethiopia*, p. 67.
39. These are discussed more fully in Chapter 5, pp. 131–5.
40. See Crummey, *Land and Society*, pp. 30–1, 88–9. Also see Chapter 5.
41. A comment made by Shiferaw Bekele, 'Monarchical Restoration and Territorial Expansion', ed. Prunier and Ficquet, *Understanding Contemporary Ethiopia*, p. 161.
42. Among many other places this statement is cited in E. Paul Balisky, *Wolaitta Evangelists* (Eugene, Oregon 209), p. 31, but see also Zewde Gebre Selassie, *Yohannes IV*, p. 53, and a comment in Ullendorff, *Ethiopia and the Bible*, p. 75, note 4.
43. Often quoted – this from Tibebe Eshete, *The Evangelical Movement in Ethiopia, Resistance and Resilience* (Waco, Texas 2009), p. 38. The 1955 constitution was the achievement of the policies of Haile Selassie who had gradually reduced the power of the hereditary nobles and affirmed an absolutist monarchy.

CHAPTER 4 SACRED SPACE AND SACRED TIME: AN APPROACH TO WORSHIP

1. J.W. McCrindle, *Christian Topography of Cosmas Indicopleustes* (Cambridge 2010), p. 120.
2. The queen's origin in Bani al-Hamwiyah is in the Egyptian chronicle, the *History of the Patriarchs of the Egyptian Church* II.171. The removal of the Ark is in an unpublished text cited by Sergew Hable Selassie. See Sergew Hable Selassie, 'The Problem of Gudit', *JEthSt* 10/1 (1972), pp. 113–24, at pp. 117, 120. The name Judith occurs in other contexts. Jeronimo Lobo tells us that Judith was the name of the Candace Queen of the Ethiopians of Acts 8.27, in Donald Lockhart (tr.), *Itinerario of Jeronimo Lobo* (London 1984), p. 156.
3. Egyptian envoys to Lalibela came to Adafa, where, according the life of Yemrha Christos, the king 'sat on his throne and ruled all according to the apostolic canons'. Taddesse, *Church and State*, p. 59.
4. See Taddesse *Church and State*, p. 56. For further comment on dating, see pp. 53–9. For arguments for a longer chronology, see Phillipson, *Ancient Churches*, pp. 196–8.
5. Beckingham and Huntingford, *Prester John of the Indies*, vol. 1, p. 226.
6. See David Phillipson, *Ancient Churches of Ethiopia* (New Haven and London 2009), pp. 37–40 for the date of construction and possible design.
7. Ibid., pp. 51–64.
8. The 'life' is generally dated to the late fourteenth or early fifteenth century. The life is edited and translated into French by J. Perruchon, as

Vie de Lalibala, roi d'Éthiopie (Paris 1892). The account of his life is at pp. 70–121.

9. For the reference to bees at his birth, see ibid., p. 78. The translation of his name from an Agaw dialect is suggested by Conti Rossini. Bees have been seen as signs of divine choice in other cultures. In 481 the Frankish king Childeric was buried in the city now called Tournai in France, with hundreds of small gold and garnet bees among the decoration. Discovery of these led Napoleon to adopt the bee as his emblem. See Diarmaid MacCulloch, *A History of Christianity* (London 2009), p. 811. Further references to bees in Conti Rossini, 'Ethiopian Hagiography', p. 335.
10. Perruchon, *Vie de Lalibala*, p. 22, translation on p. 88.
11. Phillipson, *Ancient Churches*, pp. 174–81.
12. The church of Maryam was originally dedicated to Christ.
13. David Buxton, 'The Rock-Hewn Churches and Other Medieval Churches of Tigre Province, Ethiopia', *Archaeologia* 103 (1971), pp. 33–110, at pp. 33–8, 85.
14. Phillipson, *Ancient Churches*, pp. 183–91.
15. For a picture of him doing this, and the completed church, see ibid., p. 121.
16. For a description see Phillipson, *Ancient Churches*, pp. 99–101. Buxton considers that it was excavated in the tenth or eleventh centuries.
17. Georg Gerster, *Churches in Rock: Early Christian Art in Ethiopia* (London 1970), p. 14.
18. Phillipson, *Ancient Churches*, p. 27.
19. Compare Ezekiel 44.1 and Psalm 74.7 where *mäqdäs* means temple.
20. For a description of the royal camp see Chapter 3.
21. See Chapter 2 for the Judaic features of Ethiopian Christianity.
22. The dimensions of the Temple are carefully recorded in the Old Testament in 1 Kings 6.8–22; 2 Chronicles 3.
23. For a description of the Ethiopian altar see Emmanuel Fritsch, 'The Altar in the Ethiopian Church, History Forms and Meanings', ed. Groen Bert, Steven Hawkes-Teeples and Stefanos Alexopoulos, *Inquiries into Eastern Christian Worship* (Leuven 2012), pp. 443–510, with references to the vocabulary on pp. 447–9.
24. V. Nersessian and Richard Pankhurst, 'The Visit to Ethiopia of Johannes T'ovmacean an Armenian Jeweller in 1764–66', *JEthSt* 15 (1982), pp. 79–104, and Munro Hay, *Quest*, p. 142.
25. Dimotheos, *Deux ans de séjour*, pp. 136–43, in Munro Hay, *Quest*, pp. 146–8.
26. A notorious example of western curiosity is a bestselling book by Graham Hancock, *The Sign and the Seal: A Quest for the Lost Ark of the Covenant* (London 1992), which traced a possible route which the Ark of the Covenant might have taken to go from Jerusalem to Aksum, the period of history in which this took place and the places it was kept. It is an example of journalistic imagination, and involves pyramids, Knights Templar and Freemasons among others along the way. A more sober historical analysis was given by the historian Stuart Munro Hay who researched written documents and textual sources to demonstrate the late and flimsy historical basis for the claim that the Ark is in Aksum, in Munro Hay, *Quest, passim.*
27. Cited in I. Guidi, *Annales Iohannis I, Iyasu I, Bakaffa* text 151–2, trans. 158–9, in ibid., p. 136.

28. These are from chapters 17 and 104 of the *Käbrä Nägäst*. Budge, *Queen of Sheba*, pp. 13, 197.
29. These disciplines are described in Chapter 8.
30. Sergew Selassie and Belaynesh Mikael, 'Worship in the Ethiopian Orthodox Church', in *The Church of Ethiopia: A Panorama of History and Spiritual Life* (Addis Ababa 1997), pp. 66–7.
31. Margaret Barker, *The Great High Priest* (London 2003), p. 86.
32. In some areas of the south, the fires in homesteads are allowed to become extinguished, and a new fire is lit from the communal *mäsqäl* fire. See Eike Haberland, 'The Ethiopian Orthodox Church: A National Church in Africa', in *Christian and Islamic Contributions towards Establishing Independent States in Africa South of the Sahara, Papers of the Africa Colloquium Bonn-Bad Godestag 2–4 May 1979* (Tubingen 1979), p. 163.
33. Ibid., p. 163.

CHAPTER 5 MONKS AND MISSIONARIES: THE GROWTH OF POPULAR CHRISTIANITY

1. This has already been referred to on several occasions. It is translated by Beckingham and Huntingford as *The Prester John of the Indies*.
2. There is some variation in the lists of names. For example Za Mikael Arägawi, the best known of the nine, is omitted from the list in the Gadl Gärima. Conti Rossini thinks this is a sign of rivalry between the clergy of Däbrä Damo and Däbrä Matara, the monastery of Garima. Carlo Conti Rossini, 'L'omilia di Yohannes, vescovo di Aksum, in onore di Garima', in *Actes du XI Congrès des Orientalistes, Section Sémitique* (Paris 1897), pp. 139–77. Other sources refer to the Eight Saints. For a summary see A. Brita, 'Nine Saints', in *AÉ* vol. 1, pp. 1188–90.
3. Compare the accounts of the Greek historian Evagrius Scholasticus, *Historia Ecclesiastica*, I.20; with the Palestinian monk, John Moschus, *Spiritual Meadow*, chs 19, 21, 86 etc. These are cited in John Binns, *Ascetics and Ambassadors of Christ* (Oxford 1994), pp. 108–9.
4. For discussion of the council see Chapter 7.
5. For example Carlo Conti Rossini, *Storia d'Etiopia* (Milan 1928), pp. 162–3.
6. See Taddesse Tamrat, *Church and State in Ethiopia* (Oxford 1973), pp. 29–30.
7. The social and economic pressures leading to the growth of the monastic movement are discussed in Binns, *Ascetics and Ambassadors*.
8. For a sceptical view see Stuart Munro Hay, 'Saintly Shadows', ed. Bausi, *Languages and Cultures*, pp. 221–52.
9. For the *andamta* see Chapter 7.
10. Kenneth Bailey, 'Informal Controlled Tradition and the Synoptic Gospels', *Themelios* 20 (1995), pp. 4–11, at p. 6. For oral tradition see the work of Jan Vansina, *Oral Tradition* (London 1961) and *Oral Tradition as History* (Madison Wisconsin 1985).
11. *Gädl*, plural *gädlat*, is a Ge'ez word meaning 'act' or 'struggle' and is used of saints' lives. Conti Rossini, 'Ethiopian Hagiography', pp. 329–54, at p. 331. See also Taddesse, *Church and State*, pp. 2–4; Steven Kaplan, *The*

Monastic Holy Man and the Christianization of Early Solomonic Ethiopia (Wiesbaden 1984), pp. 1–9.
12. Reported by William Dalrymple, *Age of Kali* (London 1998), pp. 182–3.
13. Conti Rossini, 'Ethiopian Hagiography', p. 331.
14. Vansina, *Oral Tradition as History*, p. 194.
15. Ibid., pp. 104–5.
16. Edition by Carlo Conti Rossini, 'L'omelia di Yohannes vescovo di Axum in onore di Garima' *in Actes du XI Congrès des Orientalistes* (Paris 1897).
17. The life of Iyasus Moa is edited by S. Kur, *Actes de Iyasus Mo'a*, CSCO Script Aeth, vols 49 and 50 (1965); and for the abbots see Taddesse Tamrat, 'The Abbots of Dabra Hayk 1248–1535', *JEthSt* 8/1 (1970), pp. 87–117.
18. For an assessment of Tekla Haymonot's influence see Taddesse, *Church and State*, p. 163. Tadesse assesses the historicity of the accounts throughout his discussion.
19. This cave can be visited, in the hill above the monastery church of Debre Libanos.
20. For the translation of the relics and growing prominence of Debre Libanos, see Marie-Laure Derat, *Le Domaine des Rois Ethiopiens (127–1527), Espace, Pouvoir et Monachisme* (Paris 2003), pp. 119–27.
21. E.A.W. Budge (tr.), *The Life of Tekla Haymonot* (London 1906), chs 36–45, pp. 75–95.
22. The saints' lives of this period present them as martyrs opposed to the lax morality of the court. See Derat, *Domaine des Rois Éthiopiens*, pp. 153–65.
23. In Carlo Conti Rossini (ed. and tr.), *Acta Sancti of Basalota Mika'el*, CSCO vol. 20 (Louvain 1905), p. 30.
24. Zara Ya'eqob, *Meshaf Birhan* ii, CSCO cclxii, p. 82, cited in Taddesse, *Church and State*, p. 210.
25. Budge, *Life of Takla Haymonot*, pp. 189–90.
26. See Derat, *Les Rois Éthiopiens*, pp. 96–109.
27. For a detailed account of royal churches see Derat, *Les Rois Ethiopiens*, pp. 209–313.
28. The continuing significance in the Gondar period is emphasised by Donald Crummey, 'Church and Nation: The Ethiopian Orthodox Tawehedo Church (from the Thirteenth to the Twentieth Century)', ed. Michael Angold, *The Cambridge History of Christianity*, vol. 5, *Eastern Christianity* (Cambridge 2006), pp. 457–77, at pp. 471–6.
29. A geographical guide to the monasteries is given in Christine Chaillot, *The Ethiopian Orthodox Tawehedo Church Tradition* (Paris 2002), pp. 158–83, who conducts the reader through the regions of Ethiopia describing the various monasteries.

CHAPTER 6 ISLAM AND CHRISTIANITY: HOW TWO FAITHS COEXISTED

1. This statement is made by UNESCO in explaining why it is a World Heritage site; see http://whc.unesco.org.
2. For this account from the Fath Madinat Harar, see the article by Ewald Wagner in *EA* vol. 2, p. 1015.

3. These events in the life and death of da Gama are in R. Stephen Whiteway (ed. and tr.), *The Portuguese Expedition to Abyssinia in 1441–1543* (London 1902), pp. 26, 68.
4. This is the account of ibn Ishaq written in the mid-eighth century. See Alfred Guillaume, *Life of Muhammad* (Oxford 1955), pp. 20–30.
5. Columns from this cathedral were used in the building of the mosque at Sana'a and can be seen today.
6. Ibid., pp. 20–30. Also Haggai Erlich, *Islam and Christianity in the Horn of Africa* (London 2010), p. 55.
7. Meles Zenawi, after his invasion and occupation of Mogadishu in 2006 was considered by some to be the new Abraha.
8. Reconstruction did not take place until the twentieth century, and a new dam was opened in 1986.
9. Guillaume, *Life of Muhammad*, pp. 150, 152.
10. One possible meaning of the use of the word *karra* or sword to describe the strict Monophysite Christological party is that Christ went in and out of the womb of Mary as a sword is drawn from a scabbard, not impacting on the scabbard, which is simply a container.
11. Ibn Hisham iii.417–18, cited in Trimingham, *Islam in Ethiopia*, p. 46.
12. Muir, *The Life of Mohammed*, p. 70, cited in Trimingham, *Islam in Ethiopia*, p. 45.
13. Qur'an, Sura 5.82.
14. Gullaume, *Life of Muhammad*, p. 155.
15. See Haggai Erlich, *Saudi Arabia and Ethiopia* (London 2007), pp. 2–3.
16. William Raven, 'Some Early Islamic Texts on the Negus of Abyssinia', *Journal of Semitic Studies* 33/2 (1988), p. 199.
17. Trimingham, *Islam in Ethiopia*, p. 102. For Muslims in Gondar, see Abussamade H. Ammad, 'Muslims of Gondar 1864–1941', *AÉ* 16 (2000), pp. 161–72.
18. Cited in Trimingham, *Islam in Ethiopia*, p. 122. For another view see Zewde Gebre-Selassie, *Yohannes IV of Ethiopia* (Oxford 1975), pp. 98–9. Zewde is the great great grandson of the emperor.
19. See Chapter 7, pp. 182–3.
20. For the career of Zakaryas see Donald Crummey, 'Shaikh Zakaryas, an Ethiopian Prophet', *JEthSt* 10/1 (1972), pp. 55–66.
21. I am grateful to Ayele Tarakegn of Imperial College London for these examples. I was unable to discover the name of the church.
22. Belay Guta Olam, *Muslim Evangelism in Ethiopia* (Fuller Theological Seminary 1997), pp. 123–6.
23. Erlich, *Saudi Arabia and Ethiopia*, p. 16.
24. René Lefort, 'The Ethiopian Economy: Developmental State vs. the Free Market', ed. Prunier and Ficquet, *Understanding Contemporary Ethiopia*, p. 381.
25. Philip Marsden, *Chains of Heaven* (London 2006), pp. 264–6.
26. Éloi Ficquet, 'The Ethiopian Muslims: Historical Processes and Ongoing Controversies', ed. Prunier and Ficquet, *Understanding Contemporary Ethiopia*, pp. 106–7 and note 23.

27. See Patrick Desplat, 'Against Wahhabism? Islamic Reform, Ambivalence and Sentiments of Loss in Harar', ed. Patrick Desplat and Terje Østerbø, *Muslim Ethiopia* (New York 2013), pp. 163–84; Erlich, *Saudi Arabia and Ethiopia*, p. 6.

CHAPTER 7 CATHOLIC MISSIONS AND CHRISTOLOGICAL DEBATE: EXPLORING DOCTRINE

1. The Oromo peoples belong within the larger ethnic grouping of the Galla. During the last century the term Galla has been used pejoratively, and as a result Oromo is the term preferred by the people themselves.
2. For the *gadaa* system see Asmarom Legesse, *Gada: Three Approaches to the Study of African Society* (New York 1973). Asmaron compares the Oromo expansion to the conquests of the Fulani in West Africa and the Nguni of South Africa as great expansions of African history.
3. Donald Levine, *Greater Ethiopia* (Chicago 1974), p. 80.
4. It was founded by Ignatius Loyola who took vows with a small group of friends in 1534, and were formally constituted by a papal bull in 1540.
5. Philip Caraman, *The Lost Empire: The Story of the Jesuits in Ethiopia 1555–1634* (London 1985), p. 2.
6. This monastery is still in existence today.
7. The letter is transcribed in Robert Silverberg, *The Realm of Prester John* (London 1972), pp. 41–5, with reference to Jacques de Vitry at pp. 71–3.
8. These lives are recounted in Caraman, *Lost Empire*, pp. 118–32 for Paez and pp. 138–56 for Mendes. Paez's journey is at pp. 21–44, and Mendes's speech at pp. 141–2.
9. See Andreu Martinez d'Alos-Moner, *Envoys of a Human God: The Jesuit Mission to Christian Ethiopia 1557–1632* (Leiden 2015), pp. 96–117, for an assessment of Paez's strategy.
10. For a discussion on Jesuit strategy see d'Alos-Moner, *Envoys of a Human God*, pp. 144–9.
11. The political dimension of the Jesuit mission has been discussed by various writers, including ibid., pp. 176–99, and Leonardo Cohen Shabot, *The Missionary Strategies of the Jesuits in Ethiopia (1555–1632)*, Aethiopistischen Forschungen, 70 (Wiesbaden 2009).
12. There is some evidence for a bishop for Adulis on the Red Sea coast; at Chalcedon he does not seem to have had contact with the church in the interior.
13. Mebratu Kiros Gebru, *Miaphysite Christology* (Piscataway, New Jersey 2010), pp. 1–4; Aymro Wondmagegnehu and Joachim Motovu, *The Ethiopian Orthodox Church* (Addis Ababa 1970), p. 96.
14. Adrian Hastings, *History of the Church in Africa* (Oxford 1994), p. 10.
15. The positions of the three schools are compared in Mebratu, *Miaphysite Christology*, pp. 36–41; Tesfazghi Uqbit, *Current Christological Positions of Ethiopian Orthodox Theologians*, Orientalia Christiana Analecta, 193 (Rome 1973), pp. 72–108.
16. Donald Crummey, *Priests and Politicians, Protestant and Catholic Missions in Orthodox Ethiopia 1830–1868* (Oxford 1972), p. 24.

17. This point re the anointing in the womb rather than at the baptism was made to me by the scholar, the late Säfa Sellassie.
18. The relationship between *karra* and *sagga lijj* is argued convincingly by Kindeneh Enedeg in several articles analysing the debates at the seventeenth-century synods. I'm grateful to Dr Kindeneh for discussing his ideas with me. The traditional view that the *sagga lijj* is a westernised account with hints of adoptionism has been assumed by many scholars; see for example Tesfazghi, *Current Christological Positions*, p. 66, or Crummey, *Priests and Politicians*, p. 24.
19. This is set out in Aloys Grillmeier, *Christ in Christian Tradition*, ii/4 (London 1996), p. 351.
20. For divisions at Waldebba, I am grateful to Dr Kindeneh Enedeg for showing me his paper on this subject.
21. Dr Ayele's thesis was revised and published in 1982: Ayele Tekle Haymonot, *The Ethiopian Church and Its Christological Doctrine* (Addis Ababa 1982). Orthodox responses include Ayalew Tamiru, *When Has Kinship with the Wolf Become Customary?* (Addis Ababa 1961) and Admasu Jembere, *A Balance of Faith* (Addis Ababa 1961). A summary of the recent debate is in Tesfazghi, *Current Christological Positions*. For an 'official' summary see Wondmagegnehu and Motovu, *The Ethiopian Orthodox Church*, pp. 95–100.
22. MacCulloch says that Armenians considered Chalcedon as 'blasphemous nonsense'. *History of Christianity* (London 2009), p. 239.
23. For the evolution of language and the use of the definite article I rely on the argument of Iain McGilchrist, *The Master and His Emissary* (New Haven and London 2009) pp. 274–86. The point is also made in McCulloch, *History of Christianity*, p. 25. Plato's *Republic*, ed. Lee, 529d–530c.
24. Objects can be objectified in Amharic by adding the suffix *u*, or *wa* in the case of feminine nouns, but these suffixes are applied to the object in its totality and not to an adjective which qualifies it.
25. For Ephrem see Sebastian Brock, *Harp of the Spirit* (Cambridge 2013), pp. 41–5. The chapter of the *Kebrä Nägäst* is ch. 68, Budge *Queen of Sheba*, pp. 110–14, and Grillmeier, *Christ in Christian Tradition*, p. 339; for the derivation from 'pearl' see J. Lössl, 'One as the Same: Elements of an Ethiopian Christology', *Östkirchliches Studien* 42 (1993), pp. 288–302, at p. 291; Claud Sumner, *Ethiopian Philosophy*, vol. 3 (Addis Ababa 1978), p. 113.
26. Admasu Jembere, *A Measure of Faith*, p. 182, cited in Tesfazghi, *Current Christological Positions*, p. 29. The extensive recent literature in Amharic is well summarised by Tesfazghi.
27. Ibid., p. 121.
28. See John Mbiti, *African Religions and Philosophy* (London 1969) p. 141.

CHAPTER 8 STUDENTS AND TEACHERS: THE ORAL TRADITION OF SCHOLARSHIP

1. See Cressida Marcus, 'Imperial Nostalgia: Christian Restoration and Civic Decay in Gondar', ed. Wendy James and Donald Donham, *Remapping Ethiopia: Socialism and After* (Oxford 2002), pp. 239–56, at 240–2.

2. Charles Beckingham, *Travels to Discover the Source of the Nile by James Bruce* (Edinburgh 1964), also Miles Bredin, *The Pale Abyssinian* (London 2000). Bruce's account describes the discovery of the source of the Nile, but in this he was claiming too much, since this place had been visited by Pero Paez in the previous century.
3. To avoid excessive italicisation, the key words of zema, qené and mäshaf will be given in non-italicised script for the rest of this chapter.
4. See Donald Levine, *Wax and Gold: Tradition and Innovation in Ethiopian Culture* (Chicago 1965), pp. 24–8.
5. Richard Pankhurst in Imbakom Kalewold, *Traditional Ethiopian Church Education* (New York 1970), p. xi.
6. I recall a conversation with a distinguished Christian missionary doctor who had worked in Ethiopia for over fifty years, who bemoaned the ignorance of Ethiopian clergy and people as an obstacle to the work of medical care.
7. For a description of Islamic schools, see Haile Gabriel Dagne, *Qur'an School System in Ethiopia* (Addis Ababa 1971).
8. Girma Amare, 'Aims and Purpose of Church Education in Ethiopia', *Ethiopian Journal of Education* 1 (1967), pp. 1–11. For a description of the traditional system see Imbakom Kalewold, *Traditional Ethiopian Church Education*, pp. 1–36, and Christine Chaillot, *The Ethiopian Orthodox Tawehedo Church Tradition* (Paris 2002), pp. 83–100.
9. Ralph Lee, *Symbolic Interpretation in Ethiopian and Ephremic Literature*, PhD thesis (SOAS London 2011), p. 15.
10. For these details from the Life of Yared, see Carlo Conti Rossini, *Acta Yared*, CSCO Scr Aeth vol. 17 (Louvain 1904), pp. 7–12.
11. For a partial version, see Lee, *Symbolic Interpretation*, pp. 67–8.
12. In this section, qené is not italicised, since it is the main topic of the enquiry, rather than an occasional term.
13. Various lists and orders of types are given. This was told to me in Gondar. For another version see Anne Damon-Guillot, 'Qene et aquaquam dans la liturgie de l'Église Chrétienne d'Éthiopie: réalisation musicale d'un texte improvisée', *AÉ* 23 (2007–8), pp. 101–14, at pp. 105–6.
14. The culture of qené is described by Levine, *Wax and Gold*, pp. 5–9.
15. Girma, 'Aims and Purpose', p. 5.
16. Levine, *Wax and Gold*, p. 7.
17. Mire Sellassie Gebre Ammanuel, 'The Bible and Its Canon in the Ethiopian Orthodox Church', *Bible Translator* 44 (1992), pp. 111–23, at p. 119.
18. R.W. Cowley, *Traditional Interpretation of the Apocalypse of John in the Ethiopian Orthodox Church* (Cambridge 1983), pp. 36–38.
19. Roger Cowley, 'The Beginnings of the Andem Commentary Tradition', *JEthSt* 10/2 (1972), pp. 1–16, at p. 1.
20. So Roger Cowley, 'Preliminary Notes on the Andam Commentaries', *JEthSt* 9/1 (1971), pp. 9–20.
21. Translation by Lee, *Symbolic Interpretation*, p. 34.
22. Steven Kaplan in *EA* vol. 2, pp. 53–4.
23. Richard Pankhurst, *Social History of Ethiopia* (Addis Ababa 1990), p. 29, and Beckingham and Huntingford, *The Prester John of the Indies*, vol. 1, pp. 127, 199, 203, 206–7, 256.

24. Plato, *Phaedrus* 276A, 274E–275A.
25. For the use of speech in the early church see Carol Harrison, *The Art of Listening in the Early Church* (Oxford 2013), pp. 4–5, 74–80.

CHAPTER 9 EVANGELICALS AND PENTECOSTALS: NEW WAYS OF BELIEVING

1. Harold Marcus, *A History of Ethiopia* (Berkeley and London 2002), pp. 78–9, and for a description of the *zamacha* see Harold Marcus, *The Life and Times of Menelik II of Ethiopia 1844–1913* (Oxford 1975), pp. 64–8.
2. Marcus, *Life and Times*, p. 135.
3. The evidence for the life of Peter Heyling is provided by Job Ludolf (1624–1704) and is summarised by Gustav Aren, *Evangelical Pioneers in Ethiopia, Origins of the Evangelical Church Mekane Yesus*, Studia Missionalia Upsaliensia, 75 (Stockholm 1978), p. 34.
4. Donald Crummey, *Priests and Politicians, Protestant and Catholic Missions in Orthodoc Ethiopia 1830–1868* (Oxford 1972), p. 3.
5. G. Annesley, *Voyages and Travels to India, Ceylon, the Red Sea, Abyssinia and Egypt in the years 1803, 1804, 1805, and 1806*, 3 vols (London 1809), vol. 3, p. 256, cited in Crummey, *Priests and Politicians*, p. 12.
6. This was Kienzlen, in ibid., pp. 124–6.
7. The story of Maqdala has often been told – including in a lively style by Philip Marsden, *The Barefoot Emperor* (London 2008), and, in a more scholarly manner, by Sven Rubenson, *King of Kings: Tewodros of Ethiopia* (Addis Ababa 1966).
8. Written from Adwa on 4 October 1843, in Crummey, *Priests and Politicians*, p. 62.
9. Written to the Propaganda Fidei on 13 June 1861, cited in ibid., p. 81.
10. For Lambie's story see T. Lambie, *Doctor without a Country* (New York 1939).
11. Gustav Aren, *Envoys of the Gospel in Ethiopia: In the Steps of the Evangelical Pioneers 1898–1926*, Studia Missionalia Upsaliensia, 75 (Stockholm 1991), p. 139.
12. See Richard Pankhurst, *Economic History of Ethiopia (1800–1935)* (Addis Ababa 1968), pp. 82–7.
13. Aren, *Evangelical Pioneers*, p. 277.
14. Gustav Aren, 'Slave Trade in Abyssinia', *Moslem World* 23/4 (1978), pp. 402–3.
15. Aren, *Evangelical Pioneers*, p. 212.
16. I am grateful to Rachel Weller who described the life of Onesimus to me in conversation. It is set out in the books of Gustav Aren. For his death, see Aren, *Envoys*, pp. 321–2. His translation of the Bible remains in use, but in 1965 work on a more scholarly version began.
17. Ibid., p. 172.
18. Donald Donham, 'Old Abyssinia and the New Ethiopian Empire: Themes in Social History', ed. Donald Donham and Wendy James, *The Southern Marches of Imperial Ethiopia* (Oxford 1986), p. 11.
19. Rachel Weller, who knew Gidada, told me about him. He wrote an autobiography: Gidada Solon, *The Other Side of Darkness* (New York 1972).

20. Aren, *Evangelical Pioneers*, p. 354.
21. E. Stock, *The History of the Church Missionary Society*, vols i–iii (London 1899), vol. 1, p. 68 in Aren, *Evangelical Pioneers*, p. 45.
22. David Stokes, *Ethiopia: Land of Outstretched Hand* (London 1948), p. 8.
23. Samuel Gobat, *Journal of a three years' residence in Abyssinia in Furtherance of the objects of the Church Missionary Society* (London 1834).
24. The approach of Gobat and other Anglican missionaries is explored in a forthcoming paper by Grant le Marquand, which he has generously let me see.
25. Refs in Gobat, *Journal*, pp. 51, 53, 94, 100, 106, 153, 190, 192, 204. Taddesse Tamrat, 'Evangelising the Evangelised: The Root Problem between Missions and the Ethiopian Orthodox Church', in Getatchew Haile et al. (eds), *The Missionary Factor in Ethiopia* (Frankfurt 1998), pp. 17–30, at p. 25.
26. Taddesse, citing CMS archives, ibid. p. 24.
27. These are collected in Philip Cousins, *Ethelstan Cheese, Saint of No Fixed Abode* (Worthing, England 1986), pp. 81, 86.
28. In a report in USPG archives, see Colin Battell, 'The Anglican Church in Ethiopia, Experiments in Co-operation with the Ethiopian Orthodox Church', in Baye Yimam et al. (eds)., *Proceedings of the VIIIth International Conference of Ethiopian Studies* (Huntingdon UK 1984) vol. 1, pp. 291–8.
29. W. Jowett, *Christian Researches in the Mediterranean from MDCCCXV to MDCCCXX in Furtherance of the Objects of the Church Missionary Society* (London 1822), p. 203; see also Aren, *Evangelical Pioneers*, pp. 42–3.
30. The life of Taye is in Aren, *Envoys*, p. 58, with ref to this conversation at p. 31.
31. Aren, *Evangelical Pioneers*, pp. 164–73, 194, 304.
32. These are set out by Brian Fargher, *The Origins of the New Churches Movement in Southern Ethiopia* (Leiden 1996), p. 26.
33. See Ingeborg Lass-Westphal, 'Protestant Missions during and after the Italo–Ethiopian War, 1935–1937', *JEthSt* 10/1 (1972) 89–102.
34. Raymond J. Davis, *Fire on the Mountains* (Grand Rapids, Michigan 1966), p. 106; Fargher, *Origins of New Churches Movement*, p. 280.
35. Tibebe Eshete, *The Evangelical Movement in Ethiopia, Resistance and Resilience* (Waco Texas 2009), pp. 172–90. As well as Mulu Wengel, a large Pentecostal denomination grew up in Mennonite missionary communities, which came to be called Meserete Kristos.
36. Ibid., p. 274.
37. See ibid., p. 30.
38. Melkamu Mengesha, *The Problem of the Conversion of Orthodox Christians to Other Religions*, senior essay, Trinity Theological College (Addis Ababa 2010).

CHAPTER 10 SURVIVAL AND GROWTH: THE ETHIOPIAN ORTHODOX TAWEHEDO CHURCH IN THE MODERN WORLD

1. Peter Gill, *Famine and Foreigners, Ethiopia since Live Aid* (Oxford 2010), p. 80.

2. For these, and statistics for Orthodox membership, see Patrick Johnstone, *The Future of the Global Church* (Milton Keynes 2011), pp. 107–9.
3. Ibid., p. 109.
4. Statistics were not kept so numbers could not be calculated accurately, but whichever figure is accepted, the disproportion in size between Egypt and Ethiopia was apparent. For newspaper reports and clergy letters see Wudu Taffete Kassu, *The Ethiopian Orthodox Church the Ethiopian State, and the Alexandrian See: Indigenising the Episcopacy and Forging National Identity 1926–1991* (University of Urbana Champaign Illinois 2006), pp. 32–3, 121.
5. See Zewde Gebre-Selassie, *Yohannes IV of Ethiopia* (Oxford 1975), p. 109.
6. Mire-Sellassie Gebre Ammanuel, *Church and Missions in Ethiopia during the Italian Occupation* (Addis Ababa 2014), pp. 315–18.
7. See Joachim Persoon, 'Between Ancient Aksum and Revolutionary Moscow: The Ethiopian Church in the 20th Century', ed. Anthony O'Mahony, *Eastern Christianity* (London 2004), pp. 160–214, at pp. 185–7.
8. For these comments, see Ephrem Isaac, 'Social Structure of the Ethiopian Orthodox Church', cited in Joachim Persoon, *Central Ethiopian Monasticism 1974–1991: Survival of an Ancient Institution in a Changing World*, PhD thesis (SOAS London 2003), p. 117, and Christopher Clapham, *Haile Selassie's Government* (Oxford 1968), p. 84.
9. For this process see Stéphane Ancel, 'Territories, Ecclesiastical Jurisdictions and the Centralisation Process of the Ethiopian Patriarchate Authority (1972–1983)', *AÉ* 26 (2011), pp. 167–78.
10. Ibid.
11. For the protests of 100,000 people see Bahru Zewde, *A History of Modern Ethiopia* (Oxford 1991), p. 123; on closure of the hospital, see Brian Fargher, *The Origin of the New Churches Movement in Southern Ethiopia 1927–1944*, Studies of Religion in Africa, 16 (Leiden 1996), p. 303.
12. We should not refer to landowners as one might naturally do in a western context. The ownership of land was passed from generation to generation – as *rist*. The nobleman did not own land but was given the right to exact tax and other charges from the peasant – *gult*. This resulted in his depending for his wealth and influence on the good will of the emperor who had granted him the *gult*, and might withdraw it. It also resulted in excessive exaction from the peasant owner as the *gult*-holder sought to gain maximum benefit from the land as long as he could, and had no interest in the long-term development of the land.
13. A more generous assessment is provided by Mersha Alehegne, who states that Tekla Haymonot was a distinguished scholar, who was also known for his support of local people to gain access to basic services. This led him to be one of the five candidates. The new bishops were part of a plan to renew the church, rather than a removal of out-of-favour postholders. See *EA* vol. 4, pp. 839–40.
14. For these see Wudu, *Ethiopian Orthodox Church*, pp. 288–9, 296, 317–29.
15. I am grateful to Alexandra Antohin for sharing her research findings on *mahabers*, and their impact on the church.
16. For the history of the Haymonote Abaw, see Haile Mariam Larebo, 'Quest for Change Haymonote Abaw, Ethiopian Students Association and the Ethiopia Orthodox Church 1959–1974', in Katsuyoshi Fukui et al. (eds),

Ethiopia in Broader Perspective, Papers of the XIIIth International Conference of Ethiopian Studies, vol. 1 (Kyoto 1997), 326–338.

17. Private communication.
18. Private communication.
19. Ginbot is the Ethiopian month which lasts from 9 May to 7 June.
20. But teachers at government schools are also poorly paid by western standards, some of them receiving 600 to 3000 birr a month – or £20 to £100.
21. One of them, Antoun Mikhail Yacoub, had a long association with the Ethiopian Church, and was Dean of Selassie College in 2001 when I got to know him and learned much from him. He had a deep commitment to building good relations with the Coptic Church and also with Islam.
22. Information from the Sunday School Department.
23. Numbers provided by the diocesan office of north Gondar in November 2014.
24. I interviewed a member of this branch of Tadiso at his bookshop in eastern Addis Ababa. He told me that he preached the gospel all over Ethiopia whenever he had opportunity, but however hard I pressed him he would not tell where or in what kinds of settings he carried out this ministry.
25. This division into three groups is based on Daniel Teshome, *The Current (1987–2007) Reformation Movement within the Ethiopian Orthodox Tawehido Church* (Addis Ababa 2007). These distinct approaches are confirmed by interviews I held in 2013–14.
26. For this see Tom Boylston, 'Orthodox Modern', *FocusOnTheHorn*, 2 July 2012, http://focusonthehorn.wordpress.com/2012/07/20/orthodox-modern-religion-politics-in-todays-ethiopia-part-1.

CONCLUSION A TRADITIONAL AFRICAN CHURCH

1. Figures in D.A. Barrett and T. Johnson, *World Christian Trends AD 30–2200* (Pasadena, California 2001), p. 17.
2. For these churches, see Bengt Sundkler, *Bantu Prophets in South Africa* (London 1948), pp. 57–65.
3. Giulia Bonnacci, 'From Pan-Africanism to Rastafari', in Prunier and Ficquet (eds), *Understanding Contemporary Ethiopia*, pp. 151–3.
4. For the story of the church in the diaspora see Chaillot, *Ethiopian Orthodox Tawehedo Church Tradition*, pp. 51–63, especially pp. 61–3.
5. A quotation form Andrew Walls, *Cross Cultural Process in Christian History* (Maryknoll 2002), pp. 90–1.
6. Adrian Hastings, *History of the African Christianity 1950–1975* (Cambridge 1979), pp. 272–4.

Bibliography

Abdussamade H. Ammad, 'The Muslims of Gondar 1864–1961', *AÉ* 16 (2000), pp. 161–72.

Adams, W.Y., *Nubia, Corridor to Africa* (Princeton 1977).

Alemayyahu Moges, *The Tradition of Church Education* (Addis Ababa 1971).

Ancel, Stéphane, 'Territories, Ecclesiastical Jurisdictions and Centralisation Process: The Improvement of the Ethiopian Patriarchate Authority (1972–1983)', *AÉ* 26 (2011), pp. 167–78.

———, and Éloi Ficquet, 'The Ethiopian Orthodox Tawahedo Church (EOTC) and the Challenges of Modernity', in Gérard Prunier and Éloi Ficquet (eds), *Understanding Contemporary Ethiopia* (London 2015), pp. 63–92.

Aren, Gustav, *Evangelical Pioneers in Ethiopia, Origins of the Evangelical Church Mekane Yesus*, Studia Missionalia Upsalensia, 32 (Stockholm 1978).

———, 'Slave Trade in Abyssinia', *Moslem World* 8/4 (1978), pp. 402–3.

———, *Envoys of the Gospel in Ethiopia: In the Steps of the Evangelical Pioneers 1898–1926*, Studia Missionalia Upsaliensia, 75 (Stockholm 1991).

Asmarom Legesse, *Gada: Three Approaches to the Study of African Society* (New York 1973).

Ayele Tekle Haymonot, *The Ethiopian Church and Its Christological Doctrine* (Addis Ababa 1982).

———, 'The Egyptian Metropolitans of the Ethiopian Church', *Orientalia Christiana Periodica* 56 (1988), pp. 175–225.

Aymro Wondmagegnehu and Joachim Motovu, *The Ethiopian Orthodox Church* (Addis Ababa 1970).

Bahru Zewde, *A History of Modern Ethiopia 1855–1991* (Oxford 1991).

———, *Pioneers of Change in Ethiopia* (Oxford 2007).

Bailey, Kenneth, 'Informal Controlled Oral Tradition and the Synoptic Gospels', *Asia Journal of Theology* 5 (1991), pp. 34–51; also in *Themelios* 20 (1995), pp. 4–11.

Balisky, E. Paul, *Wolaitta Evangelists: A Study of Religious Innovation in Southern Ethiopia 1937–1975* (Eugene, Oregon 2009).

Barker, Ernest, *Social and Political Thought in Byzantium* (Oxford 1957).

Barker, Margaret, *The Great High Priest* (Edinburgh 2003).

Barrett, D.A., and T. Johnson, *World Christian Trends AD 30–2200* (Pasadena, California 2001).

Battell, C., 'The Anglican Church in Ethiopia: Experiments in Co-operation with the Ethiopian Orthodox Church', in Baye Yimam et al. (eds), *Proceedings of the VIIIth International Conference of Ethiopian Studies* (Huntingdon, UK 1984), vol. 1, pp. 291–8.

Bausi, A. (ed.), *Languages and Cultures of Eastern Christianity: Ethiopian*, Worlds of Eastern Christianity 300–1500, 4 (Ashgate 2012).

Beckingham, Charles F., *Travels to Discover the Source of the Nile by James Bruce* (Edinburgh 1964).

———, and G.W.B Huntingford, *The Prester John of the Indies* (Cambridge 1961).

Belay Guta Olam, *Muslim Evangelism in Ethiopia* (Fuller Theological Seminary 1997).

Binns, John, *Ascetics and Ambassadors of Christ: The Monasteries of Palestine, 314–631* (Oxford 1994).

———, *Introduction to the Christian Orthodox Churches* (Cambridge 2002).

———, 'Theological Education in the Ethiopian Orthodox Church', *Journal of Adult Theological Education* 2/2 (2005), pp. 103–13.

———, 'Out of Ethiopia – A Different Way of Doing Theology', *International Journal for the Study of the Christian Church* 13/1 (2013), pp. 33–47.

Bonacci, Giulia, 'Ethiopia, Religious Policy of the State and Its Consequences for the Orthodox Church', in Baye Yimam et al. (eds), *Proceedings of the VIIIth International Conference of Ethiopian Studies* (Huntingdon UK 1984), vol. 1 pp. 593–605.

Boylston, Tom, 'Orthodox Modern', *Focus On The Horn*, 2 July 2012, http://focusonthehorn.wordpress.com/2012/07/20/orthodox-modern-religion-politics-in-todays-ethiopia-part-1/.

———, *The Shade of the Divine: Approaching the Sacred in an Ethiopian Orthodox Christian Community*, PhD thesis (London School of Economics 2012).

Bredin, Miles, *The Pale Abyssinian* (London 2000).

Brock, Sebastian, *Harp of the Spirit* (Cambridge 2013).

Bruce, F.F., 'Philip and the Ethiopian: The Expansion of Hellenistic Christianity', *Journal Semitic Studies* 34/2 (1989), pp. 377–80.

Budge, E.A.W. (ed. and tr.), *The Life and Miracles of Takla Haymonot* (London 1906).

——— (ed. and tr.), *The Queen of Sheba and Her Only Son Menyelek* (London 1922).

Buxton, David, 'The Christian Antiquities of Northern Ethiopia', *Archaeologia* 92 (1947), pp. 1–42.

———, 'The Rock-Hewn Churches and Other Medieval Churches of Tigre Province Ethiopia', *Archaeologia* 103 (1971), pp. 33–100.

Caraman, Philip, *The Lost Empire: The Story of the Jesuits in Ethiopia 1555–1634* (London 1985).

Cerulli, Enrico, *Storia della litteratura etiopica* (Milan 1956).

———, 'Monasticism in Ethiopia', in A. Bausi (ed.), *Languages and Cultures of Eastern Christianity*, vol. 4, *Ethiopia* (Ashgate 2012), pp. 355–70.

———, 'Perspectives on the History of Ethiopia', in A. Bausi (ed.), *Languages and Cultures of Eastern Christianity*, vol. 4, *Ethiopia* (Ashgate 2012), pp. 1–26.

Chaillot, Christine, *The Ethiopian Orthodox Tawehedo Church Tradition* (Paris 2002).
———, 'Traditional Teaching in the Ethiopian Orthodox Church, Yesterday, Today and Tomorrow', in Harald Aspan et al. (eds), *Research in Ethiopian Studies, Selected Papers of the 16th International Conference of Ethiopian Studies, Trondheim July 2007* (Wiesbaden 2010), pp. 240–7.
Clapham, Christopher, *Transformation and Continuity in Revolutionary Ethiopia* (Cambridge 1988).
Cohen Shabot, Leonardo, *The Missionary Strategies of the Jesuits in Ethiopia (1555–1632)*, Aethiopistischen Forschungen, 70 (Wiesbaden 2009).
Conti Rossini, Carlo, 'L'omilia di Yohannes, vescovo di Aksum, in onore di Garima', in *Actes du XI Congrès des Orientalistes, Section Sémitique* (Paris 1897), pp. 139–77.
———, *Acta Yared*, CSCO, 17 (Louvain 1904).
———, *Acta Sancti Basalaota Mika'el*, CSCO, 20 (Louvain 1905).
———, *Storia d'Etiopia* (Milan 1928).
———, 'Ethiopian Hagiography and the Acts of Saint Yafqeranna Egzi' (14th Century)', in A. Bausi (ed.), *Languages and Cultures of Eastern Christianity*, vol. 4, *Ethiopia* (Ashgate 2012), pp. 329–54.
Cotterell, Peter, *Cry Ethiopia* (Eastbourne 1988).
Cousins, Philip, *Ethelstan Cheese, Saint of No Fixed Abode* (Worthing 1986).
Cowley, Roger, 'The Ethiopian Church and the Council of Chalcedon', *Sobornost* 6/1 (1970), pp. 33–8.
———, 'Preliminary Notes on the Andem Commentaries', *JEthSt* 9/1 (1971), pp. 9–20.
———, 'The Beginnings of the Andem Commentary Tradition, *JEthSt* 10/2 (1972), pp. 1–16.
———, 'Old Testament Introduction to the Andemta Commentary Tradition', *JEthSt* 12/1 (1974), pp. 133–75.
———, *The Traditional Interpretation of the Apocalypse of St John in the Ethiopian Orthodox Church* (Cambridge 1983).
———, *Ethiopian Biblical Interpretation* (Cambridge 1988).
Crummey, Donald, 'The Violence of Tewodros', *JEthSt* 9/1 (1971), pp. 107–25.
———, *Priests and Politicians: Protestant and Catholic Missions in Orthodox Ethiopia, 1830–1868* (Oxford 1972).
———, 'Shaikh Zakaryas: An Ethiopian Prophet', *JEthSt* 10/1 (1972), pp. 55–66.
———, *Land and Society in the Christian Kingdom of Ethiopia* (Chicago 2000).
———, 'Church and Nation: The Ethiopian Orthodox Tawahedo Church', in Michael Angold (ed.), *The Cambridge History of Christianity*, vol. 5, *Eastern Christianity* (Cambridge 2006), pp. 457–87.
D'Alos-Moner, Andreu Martinez, *Envoys of a Human God: The Jesuit Mission to Christian Ethiopia, 1557–1632* (Leiden 2015).
Dalrymple, William, *The Age of Kali* (London 1999).
Damon-Guillot, Anne, 'Qene et aquaquam dans la liturgie de l'Église Chrétienne d'Éthiopie: réalisation musicale d'un texte improvisée', *AÉ* 23 (2007–8), pp. 101–14.
Daniel Teshome, *The Current (1987–2007) Reformation Movement within the Ethiopian Orthodox Tewahido Church* (Addis Ababa 2007).
Daoud, Marcus, *The Liturgy of the Ethiopian Church* (Cairo 1959).

Davis, Raymond J., *Fire on the Mountains: The Story of a Miracle: The Church in Ethiopia* (Grand Rapids Michigan 1966).

Derat, Marie-Laure, *Le Domaine des Rois Éthiopiens (1270–1527): Espace, Pouvoir et Monachisme* (Paris 2003).

———, 'Roi prêtre et Prêtre Jean: analyse de la Vie d'un souverain éthiopien du XIIe siècle Yemrahanna Krestos', *AÉ* 27 (2012), pp. 127–48.

Desplat, Patrick, 'Against Wahhabism? Islamic Reform, Ambivalence and Sentiments of Loss in Harar', in Patrick Desplat and Terje Østerbø (eds), *Muslim Ethiopia* (New York 2013), pp.163–84.

———, and Terje Østerbø (eds), *Muslim Ethiopia: The Christian Legacy, Identity Politics, and Islamic Reformism* (New York 2013).

Donham, Donald, 'Old Abyssinia and the New Ethiopian Empire: Themes in Social History', in Donald Donham and Wendy James (eds), *The Southern Marches of Imperial Ethiopia* (Oxford 1986), pp. 3–48.

———, *Marxist Modern: An Ethnographic History of the Ethiopian Revolution* (Oxford 1999).

Douglas, Mary, *Purity and Danger* (London 1966).

Eide, Øyvind, *Revolution and Religion in Ethiopia: The Growth and Persecution of the Mekane Yesus Church, 1974–1986* (Oxford 2000).

Ephraim Isaac, *The Ethiopian Church* (Boston 1968).

Erlich, Haggai, *Saudi Arabia and Ethiopia: Islam, Christianity and Politics Entwined* (London 2007).

———, *Islam and Christianity in the Horn of Africa* (London 2010).

Fantini, Emanuele, 'Go Pente! The Charismatic Renewal of the Evnagelical Movement in Ethiopia', in Gérard Prunier and Éloi Ficquet (eds), *Understanding Contemporary Ethiopia* (London 2015), pp. 123–46.

Fargher, B.L., *The Origins of the New Churches Movement in Southern Ethiopia 1927–1944*, Studies of Religion in Africa, 16 (Leiden 1996).

Ficquet, Éloi, 'The Ethiopian Muslims: Historical Processes and Ongoing Controversies', in Gérard Prunier and Éloi Ficquet (eds), *Understanding Contemporary Ethiopia* (London 2015), pp. 93–122.

Friedlander, Maria-Jose, and Bob Friedlander, *Hidden Treasures of Ethiopia* (London 2015).

Fritsch, Emmanuel, 'The Liturgical Year and the Lectionary of the Ethiopian Church', *Warsawskie Studia Teologiczne* 12/2 (1999), pp. 71–116.

———, *The Liturgical Year of the Ethiopian Church: The Temporal Seasons and Sundays* (Addis Ababa 2001).

———, 'The Altar in Ethiopian Church History: Forms and Meanings', in Groen Bert, Steven Hawkes-Teeples and Stefanos Alexopoulos (eds), *Inquiries into Eastern Christian Worship* (Leuven 2012), pp. 443–510.

Fukui, Katsuyoshi, and Shigata Kurimoto (eds), *Ethiopia in Broader Perspective*, Papers of the XIIIth International Conference of Ethiopian Studies, 3 vols, Kyoto 12–17 December 1997 (Kyoto 1997).

Gerster, Georg, *Churches in Rock: Early Christian Art in Ethiopia* (London 1970).

Getatchew Haile, A. Lane and S. Rubenson (eds), *The Missionary Factor in Ethiopia* (Frankfurt 1998).

Gidada Solon, *The Other Side of Darkness* (New York 1972).

Gill, Peter, *Famine and Foreigners, Ethiopia since Live Aid* (Oxford 2010).

Girma Amare, 'Aims and Purpose of Church Education in Ethiopia', *Ethiopian Journal of Education* 1 (1967), pp. 1–11.

Gobat, Samuel, *Journal of a Three Years' Residence in Abyssinia in Furtherance of the Objects of the Church Missionary Society* (London 1834).

Grillmeier, Aloys, *Christ in Christian Tradition*, vol. 2, part 4 (London 1996).

Guillaume, Alfred, *The Life of Muhammad* (Oxford 1955).

Haberland, Eike, *Untersuchungen zum Athiopischen Königtum* (Wiesbaden 1965).

———, 'The Ethiopian Orthodox Church – A National Church in Africa', in *Christian and Islamic Contributions towards Establishing Independent States in Africa South of the Sahara: Papers of the Africa Colloquium Bonn-Bad Godestag 2–4 May 1979* (Tübingen 1979).

Haile Gabriel Dagne, *Quran School System in Ethiopia* (Addis Ababa 1971).

———, *Selected Articles on Society and Education in Ethiopia* (Addis Ababa n.d.).

Haile Mariam Larebo, 'Quest for Change: Haymonote Abaw Ethiopian Students Association and the Ethiopian Orthodox Church 1959–1974', in Katsuyoshi Fukui et al. (eds), *Ethiopia in Broader Perspective, Papers from the XIIIth International Conference of Ethiopian Studies* (Kyoto 1997), pp. 326–38.

Hammerschmidt, Ernst, 'Jewish Elements in the Cult of the Ethiopian Church', *JEthSt* 3/2 (1965), pp. 1–12.

Hancock, Graham, *The Sign and the Seal: A Quest for the Lost Ark of the Covenant* (London 1992).

Harrison, Carol, *The Art of Listening in the Early Church* (Oxford 2013).

Hastings, Adrian, *The History of African Christianity 1950–1975* (Cambridge 1979).

———, *The Church in Africa, 1450–1950* (Oxford 1994).

Heldman, Marilyn E., 'Architectural Symbolism, Sacred Geography and the Ethiopian Church', *Journal of Religion in Africa* 22/3 (1992), pp. 222–42.

Heyer, Friedrich, *Die Kirche Aethiopiens* (Berlin 1971).

Honigmann, Ernst, 'Un évêque d'Adulis au concile de Chalcedoine', *Byzantion* (1950), pp. 295–301.

Hubbard, David, *The Literary Sources of the Kebra Negast*, PhD thesis (St Andrews University 1956).

Huntingford, G.W.B., 'The Lives of Tekla Haymonot', *JEthSt* 4/2 (1966), pp. 35–40.

Imbakom Kalewold, *Traditional Ethiopian Church Education* (New York 1970).

Johnson, David, 'Dating the Kebra Negast: Another Look', in T. Miller and J. Nesbitt (eds), *Peace and War in Byzantium* (Washington D.C. 1995), pp. 197–208.

Johnstone, Patrick, *The Future of the Global Church* (Milton Keynes 2011).

Kaplan, Steven, 'Hagiographies and the History of Medieval Ethiopia', *History in Africa* 8 (1981), pp. 107–23.

———, 'Ezana's Conversion Reconsidered', *Journal of Religion in Africa* 13 (1982), pp. 101–9.

———, *The Monastic Holy Man and the Christianization of Early Solomonic Ethiopia*, Studien zur Kulturkunde, 370 (Wiesbaden 1984).

———, *The Beta Israel (Falasha) in Ethiopia from the Earliest Times to the Twentieth Century* (New York 1992).

Kefyalew Merahi, *The Meaning of Quine, the River of Life* (Addis Ababa 2006).

Kindeneh Endeg Mihretie, 'The Eighteen Million Tawehedo Victims of the Martyr-Saint Adyam Seged Iyasu: Towards a Better Understanding of Lasta-Tigray Defiance of the Royal Court of Gondarine Ethiopia 1930s–1760s', *Aethiopica* 16 (2013), pp. 45–73.

Kinfe Rigb Zelleke, 'Bibliography of the Ethiopic Hagiographical Tradition', *JEthSt* 13/2 (1975), pp. 57–102.

Knibb, Michael, *Translating the Bible: The Ethiopic Version of the Old Testament* (Oxford 1999).

Kur, Stanislaw, *Actes de Iyasus Mo'a*, CSCO, 259–60 (Louvain 1963).

Lambie, Thomas, *Doctor without a Country* (New York 1939).

Lass-Westphal, Ingeborg, 'Protestant Missions during and after the Italo-Ethiopian War, 1935–1937', *JEthSt* 10/1 (1972), pp. 89–102.

Lee, Ralph, *Symbolic Interpretation in Ethiopian and Ephremic Literature*, PhD thesis (SOAS London 2011).

Lefort, René, 'The Ethiopian Economy: Developmental State vs. the Free Market', in Gérard Prunier and Éloi Ficquet (eds), *Understanding Contemporary Ethiopia* (London 2015), pp. 357–93.

Levine, Donald, *Wax and Gold: Tradition and Innovation in Ethiopian Culture* (Chicago 1965).

———, *Greater Ethiopia* (Chicago 1974).

Lewis, H.S., 'Spirit Possession in Ethiopia', in S. Segert and J. Bodrogligeh (eds), *Ethiopian Studies* (Harrassowitz 1983), pp. 466–80.

Lewis. I.M. Ahmed Al-Safi, and Sayyid Hurreiz (eds), *Women's Medicine: The Zar-Bori Cult in Africa and Beyond* (Edinburgh 1991).

Lockhart, Donald (tr.), *Itinerario of Jeronimo Lobo* (London 1984).

Lössl, Joseph, 'One as the Same: Elements of an Ethiopian Christology', *Östkirchliches Studien* 42 (1993), pp. 288–302.

McCrindle, J.W., *The Christian Topography of Cosmas Indicopleustes* (Cambridge 2010).

MacCulloch, Diarmaid, *A History of Christianity* (London 2009).

McGilchrist, Iain, *The Master and His Emissary* (New Haven and London 2009).

Marcus, Cressida, 'Imperial Nostalgia: Christian Restoration and Civic Decay in Gondar', in Wendy James and Donald Donham (eds), *Remapping Ethiopia: Socialism and After* (Oxford 2002), pp. 239–56.

Marcus, Harold, *The Life and Times of Menelik II Ethiopia 1844–1913* (Oxford 1975).

———, *A History of Ethiopia* (Berkeley and London 2002).

Markakis, John, *The Last Two Frontiers* (Oxford 2011).

Marrassini, Paolo, 'A Hagiographic Text, the Royal Chronicle', in A. Bausi (ed.), *Languages and Cultures of Eastern Christianity*, vol. 4, *Ethiopia* (Ashgate 2012), pp. 389–97.

Marsden, Philip, *The Chains of Heaven: An Ethiopian Romance* (London 2006).

———, *The Barefoot Emperor: An Ethiopian Tragedy* (London 2008).

Mbiti, John S., *African Religions and Philosophy* (London 1969).

———, *Concepts of God in Africa* (London 1970).

Mebratu Kiros Gebru, *Miaphysite Christology* (Picataway New Jersey 2010).

Meinardus, O.F.A., 'Ecclesiastica Aethiopica in Aegypto', *JEthSt* 3/1 (1965), pp. 23–35.

Melkamu Mengesha, *The Problem of the Conversion of Orthodox Christians to Other Religions*, senior essay, Trinity Theological College (Addis Ababa 2010).

Merid Wolde Aregay, 'The Legacy of Jesuit Missionary Activities in Ethiopia', in Getatchew Haile et al. (eds), *The Missionary Factor in Ethiopia* (Frankfurt 1998), pp. 31–56.

Messay Kebede, *Survival and Modernisation Ethiopia's Enigmatic Present: A Philosophical Discourse* (Asmara 1999).

Mire Sellassie Gebre Ammanuel, 'The Bible and Its Canon in the Ethiopian Orthodox Church', *Bible Translator* 44 (1992), pp. 111–23.

———, *Church and Missions in Ethiopia during the Italian Occupation* (Addis Ababa 2014).

Moberg, Axel, *The Book of the Himyarites* (London 1924).

Mohammed Girma, *Understanding Religion and Social Change in Ethiopia* (New York 2012).

Munro Hay, Stuart, 'The Dating of Ezana and Frumentius', *Rassegna di Studi etiopici* 32 (1988), pp. 111–27; repr. in A. Bausi (ed.), *Languages and Cultures of Eastern Christianity*, vol. 4, *Ethiopia* (Ashgate 2012), pp. 57–73.

———, *Ethiopia and Alexandria: The Metropolitan Episcopacy of Ethiopia* (Warsaw 1997).

———, 'A Sixth Century Kebra Negast?' *AÉ* 17 (2001), pp. 43–58.

———, *Ethiopia, the Unknown Land: A Cultural and Historical Guide* (London 2002).

———, *Ethiopia and Alexandria: The Metropolitan Episcopacy of Ethiopia from the Fourteenth Century to the Zemana Mesafint* (Warsaw 2005).

———, *The Quest for the Ark of the Covenant* (London 2005).

———, 'Saintly Shadows', in A. Bausi (ed.), *Languages and Cultures of Eastern Christianity*, vol. 4, *Ethiopia* (Ashgate 2012), pp. 221–52.

Nersessian, V., and Richard Pankhurst, 'The Visit to Ethiopia of Johannes T'ovmacean an Armenian Jeweller in 1764–66', *JEthSt* 15 (1982), pp. 79–104.

Pankhurst, Richard, *Travellers in Ethiopia* (London 1965).

——— (ed.), *A Social History of Ethiopia* (Addis Ababa 1990).

Perruchon, J., *Vie de Lalibala, roi d'Éthiopie* (Paris 1892).

Persoon, Joachim, 'The Monastery as a Nexus of Ethiopian Culture: A Discourse of Reconstruction', in Katsuyoshi Fukui and Shigata Kurimoto (eds), *Ethiopia in Broader Perspective*, Papers of the XIIIth International Conference of Ethiopian Studies, 3 vols, Kyoto 12–17 December 1997 (Kyoto 1997), pp. 679–86.

———, *Central Ethiopian Monasticism 1974–1991: Survival of an Ancient Institution in a Changing World*, PhD thesis (SOAS London 2003).

———, 'Between Ancient Axum and Revolutionary Moscow: The Ethiopian Church in the 20th Century', in Anthony O'Mahony (ed.), *Eastern Christianity* (London 2004), pp. 160–214.

———, 'The Ethiopian Monk: A Changing Concept of Masculinity', *JEthSt* 35/1 (2007), pp. 43–66.

Phillipson, David W., *Ancient Ethiopia* (London 1990).

———, *Ancient Churches of Ethiopia* (New Haven and London 2009).

Prunier, Gérard, and Éloi Ficquet (eds), *Understanding Contemporary Ethiopia* (London 2015).

Reader, John, *Africa: A Biography of the Continent* (London 1997).

Rodinson, Maxime, 'On the Question of "Jewish Influences" in Ethiopia', *Journal of Semitic Studies* 9 (1964), pp. 11–19.

———, 'Review of Edward Ullendorff', in *Bibliotheca Orientalis* 21 (1964), pp. 238–45.

Rubenson, Samuel, 'The Interaction between the Missionaries and the Orthodox: The Case of Abune Salama', in Getatchew Haile et al. (eds), *The Missionary Factor in Ethiopia* (Frankfurt 1998), pp. 71–84.

Rubenson, Sven, *King of Kings: Tewodros of Ethiopia* (Addis Ababa 1966).

Sergew Hable Selassie, 'The Problem of Gudit', *JEthSt* 10/1 (1972), pp. 113–24.

——— and Belaynesh Mikael, 'Worship in the Ethiopian Orthodox Church', in *The Church of Ethiopia: A Panorama of History and Spiritual Life* (Addis Ababa 1997), pp. 66–7.

Shahid, Irfan, 'The Kebra Negast in the Light of Recent Research', *Le Museon* 89 (1976), pp. 133–78.

Shelemay, K.K., 'The Musician and Transmission of Religious Tradition: The Multiple Roles of the Ethiopian Dabtara', *Journal of Religion in Africa* 22/3 (1992), pp. 242–60.

Shenk, Calvin, *The Development of the Ethiopian Orthodox Church and Its Relationship with the Ethiopian Government from 1930–1970*, PhD thesis (New York University 1972).

Shiferaw Bekele, 'Monarchical Restoration and Territorial Expansion: The Ethiopian State in the Second Half of the Nineteenth Century', in Gérard Prunier and Éloi Ficquot (eds), *Understanding Contemporary Ethiopia* (London 2015), pp. 159–81.

Silverberg, R., *The Realm of Prester John* (London 1972).

Stokes, David, *Ethiopia: Land of Outstretched Hand* (London 1948).

Strauss, Steven, *Perspectives on the Nature of Christ in the Ethiopian Orthodox Church: A Case Study in Contextualised Theology* (Pasadena California 1997).

Sumner, Claud, *Ethiopian Philosophy*, vol. 3 (Addis Ababa 1978).

Sundkler, Bengt, *Bantu Prophets in South Africa* (London 1948).

———, and Christopher Stead, *A History of the Church in Africa* (Cambridge 2000).

Taddesse Tamrat, 'The Abbots of Dabra Hayq 1248–1535', *JEthSt* 8/1 (1970), pp. 87–117.

———, 'A Short Note on the Traditions of Pagan Resistance to the Ethiopian Church (14th and 15th Centuries)', *JEthSt* 10/1 (1972), pp. 137–50.

———, *Church and State in Ethiopia* (Oxford 1973).

———, 'Evangelising the Evangelised: The Root Problem between Missions and the Ethiopian Orthodox Church', in Getatchew Haile et al. (eds), *The Missionary Factor in Ethiopia* (Frankfurt 1998), pp. 17–30.

Taylor, John V., *The Primal Vision* (London 1963).

Tesfazghi Uqbit, *Current Christological Positions of Ethiopian Orthodox Theologians*, Orientalia Christiana Analecta, 193 (Rome 1973).

Teshome Wagaw, *Educational Developments in Ethiopia* (Addis Ababa 1979).

Tibebe Eshete, *The Evangelical Movement in Ethiopia: Resistance and Resilience* (Waco, Texas 2009).

Trimingham, J. Spencer, *Islam in Ethiopia* (Oxford 1952).

Tubiana, Joseph, 'Zar and Buda in Northern Ethiopia', in I.M. Lewis et al. (eds), *Women's Medicine: The Zar-Bori Cult in Africa and Beyond* (Edinburgh 1991).

Uhlig, S. (ed.), *Encyclopedia Aethiopica*, 5 vols (Wiesbaden 2003–14).

Ullendorff, Edward, 'Hebraic-Judaic Elements in Abyssinian (Monophysite) Christianity', *Journal of Semitic Studies* 1 (1956), pp. 215–56.

———, *The Ethiopians: An Introduction to Country and People* (Oxford 1960).

———, *Ethiopia and the Bible* (Oxford 1968).

Vagnon, Emmanuelle, 'Comment localiser l'Éthiopie: La confrontation des sources antiques et des témoignages modernes au XV^{è} siècles', *AÉ* 27 (2012) pp. 21–48.

Vansina, Jan, *Oral Tradition: Study in Historical Methodology* (London 1965).

———, *Oral Tradition as History* (Madison, Wisconsin 1985).

Walls, Andrew, *Cross Cultural Process in Christian History* (Maryknoll 2002).

Whiteway, R. Stephen (ed. and tr.), *The Portuguese Expedition to Abyssinia in 1441–1543* (London 1902).

Witakowski, Witold, 'Syrian Influences in Ethiopian Culture', *Orientalia Suecana* 38–9 (1989–90), pp. 191–202.

Wudu Taffete Kassu, *The Ethiopian Orthodox Church, the Ethiopian State and the Alexandrian See: Indigenizing the Episcopacy and Forging National Identity 1926–1991*, PhD thesis (University of Urbana Champaign Illinois 2006).

Yeshaq, *The Ethiopian Tawehedo Church: An Integrally African Church* (Nashville 1997).

Zewde Gebre-Sellassie, *Yohannes IV of Ethiopia* (Oxford 1975).

Index

www.ingramcontent.com/pod-product-compliance
Ingram Content Group UK Ltd.
Pitfield, Milton Keynes, MK11 3LW, UK
UKHW020731280225
455688UK00012B/605